The
Law of Attraction

and Other Secrets
of Visualization

© Second Printing March, 2008
First Printing May, 2007
by the School of Metaphysics No. 100189

Cover design and photo by Aisha Causey

ISBN: 0-944386-39-3

Library of Congress Control No. 2007925213
PRINTED IN THE UNITED STATES OF AMERICA

If you desire to learn more about the research
and teachings in this book, write to

School of Metaphysics World Headquarters,
Windyville, Missouri 65783
or call us at 417-345-8411

Visit us on the internet at www.som.org

The
Law of Attraction

and Other Secrets
of Visualization

Laurel Clark, D.M., D.D.

SOM Publishing
Windyville, MO 65783

By the same author

Dharma: Finding Your Soul's Purpose

Karmic Healing

Interpreting Dreams for Self Discovery

Concentration

Vital Ingredient: Healing for a Higher Purpose

Shaping Your Life

I would like to express my appreciation for my parents who taught me to think in pictures by reading to me, telling stories, playing music, taking me to art museums, and encouraging my love of reading. I am also deeply grateful for all of my teachers in the School of Metaphysics who have taught me the science and application of Universal Law.

Thank you, Aisha Causey, for your generosity in preparing the layout and design of this book and for your willingness to learn and teach.

Contents

As irrigators lead water where they want,
as archers make their arrows straight,
as carpenters carve wood,
the wise shape their minds.
-- The Dhammapada

Preface

It was a beautiful sunny day. Jay, Rick, Sheila and Deborah were burning piles of brush that they had cleared from a wild tract of land in mid-Missouri. They were pioneers, removing the brushy tangle of scrub oak so the area would be tamed for fields and pasture. Suddenly, the wind picked up. The pile of brush that was burning nestled in a small valley immediately burst into a rapidly spreading wildfire.

Tiny five-foot-tall Deborah screamed and grabbed a shovel to try to pound out the flames. Jay and Rick stood there, paralyzed for a second, wondering whether they had time to run to get help. Sheila rapidly assessed the situation. She respected the tremendous power and swiftness of fire and knew that they had to respond at once. She could see that physical manpower would not stop the flames which were escalating in size and speed. By the time the local volunteer fire department arrived from the outlying country areas, the fire would have already consumed half of the thousand-acre property. The fire was rapidly spreading toward the woods and once it reached the trees they would never be able to control it. Sheila had to do something. She and many other people had worked long and hard to buy this land and to tend it for the purpose of building a spiritual community. She felt sick to her stomach foreseeing the possibility of one small fire spreading to destroy a thousand acres.

Sheila said to herself, "If I really am a mental creator, I can stop this." She quickly centered herself and said, "Wind! I command you to be still." She visualized the wind calming down, the fire subsiding, and the brush pile burning itself out in a small area. Within seconds the wind died down. The fire ceased running rampant and Sheila contained it in one place.

Deborah, Jay and Rick stopped their frantic and futile attempts to beat out the flames and gaped in wonder. Then they all cheered and hugged one another with joy.

This is a true story. It is not a fairy tale, nor allegory, nor fabricated fable. Sheila is a friend of mine who had been studying metaphysics and practicing concentration and visualization for about five years when this incident occurred. It seems like a miracle to be able to stop the wind, and yet, this miracle occurred in the twentieth century. Through the power of creative imagery, directed with concentration and will, one woman stopped a fire and saved a newly-forming community from vast destruction.

People throughout the world use visualization on a daily basis, to create wondrous projects, to build cities, to compose inspiring music. People use visualization to heal themselves of cancer, AIDS, and other life-threatening diseases. Others use it in emergencies — a 120-pound woman has been known to lift a car by herself to save her child trapped underneath. Creative imagery has been used throughout the ages by inventors, scientists, and innovators to develop new ways of life. The telephone, electrical light bulb, radio, television, automobile, and airplane all resulted from the imagination and will of their creators.

Now you can learn about the power of your creative mind. You can learn how to design your life dreams, how to change annoying habits, how to improve relationships. You can learn how to draw upon the wellspring of creativity which is at the very essence of your being. You can truly have anything you desire in the mental, emotional and spiritual realm by developing your imagination and will power.

This is your life. It is yours to create. Listen to that inner voice, the one that whispers to you, inspiring you to become your highest and best Self. When you give of your Real Self, the world will be a better place for all.

The
Law of Attraction

and Other Secrets
of Visualization

In learning to harness the power of your mind, I encourage you to be discerning in your choices. Create for the good of all. Create for something greater than yourself, to help others, to share your abundance. When you gain mastery of attention, you become a thinker. When you master visualization you become a mental creator. Ask yourself, "For whom am I creating?" When you create for the benefit of other people as well as yourself, you become personally enriched.

Visualization will enable you to free your consciousness from limitations and restrictions. You will become more hopeful, more gracious, and more generous as you discover more and more of your creative power. Share what you are learning with others so that your benefits may continue beyond you!

The second part of the book that was *Shaping Your Life* will be another volume describing in greater depth the universal laws of self mastery. You will learn more about how to unlock your innate genius. You'll be educated about the science and mechanics of the mind. There are universal principles that govern the process of visualization that you can learn, understand, and put into practice. This knowledge will aid you to live with the highest ideals in mind. I look forward to sharing this insight with you soon.

If you want to learn directly how your own creative mind functions, contact us at the College of Metaphysics and inquire about the Spiritual Focus Weekend called *The Genius Code*. This session is offered by special request, an opportunity for you to receive your own Creative Mind intuitive report.

I send you my circle of love,
Dr. Laurel Clark, January 2007

the one who expects disaster at every turn. Listen to your own thoughts and you may be able to discern why you are fortunate or not.

We each have the ability to imagine, and through using imagination and will power we can create the life of our dreams. Every time we create we learn that we are a part of something much greater than ourselves. All the forces of the universe draw to us seemingly mystical and magical experiences. When we create with the purpose of learning *how creation occurs* we can begin to understand these universal forces called universal laws. They are universal because they apply to anyone, anywhere, any place.

This means that no one person is favored by the universe. We can all receive its bounty. As we create for the good of all and share what we learn with others, the more abundance we each have. When we teach what we learn about creation to other people, we gain deeper understanding. The more people there are who know how to harmonize with universal law, the more harmonious our world will be!

When we read books by or about successful people, we find that there are similar ideas which permeate the literature. Studying the lives of these men and women, we discover that it doesn't matter what field of endeavor the notable person pursues — business, art, music, science, religion, communication — the same principles work. People who accomplish their ideals are cooperating with the universal laws whether they know it or not. Just as gravity functions even if someone does not know how it works, the universal laws operate with or without one's conscious awareness.

Knowing how the universal laws operate will make you more effective in your visualizing. You will be able to expend less energy and direct it more efficiently, enabling you to create always higher and greater achievements. You will become more purposeful and self aware.

Mysterious Coincidence

A few years ago I was attending an exercise class at a health club near my home. I really enjoyed the instructor because her love for teaching and concern for her students was evident. After the class ended, I thanked her for teaching and asked when she taught other classes. I let her know that I travelled quite a bit so I was not always in town to come to her classes. She asked me what I did. I told her that I am a teacher at the School of Metaphysics and described what metaphysics is.

Her eyes grew wide. She said, "Wow! That's amazing! I love that stuff. In fact, a couple of the other girls who work here keep a book behind the counter that lists dream symbols. When we have free time we talk about each others' dreams but we're never sure if we're interpreting them correctly."

One of the other women in the exercise class overheard us. She joined in excitedly, remarking, "I just heard someone on the radio yesterday morning interpreting dreams. What she said made more sense than anything I had ever heard before about dreams." I asked her what station she was listening to. When she responded I smiled, saying, "That was me you heard on the radio."

She exclaimed, "Really? I can't believe it! I've never met anyone who I've heard on the radio."

Several of us discussed dreams and their interpretations for about an hour. Susan, the instructor of the exercise class, came over to the School of Metaphysics that evening to register for a class.

Was this some divine accident that caused all of us to be in the same place at the same time? Or was it a response to some mysterious plan? This meeting of minds shows a universal law at work, bringing together people with corresponding needs and desires.

What causes a coincidence? How do seemingly miraculous events take place? The action of attraction is one of the forces at work! Attraction is a universal principle, the drawing together in the subconscious mind is imperceptible to the physical senses. When a seed is within the earth, you tend it and care for it although you cannot yet see, touch, feel, or smell it.

In the same way, there is a time to watch expectantly for a developing thought form to manifest in physical form. Knowing that you have created a clear and complete image, you watch for the signs that your desired object is coming to fruition. The Law of Attraction operates even when you do not know exactly how you will fulfill a desire. It ensures that you will be in the right place at the right time for things to "click" into place.

Your job is to create the clear thought form which initiates the process, then to move toward it with activity. The conscious mind needs to decide, to be definite. **Out of infinite possibilities choose exactly what you want.**

Once you have created the clear and definite thought form, the subconscious mind can do its work of *drawing to you* the people, place, and things which are compatible. Or *you will be drawn to* people, places, and things which match your desire.

This is why it is important to maintain an attitude of expectation, watching for signs of your desire, responding to the opportunities to bring it to fruition. Attentiveness, expectation, love, and responsiveness are keys for cooperating with your developing thought form.

The following story illustrates how Lynn used these principles to find a job that matched all the conditions she wanted. She was a student of metaphysics at the time and applied what she was learning to visualize a teaching position when she moved to a new state.

"When I moved out to Colorado from Wisconsin, my friends thought I was taking a big risk to be moving without having a job lined up, a place to

move into, and knowing only one family who lived out there. I saw it as an 'adventure'! I hadn't had an adventure for so long, I needed to create one and move on. So I packed up all my things in a Ryder truck, towing my car behind and left 'security' behind.

Having been an elementary school teacher for ten years, I was still in the 'August is summer vacation' mode of thinking. I wasn't too anxious to get a job right away. Soon September came along and I began to feel the pull of the familiar educational system toward school buildings and children; I began getting my resumé printed up. I applied to private schools or teaching centers that were different from the public school setting.

I made out a list of the things I wanted most in my life. Number one on the list was a teaching job in a motivating environment, enthusiastic staff of people to work with, a place where I could be very creative, yet flexible with my teaching and hours. Teaching many ages, multi-disciplinary (all subjects), for a salary. I wanted something new and different compared to what I had come from. I could feel what it would be like.

I sent letters to tutoring centers and schools that had programs unlike the public systems. I also read my list daily and September rolled on. I began to get anxious. Toward the end of September I decided to look through the yellow pages again and a school's name, Rivendell, popped out from the page. The ad said, 'Using the British primary and Montessori techniques.' I had visited a school in Britain and I was curious about how this school had adopted their teachings. So I called them up and made an appointment to visit.

When I walked into the huge classroom that had five teachers and one hundred kids, a bunch of tables with chairs and a huge open play area, I knew this would be different. After observing for about an hour — watching four-year-olds and twelve-year-olds side by side, working independently or in small groups, I realized that something here works!

By the next hour the head teacher told me that one of the teachers would be taking a maternity leave in a couple of weeks, that they hadn't advertised yet for the position, and if I was interested they would accept my application. I did not hesitate in saying yes. I knew this was the place I had projected for. By the end of the week I had the job and could start right away so that Ann could teach me the ropes of her job before leaving.

I felt as if I walked right in to the very place I projected to be working at. The secretary joked about how worried she was the job wasn't posted and filled earlier and how Terri, the head teacher, wasn't in the least concerned. Maybe she knew I'd be there even before I did!" — L.R.

Lynn's story shows how many minds come together. Her desire to teach in an alternative setting drew her from several states away to the school that needed a teacher with her qualifications. Terri's positive expectation was a match for Lynn's enthusiasm and interest.

The Power of Expectation

I heard a minister named John relate a story describing his faith in divine providence. John had recently moved from a city to a rural area with his family. A hardworking man, he had not yet obtained a full time job to support his family although he willingly accepted any work which was available. One evening as dinnertime approached, John knew that there was no food to feed his family, but he instructed his daughter to set the table nonetheless.

John believed that his efforts would pay off in some way at some time. He knew that he was a good person, and he knew that his family was worthy of being fed. He had had miraculous events occur at other times in his life so he trusted that the universe would not let his family go hungry.

The family gathered together around the table and John led them in prayer. As they sat holding hands, there was a knock at the door. John finished the prayer and answered the knock. There stood his landlord with two grocery sacks in his arms. The landlord was a gruff man who usually said very little and rarely smiled. John greeted him, and the landlord said,

"Our garden is producing so many vegetables, my wife and I can't keep up. I hate waste, so I was wondering if you would use any of these things. Oh, and we just butchered a steer and there are certain cuts my kids won't eat. If you think yours would eat them, you can have these, too." John smiled gratefully and thanked his landlord, assuring him that the food would be put to good use.

This story demonstrates the action of several universal laws, including the "match" of compatible desires — John's desire to feed his family and the landlord's desire to insure that the food was used and not wasted.

When events "just happen" to occur fortuitously, the Law of Attraction is at work. Here is an example. When I was directing a School of Metaphysics branch in Ann Arbor, Michigan, I set a goal to teach a new class in applied metaphysics. I created a very clear image of the benefits of the lessons — learning concentration to become calm and centered, dream interpretation for self awareness, mental relaxation, greater direction in life, peace of mind. I imagined new students learning undivided attention, how to improve memory, how to develop imagination, reasoning, and intuition, all part of the course of study.

I created a strong idea of love, for I loved what I was learning and wanted to share it with others. I made telephone calls to people who had come to lectures at the school, put announcements in the newspaper, told all my students and asked them to invite their friends to the class, posted flyers around the local university campus.

One day, as I returned from work, the phone rang. It was a woman who was asking all kinds of questions about the school and its services. I answered her questions, and then asked her how she had heard about the school.

"That's the funniest thing," she replied. "I had just been thinking about how it was time to make a change in my life and I didn't know exactly what to do. One thing I've always found is that when I need to clear my mind I'll clean the house. It gives me a way to get my mind off my problems. Well, I was dusting the bookshelf, and I knocked the phone book off the shelf. It fell open to the yellow pages and I saw your ad there. What a coincidence!"

This shows the Law of Attraction at work. I had formed a clear image of my desire to teach and this woman had formed a clear image of her desire to learn. Both of our minds were reaching out, and the desires "met" in Universal Mind. It didn't just happen by chance. Both of us put forth some physical activity. In my case, I was talking, putting out flyers, and placing notices in the newspaper. Someone before me had made sure that the School of Metaphysics was listed in the yellow pages. The woman was attentive so that she saw the ad. She could have just put the book back on the shelf without even looking at it. She responded to her desire by picking up the telephone and calling once she read the advertisement. At any stage, this match could have been thwarted if one or both of us had been passive or thought defeatedly, "Why bother. It's not going to work anyway."

This is a very important key. The person who lives a charmed life is one who expects to have what he wants. She is not afraid to reach out and go after her desire. People who never seem to have what they want usually think that way. They are afraid of being rejected or disappointed or they fear that they will fail, so they don't even try. They make excuses for not taking action. These excuses can take the form of "not enough time," or "that person won't be interested so I won't ask them," or "this always happens to me."

Cooperating with universal law means that you create the desire in your mind and respond with physical activity. The Law of Attraction is fun because you must watch expectantly in order to harmonize with it. The thrill of discovery is apparent in every book you read, every corner you turn, every letter you open.

Every time the phone rings, the expectant teacher will think, "Is this someone calling to come to my class?" The person who is looking for a job will open the newspaper attentively watching for his or her job that will be advertised that day. Whatever you desire, instead of wondering *if* it will happen, look for when and where the signs of its manifestation are occurring. This makes living a joy. Everyday experience becomes fulfilling and rewarding.

The Secret of Aladdin's Lamp

Do you remember the story of Aladdin? The genie appears when he rubs the lamp, and Aladdin's wishes are granted. The Law of Attraction exists as everyone's genie, bringing to us what we desire in the form of conditions that enable us to create.

When you expect life to be rewarding and look for the ways to accomplish what you want, you will see opportunities everywhere. When you have imagined a desire for a long time, everything seems to fall in place when it is fulfilled. Several years ago, I decided that I wanted to earn some extra money and I also wanted to write every day. I visualized both desires and wrote them down. I did not set limits on how I would earn the money, I just wrote that I wanted to earn about $300 extra. I also did not define what kind of writing I wanted to do. I just decided that because I love to write, I wanted to include that in my daily activities.

I met an artist who had come to the School of Metaphysics to learn about dream interpretation, since she often used images from her dreams in her paintings. We developed a friendship and often talked about our creative pursuits. One day we were eating breakfast at a local café, and she told me that she had been considering adding verbal phrases to her line of greeting cards. Prior to this time she had been producing a line of greeting cards that featured her paintings. They were blank inside. This got my attention, because I had often thought about writing greeting card verses. I love to send cards and often buy them; in my search for the appropriate card I have thought, "I could write cards like these," or "I could write better verses than these." I had even written to some greeting card companies to find out their procedures for obtaining new sayings but hadn't followed through with any subsequent action.

I told Barbara that I would love to write some verses for her cards, and she said that she would love to see what I wrote. I asked her what she had in mind, and she said she really didn't know. She explained that her form of expression was visual and she had difficulty putting her thoughts into words. She suggested that I look at her cards and write verses as the spirit moved me. Then she would consider them. She gave me about fifteen or twenty different designs and I went home to try my hand at it. I sat down at the typewriter and reeled off thoughts that were inspired by the images on her cards. The more I wrote, the more inspired I became. I thought about particular people I love and the most heartfelt sentiments I wanted to share with them. When I finished, I had written about one hundred different poetic phrases for the cards. I was happy to write from my heart, but I was somewhat insecure about showing the verses to Barbara. I did not know if she would like them, especially because she had not given me any idea what she wanted for her cards.

When I showed Barbara what I had written, her face lit up. "This is great! This is beautiful! This is exactly what I would have wanted to say but I wouldn't have even thought of it!" She wanted to use all the verses I had written but had only planned on putting writing inside ten of her designs. She decided to purchase twenty of the phrases because she had another line of cards coming out the following season. She could make use of the extra verses with her new line. She paid me $15 apiece for the one-sentence phrases to go in her cards and bought twenty. As a result, I received a check for $300 for a couple of hours of my time spent doing what I love to do — writing from my heart. Two desires fulfilled at once with clearly visualized thought forms.

This story shows the Law of Attraction at work. Barbara was attracted to the School of Metaphysics because of her love for art, her understanding that images have meaning, and her desire to understand the Universal Language of Mind. The friendship that developed between us was based on a mutual desire to learn, to explore and understand the nature of creativity. My desire to write matched her desire for words in her greeting cards. Her desire for written verses matched my long-standing desire to contribute to greeting cards.

The universal laws brought us together, and we responded with communication and action. The beauty of cooperating with universal law is that everyone receives what they want and together people can create something greater than one person can by themselves. We grow when we create with others. This is one of the secrets of visualization: when we create with the goodness of all concerned, everyone's life is enriched.

Changing Habits

Addictive Behavior

After sixteen years of being a heavy (two packs a day) smoker, I quit. I can report happily that I have never touched a cigarette in the sixteen years following, nor have I gained weight, nor do I regret it, nor do I miss smoking. I didn't force myself to change and I did not resort to nicotine patches, drugs, or hypnosis.

Anyone can learn to change addictive habits. The key is not, as some people suppose, the exercise of will power. The secret lies in the effective use of visualization. Every physical habit starts with a thought. At one time, I had imagined myself being a smoker and practiced a particular image while learning to hold a cigarette and breathe smoke into my lungs. As I created a strong thought-form image of smoking, my body also became accustomed to the nicotine. So when the time came to quit, I had to change not only the visualized image of myself as a smoker, but also the physical condition of addiction.

Changing a habit starts with *wanting* to do it. How do you create a desire for something you are going to leave? When you are attached to an idea it becomes a part of you. Therefore, losing it means losing a part of your identity. It is an art to create a different image that involves productive gain rather than deprivation or denial and loss. For a long time I tried unsuccessfully to quit smoking because my image of quitting was like seeing a cigarette with a red "don't" line through it. Every time I thought about quitting, I thought about cigarettes until my mind was filled incessantly with the thought of smoking!

The first step in creating a desire for change is to identify what the habit gives you, how it benefits you. In my case, I had to remember when I started thinking about smoking. When I was fifteen years old I admired my older sister. She seemed so mature to me. She smoked and my parents had smoked when I was a child. Although they no longer smoked by the time I was fifteen, my earliest images of adulthood included smoking. I read magazines that showed glamorous pictures of worldly women holding cigarettes. I had seen old movies with Lauren Bacall looking sexy and sophisticated expectantly waiting for Humphrey Bogart to light her cigarette. In my adolescence I associated smoking with the idea of being mature, adult, sophisticated, sexy, alluring, and womanly.

I remember buying my first pack of cigarettes and going to my room, locking the door, sitting in front of the mirror and practicing holding the cigarette and inhaling it. I experimented with different ways of holding the cigarette until I achieved the look I wanted. At first the smoke was acrid and tasted terrible, but my desire for maturity and sophistication was so strong I was able to keep inhaling until I had overcome my body's resistance to the poison.

As I cultivated this new image, I became attached to the cigarette as a symbol of my new-found and developing adulthood. Years later, as an adult, I didn't remember the thought which originated my desire to smoke, but I still found myself smoking more during the times when I felt my authority challenged. It was enlightening to explore these early memories and to discover the thought-image which motivated me to pick up a cigarette.

As I developed the habit, I learned to relate other images with cigarettes. Moments of intimacy, after sexual encounters, sharing secrets over a cup of coffee, long talks on the phone, all of these events became associated with smoking. As I explored these connections, I found out that I had been using cigarettes as a form of protection. When I was revealing my deepest "private" self, I would light a cigarette to keep myself at a distance from the person with whom I was becoming intimate. Smoking cigarettes was a way to repress my emotions.

I also used cigarettes to procrastinate. Waiting for a bus, lingering after a meal, between projects at work, I would smoke. I often drank a cup of coffee and smoked a cigarette or two to start my day — first at home, and again when I arrived at work. Lighting a cigarette was a way to literally kill time. When I was being indecisive or non-committal or insecure about what to do next, I'd think, "I'll do this after I have a cigarette" and thus put off the decision for a few more minutes.

Changing the habit of smoking meant changing all these mental habits. By stilling my mind I became aware of these thoughts — the real desires which stimulated the decision to light up. This growing awareness became like a treasure hunt. Unlocking unconscious patterns of thinking was a thrill!

In addition, after years of smoking my body had become addicted to the nicotine. So the decision to quit smoking was a multi-faceted one which involved re-thinking many activities in my life. I had to become conscious of thoughts that had been submerged in unconsciousness, and discipline my physical senses and physical body. It was scary to think about giving up my protection, giving up this constant companion, giving up the cigarettes that I clung to when I was being insecure. Cigarettes had infiltrated every area of my life. Anywhere I went — at home, in my car, at work, in bed — there were stimuli to draw my attention to my attachment. I needed a positive, attractive reason to quit smoking because I had actually developed a sixteen-year relationship with cigarettes!

I knew people who wanted to quit smoking because they were afraid of getting cancer or emphysema. This seemed too far away to motivate me, although my father had died of cancer and my aunt from emphysema. I seemed to breathe all right and cigarettes weren't affecting my health. My desire to change this habit began when I realized that I had become a slave to cigarettes. I hated seeing myself in this light. The relationship that at one time seemed so appealing was now abusive and masochistic.

One evening, at midnight, dressed only in pajamas and almost ready for bed, I found myself frantically searching the house for a cigarette. When I couldn't find one, rather than saying, "Oh, well, I'll get some tomorrow," I stooped to rummaging through the trash for a long "butt" which was still smokable — looking and feeling like a common bum! I was appalled when I saw what I was doing to myself.

Every place I went, I would look for the areas where smoking was permitted, I was always checking to make sure I had my cigarettes with me, and I would gauge time by how long it had been since I had had a cigarette. Much of my attention was consumed by thinking about smoking.

In every other area of my life I was striving for mastery. As a serious student of metaphysics, I had practiced concentration exercises for years. I had practiced a weekly discipline of eating only fruit for two days in a row to be in command of my body. I sat still for hours in meditation. I was teaching people how to control their lives, teaching them how powerful their minds were, and here I was being enslaved by cigarettes! This idea was offensive to me, for it conflicted with everything I believed and the principles on which I based my life. I do not like hypocritical behavior in others, and here I was being a hypocrite myself. The urge to be a good example to my students and to live up to my own ideals motivated me to form a new desire.

I decided that I was tired of being a slave. I wanted to be a master. The positive thought-form image I created to replace the old one was this: being the master of my life, my circumstances, my thoughts, and my senses. I imaged myself having command of my attention and having command of mySelf. Because the addiction to the nicotine was strong, I still had to deal with the physical withdrawal. I used various methods to help with this. I bought some herbal tablets at a health food store with an herb called lobelia which helps reduce the craving for nicotine without creating a new addiction. I read books which said that the actual physical craving for nicotine lasts about sixty seconds. When I felt the irritating sensation of crawling out of my skin and being immeasurably agitated and restless, I would breathe deeply, go for a walk, drink lots of water, direct my attention elsewhere, and indeed in a minute or so the most acute physical discomfort was gone.

When I was tempted to pick up a cigarette I'd ask myself, "Laurel, what do you want? Do you want to be the slave or do you want to be the master?" Every time I considered this question carefully, for I realized that I did not have to quit. I could still smoke if I wanted to, but if I smoked I would once again be enslaved. And so I would answer, "I want to be the master."

This kind of self determination was especially important when no one was around and I could rationalize that no one would know if I smoked. Every time I practiced mastery I was proud of myself, and at the close of each day I would mark off how many days I had accomplished this mastery. Every time I was tempted to smoke just one drag, I would think about the amount of time and energy I had already invested in this change. I wanted the investment to pay off. If I smoked even one drag I knew I would have to start all over again from the beginning and I wanted to add on to what I had already invested.

Gradually, I became less attached to the idea of being a smoker and more and more attached to the pride and security that came from knowing that I was the master of my mind and body. In time, the physical cravings lessened. As I gave conscious attention to my thoughts and why I craved cigarettes at certain times, I learned how I had used cigarettes to protect myself from being vulnerable in intimate moments and to pretend to be mature when I doubted my authority. I practiced being inwardly calm, learning to receive and to give rather than reaching for a smoke. These experiences were very enriching, for I built strength and confidence in areas where I had used cigarettes as a crutch.

I know that this change is a permanent one because I practiced consciously changing my image and cultivating a new, productive, powerful image to replace the old one. I do not miss cigarettes, and I never replaced that habit with another one such as gum chewing or eating compulsively. The change was in my thoughts and attitudes, not in the physical behavior alone. Changing behavior while thinking the same thoughts leads to new compulsive behavior with a different object of attachment. "Behavior modification" works when there is conscious attention given to the thoughts that are causing the behavior and those thoughts are changed with visualization.

Thinking in Pictures

The secret to changing your thoughts is understanding how thinking occurs. We communicate in pictures. This is why most street signs have pictures or images rather than words. For example, a pedestrian crossing sign features a silhouette of a man walking between two lines. A no smoking sign shows a drawing of a cigarette in a red circle with a red line through it. In a car, there are picture symbols for the driver: an image of a person with a diagonal line shows that the driver needs to put on a seat belt, a picture of an oil can is used for the oil gauge.

Many people are unconscious of this fact. They say words without knowing what picture those words describe. They may be unaware that they even hold mental images. When I was changing the smoking habit, I was amazed to discover how many mental images I associated with it. It was only by paying attention to my thoughts that I remembered the *image* of Lauren Bacall smoking in the movies, and then realized my associated thought of being sophisticated and adult.

Changing habit patterns means becoming aware of the images we formed at one time. Then we can choose images we want to create and manifest, rather than unconsciously operating from old images that served a purpose in the past but hinder our growth in the present.

When we observe children we can see the natural tendency to think in pictures. I have been with young children who can tell a story and draw it long before they develop verbal writing skills. When children act out a story or a play, they are creating a moving image. As we learn to use words through speaking and writing, it is important to keep alive this ability to think in pictures.

Many advertisers capitalize on the power of images to communicate. Filmmakers intentionally use this knowledge to convey meaning in films. Anyone can become intentional in the use of mental imagery. It is one of the secrets to charisma -- creating clear mental images and describing them with words.

How do you create a mental image? You can practice by gazing at a simple object, closing your eyes, and then recalling the picture in your mind. Start now. Choose an object in your immediate environment, such as a coffee cup. Look at it, observe its shape and size. Hold it in your hand. Feel the weight, the curves, whether the surface is rough or smooth. Smell it. Use as many of your senses as you can to identify it. Now, close your eyes and recall to mind the picture, the mental image of the coffee cup. Can you see the details in your mind? The color, the size, the weight, and texture? Did it have a smell? Can you recall the smell in your mind?

Once you have pictured the object as it is, with your eyes closed, imagine that you are on top of it looking inside of it. See the curves of the cup from this angle. You can practice viewing the object in your mind from different angles.

Open your eyes now. Were you able to envision the object? Try this with several objects until you are familiar with seeing pictures in your mind. Now you can practice creating new images. Start with the object you chose for the previous exercise. Imagine it growing bigger. Now imagine it growing smaller. Now, imagine it disappearing. In its place, create something else. A different cup, made of a different material, of a different size and shape. Keep practicing until you have confidence creating images in your mind.

The next practice is to image your *self* as you desire to be. If you are strongly attached to an old image, such as smoking, or feeling awkward in social situations, or having difficulty saying what is on your mind, you might call this image to mind and then see it disappear. You might put it in a bubble, like a soap bubble, and see it floating away in the wind, then poof! it dissolves like a soap bubble dissolves. You can have fun imagining how to replace your old image with a new one.

When we want to make a change, it is helpful to draw a picture of the ideal self we want to cultivate. Some people will go through magazines and cut out pictures to form a collage that exemplifies the changed condition they want. Both of these methods are helpful to stimulate the imagination to create a picture image of the desired end result.

Body Image

Some people use this idea to visualize creating the kind of body they desire. They will find a magazine picture of a person with the ideal body shape and size. Then they find a photograph of themselves. They cut out the head and place their own face on top of the ideal body they want! This helps them visualize themselves looking the way they want to.

Why do people spend so much time engrossed in thinking about the kind of body they want to have? Many women in this country have the idea that they are fat, even when they are remarkably skinny. Hopefully, one day society will learn to respect and appreciate the female form with its curves. In today's media, models are skinny, with chiseled features, sunken cheeks, and protruding hip bones. Both men and women spend an inordinate amount of time consumed with their physical appearance, thinking about diet, exercise, and weight-loss supplements. Commercials tell women that they will be happy when they are pencil thin; men are told that they need to have washboard stomachs.

We are led to believe that food makes us fat. At the same time, we are taught that certain foods are soothing, we build many social gatherings around food and learn to associate being fed with being loved. Some mothers feed babies to keep them quiet or reward their children for good behavior with cookies and candy. We turn to ice cream and chocolate to assuage our emotional upsets, and then hate ourselves for eating!

This kind of thinking will change as more and more people discover the purpose of the physical form. Our bodies serve us so that we can live and learn and love and grow. As we discover how to live a more purposeful life, it helps us to put into perspective the body we have. As we become more confident and self assured through creating what we want in life, we can be less attached to having to look a certain way to gain approval or acceptance.

I knew a young woman who battled overweight throughout her childhood, adolescence, and early adulthood and finally conquered the "fat demon" through practicing creative imagery. Rachel was very intelligent and shy. She loved to read and would spend long hours inside the house, devouring books. Her sports-loving mother kept telling Rachel, "You're not athletic" and the child believed it. When she did venture outside to play kickball or softball, she held the image that she was awkward and clumsy, so she was picked last to be on the neighborhood kids' team. This reinforced her dislike of her body and her discomfort with the idea of physical activity.

Rachel's mother was health conscious and served meals that were low in fat and sugar. She had waged her own battles with overweight and was afraid of foods that were "fattening." She often spoke disapprovingly of such foods. On special occasions, she would serve desserts as a treat, so Rachel learned that sweets were something to be highly prized but avoided on a daily basis. Rachel grew up with the idea that food had power over her, that she would gain weight from eating any food with sugar or fat in it. She denied herself some of the foods she enjoyed, like chocolate and ice cream, and then in fits of rebellion, she would gorge herself with large quantities of both. Rachel used food as a form of comfort, when she was sad, or anxious, or lonely. She also used eating as a way of asserting her will, thinking, "No one's going to tell me what I shouldn't eat!"

Rachel hated having to worry about every bit of food she put into her mouth. She hated being at odds with her body. She wanted to enjoy eating instead of feeling guilty about it, and she wanted to like her body rather than viewing it as her enemy. She had a friend who was skinny, who ate a lot of anything she wanted and stayed thin. Her friend was always saying, "I can eat anything I want and never gain an ounce." This was true! Rachel was always dieting and as she listened to her thoughts and fears about gaining weight, she heard herself thinking, "If I even *look* at a piece of chocolate cake I gain five pounds." When she watched the people around her, she discovered that those who were lean thought of themselves as slim; those who were always afraid of gaining weight talked and thought of themselves as chubby, chunky, or fat.

"I wonder what it would be like to be thin?" she pondered. This was a new thought for her. Previously, she had tried to keep her weight down, to stem the tide of increasing weight gain. She had imaged herself being clumsy, awkward, and uncomfortable with her physical form. But now she started imagining how it would feel to move easily and gracefully. She stood in front of a mirror with her clothes off and examined her body. It wasn't so bad, but, like a sculptor with a critical eye she pictured how her body would look if she sculpted it differently — if her stomach were flat, if her thighs were firm. She tightened her muscles to define their shape and viewed her body as she wanted to be. As she looked in the mirror she began to develop some objectivity — this body was not *her*, it was a body. So even though her body might have some extra fat, that didn't mean that *Rachel* was fat. Rachel had never before realized how pervasive was her dislike for herself and her image of fat — lazy, slothful, sluggish, awkward, unable to coordinate with the rest of the world.

Rachel started to develop a new respect for herself. She eyed this body's bone structure and began to appreciate its strength and balance and proportion. She decided to learn how to get acquainted with her body so she could cooperate with it rather than fighting it. Every time she moved, whether it was bending down to pick up a pencil, walking up a flight of stairs or lifting a sack of flour, she visualized her muscles being toned, her body tight and firm. She found out that her thoughts could command her body. This stimulated her to speed up the process with exercise. She experimented with walking, bicycle riding, swimming, aerobics, and yoga and found that she enjoyed walking and stretching with yoga, so she incorporated these activities into her life. By visualizing her body becoming fit, toned, graceful, and fluid, even a minimal amount of physical exercise produced tremendous results.

As Rachel harmonized with her body, learning to cooperate with its need for movement, she also learned to be attentive to the process of eating. She visualized food nourishing her body, being used efficiently by all the cells and organs, causing them to sing with health and vigor. She imaged the waste products being sloughed off and carried away, drinking lots of water to facilitate the process. She appreciated the food and started giving her full attention to the tastes and textures rather than sneaking food with guilt or grabbing it with rebellion. She practiced listening to herself to choose the foods that her body needed. When Rachel shoved food into her mouth without thinking, she might eat chocolate when her physical system needed iron or choose salty chips when her body needed water.

She became more attentive to her body's needs and requirements. She imaged her body perking up with renewed energy and life, the cells saying, "Thank you for feeding me well." By loving her meals, chewing the food, enjoying its flavor and feel, Rachel found that she was satisfied eating smaller quantities. She learned to more accurately interpret the cravings and signals from her appetite.

This process helped Rachel to become aware of her motivation for eating. At times she ate when she was physically hungry. But often she ate because she was lonely and wanted comfort. Sometimes she found she would turn to the refrigerator when she was angry and suppressing the anger. Rachel also discovered that she used eating as a way to concentrate and slow down. Sometimes she had lots of ideas and didn't know what to do. When she found herself being scattered or indecisive, she would often eat to give her mind a physical focal point.

Rachel began keeping a journal to write down her thoughts when she wanted to eat. She discovered that when she ate out of defiance or anger or to soothe a hurt, the food settled on her body as a fat barrier from the cold, cruel world. Self examination brought her to the realization that she was trying to feed an inner hunger with physical food. No wonder she could eat and eat and still feel unsatisfied! It wasn't so much the taste of chocolate she craved, it was the comfort it represented. Her mother used to give her cake on special occasions, so she associated it with being good and feeling loved. As a child she felt deprived because her friends could eat candy any time they wanted, and she was taught to restrict her intake. So sometimes she would go overboard eating sweets to prove that she could do what she wanted in life. She once had a boyfriend who badgered her to lose weight, and some of her dieting was an attempt to please him. So when she was angry with him, she ate more to defy him. Even after the relationship ended she resorted to food as a statement of self-assertion.

As Rachel learned to discern when she was eating to satisfy an inner need, she began to image different methods of fulfilling those needs. For example, she had always wanted to write a book, but every time she attempted it, her mind was flooded with self-deprecating messages like, "You'll never be able to complete anything you start. You won't amount to much." Instead of approaching the computer, she would walk over to the refrigerator and eat until she felt better. Changing the behavior meant changing the accompanying thoughts. She started thinking loving, positive thoughts about herself. She reminded herself that she had started respecting her body with exercise and gave herself a compliment. She set goals to commit herself to writing for one hour each day. As she acted on these goals, she was less inclined to feed her body for comfort because she was feeding her soul with productive activity.

Visualization helped Rachel to enjoy food and to end her "love-hate" relationship with it. She developed a more healthy respect for her body and its needs. She stopped eating in secret and trying to hide her desire for food, which had only perpetuated the self-hatred and compulsive behavior. She felt better about herself as she learned to appreciate physical movement. She formed an image of being strong and graceful, toning her body so that it could more readily respond to her desires for action. This was a big change from her previous desire to look a certain way so she could receive approval or attention.

Because she used visualization to change her thinking, Rachel no longer had to turn to eating to find satisfaction. She visualized herself communicating with people whom she felt controlled her rather than rebelling by stuffing herself with food. Then she practiced initiating communication, learning that it was she who needed to control her own thoughts. She learned to be more open and direct. As she gave more of herself, being more genuine and sincere, she felt less of a need to protect herself. She imaged a new Rachel who was strong, secure, productive, happy, healthy, in control of herself and her world, and easily able to respond to life's challenges.

Intuitive Research

There is a unique resource available for people who want to learn alternative methods for changing habits like smoking or overeating. An Intuitive Health Analysis offered by the School of Metaphysics describes attitudes and emotions that interfere with an individual's innate wholeness, giving suggestions for correction of any disorder. Some people who request health analyses ask how they can lose weight or quit smoking.

For example, a young man who gained a lot of unwanted weight in a short period of time asked, "Any suggestions for weight loss?" His Intuitive Health Analysis gave the following counsel:

> *Would suggest to this one to formulate an image of the Self as an eternal being, to decide how this one wants to exist beyond the physical form within a physical form, using a physical form; however, for the consciousness to be above and beyond that. It is in this one living for more than physical reasons, in this one having spiritual purposes, that there will be a more fluid movement of energy within the physical form itself." (05-04-2004-LJC-4)*

It's interesting to note that he was given advice to pay less attention to the body itself and more attention to the purpose for even having a body. This is much different from being attached to how the body looks, which is what most people do who are concerned about weight loss.

A young woman also asked about her weight in a health analysis. She said, "Why have I put on excess weight and how can I reach my ideal body weight?" She learned that she had gained weight to protect herself from feeling too vulnerable:

> We see that part of this is a protection ... against this one's self. We see that this one has experienced [an] emotional opening, and therefore is experiencing a sense of vulnerability. Would suggest to this one to embrace it as an infant embraces each situation in their existence. Would suggest this would aid this one in being able to cultivate the wonder and curiosity that is present within this one. (06-24-2004-SMB-1)

Another young woman was trying to quit smoking. She felt as if she needed to smoke, and wanted to understand how to be released from this compulsion. She asked in her health analysis, "Any suggestions on releasing the emotional attachment to smoking?" Her intuitive report said:

> To recognize the benefit of the action. And in doing so, to begin to image, create that which will fulfill the intent of the action. To, in essence, to create a new action that will fulfill the same purpose. (01-24-2004-BGC-2)

This counsel has universal applications. When we are attached to a habit, even if we know it is not good for us, there is still some kind of benefit we derive from it. Whether it is feeling loved when we eat, thinking we are more mature when we smoke, being protected from hurt and vulnerability by holding onto excess weight, there is an intent motivating the habit-action. By identifying the thought-desire, we can then create a more productive action to fulfill it.

Mind over Matter

If you wonder how it is possible to use mental imaging to change the dense physical matter of your body, consider the idea that the nature of the physical world is change. The molecules which make up the physical body are a whirling bundle of activity. They are fluid, changeable, and responsive to your mental direction. Have you ever thought about what happened to your five-year-old body? Did it disappear? If not, where is it now? The answer is this: your five-year-old body has changed. The body you use now has the same genetic makeup it had when you were born. It still has two hands, two feet, face, trunk, and so forth. But it is a structure that has evolved from the one you inhabited when you were five years old. Your body evolved as you evolved. As you imaged yourself being six years old, your body changed. Similarly, as you image yourself being lithe, lean, fit, and toned, your body will follow suit.

If this still seems unreal, think about a time when you were facing an important project and were so excited about it you didn't want to sleep. Even though you may have been accustomed to a particular bedtime, your body stayed in motion because your mind was still active. Probably you remained energized until you had accomplished your goal (completed the important meeting, went on the anticipated date) and then, when it was over, you were refreshed and ready for restful sleep. How did this happen? Your mental alertness, the desire to complete the project and your thoughts on the expected event, caused your metabolism to remain active and your body stayed energized. The learning you gained from accomplishing your goal actually fed your inner mind with energy. (To learn more about how the chakras return energy to the mind, read Dr. Barbara Condron's book *Kundalini Rising*.)

Or think about a time when you were depressed. You had no goals. You had a list of things to do but no motivation to do any of them because everything seemed purposeless. There was nothing in your life to which you could look forward. Maybe you dreaded going to work in the morning. When your alarm rang, you felt exhausted even though you slept well over eight hours. All your attention was on avoiding your day. You did not want to face the events, so your body slowed down in response, ready for sleep. The sleep was not needed for rest; it was an escape from life.

These are two examples of how your body can respond to the thoughts you create. If you review your life, you will probably recognize when you have commanded your body to follow your mental direction. Believe in your power to create with thought, and you will change your life for the better. Creative imaging can be used to change any habits you desire. Whether it is smoking, eating, gum chewing, nail biting, the process is the same. To change addictive behaviors you must draw out and face the images that initiated the behavior in the first place. If you have difficulty with this, counseling may be beneficial to aid you to become more Self aware.

The causal thought is the image you created when you first started practicing the addictive behavior and which you have repeated since then. Once you identify this causal thought and its associated images, you are on your way to creating new, productive, healthy images. Practice thinking in these new ways, follow by making healthy choices, and you have productive change.

Changing Your Moods

These same principles work for changing emotional habits as well. Have you ever felt depressed or angry and didn't know how to get out of it? I have known people who have trouble being motivated or feel as if they have lost the inspiration to create. They say things like, "I don't know why I don't want to do that.

I just don't feel motivated." Or, "I don't feel like I can do that. I just feel helpless." "I'm not very excited about that." When you don't feel like you can do something, it is very difficult to cause change. All you can do is wait for the feeling to change. This could take a few minutes, days, or years.

Through intuitive research, the School of Metaphysics has discovered that thought patterns create emotional responses and reactions. Learning to identify the thought patterns that cause emotional states brings self awareness. Feelings (whether positive or negative) can help us become aware of something that needs our attention.

For example, you might be angry because you think that you have failed at accomplishing a goal. Or you become depressed when you lose sight of your purpose for a project you've initiated. Once you have identified these causal thoughts, then the key to causing change is to change the thoughts that produce these feelings. You see how you need to adjust or give more or be more creative to accomplish your goal, you re-awaken or formulate a new purpose for the project.

> Once you have identified the causal thoughts, the key to causing change is to change the thoughts that produce the feelings

When I described this process to a student of mine, he said that he couldn't just change his thoughts. After asking more questions, I discovered that he thought that "changing his thoughts" meant saying new words while holding the same picture in mind. When I asked him to describe in picture form how he felt, he said it was like being at the bottom of a hole. Everything around him was dark, he couldn't breathe and couldn't get out. That's what it felt like to him when he was depressed.

He knew that he fell into the hole when he felt like someone was criticizing him. His own judgements are very harsh. When he thought that he had made a mistake or disappointed someone else, he just wanted to hide. Thus, he found himself at the bottom of the dark hole. Upon discovering this mental image, he could then form a new image to replace it.

At one time he had had visions of the kind of society he wanted to live in, a world in which people were open with each other, were creative, deep thinkers, with spiritual consciousness. He had gotten disappointed over and over when he found that people laughed at these ideas. So he had retreated into a kind of shell, keeping his ideas to himself. Over time, he lost sight of this vision.

Once he re-awakened this image of an ideal future, he gave it much more attention, lovingly envisioning it each day. He got out some markers and pens and drew a picture of his ideal world. He talked about it, tentatively at first, and then with more confidence and security as he practiced being the kind of person he imagined in his ideal future world. It gave him something to which he could look forward. He had a purpose for climbing out of the hole — to walk into this bright scenario and bring other people with him. In a short time, his feelings of depression and hopelessness changed to those of hope and optimism.

> We have the power to choose
> what to embrace in our
> consciousness

The power of creative imagery helped him to move from feeling lost and stuck to knowing his value and power. It begins with the thoughts.

The Creative Mind

Within each one of us there lies an incredible potential to create, to learn and change and grow. Why is it, then, that so few people really realize their great potential? Why are there so few known geniuses like Michelangelo or Leonardo da Vinci or Einstein? Many people have learned to accept limitations, often learned in childhood. Because our thoughts are so powerful, we can create fear and limitation as well as hope, creativity, and love. We have the power to choose what to embrace in our consciousness.

The School of Metaphysics has developed a method of intuitive research, drawing upon the subconscious mind to access universal wisdom. This is given in intuitive reports. A Creative Mind report aids a person to bring forth his or her genius potential. The following excerpt from a Creative Mind intuitive report shows how one can imagine fear into existence and, by the same process, imagine creativity and productivity.

How can this one overcome the fear, therefore become more creative and productive?

This one will need to admit that the fear has been Self-created. *That it does not exist independent of this one. By taking ownership of the creation of the fear, this one then can become more reasonable in the approach toward the creativity itself. Since it does not make sense to this one to want to be fearful, the ownership will cause the fear to be seen in a different light, and therefore, this one will be able to become powerful rather than weak in the face of the idea that she herself created. This is all.*

This one says, "How can I use my creativity to help heal myself and others?"

There is the capacity to use creative energy toward that which would make something whole, which is the essence of healing. In order for this to transpire there must be the willingness to envision the whole and to cause the energies to move toward that kind of arrangement. This is universally true. Therefore, in regards to this one, there would need to be the capacity cultivated to envision that which is complete and is sustaining and is in harmony. This one holds within the mind a line of attachment to disharmony. This is part of the construction of fear that has already been described, therefore, again it will necessitate this one admitting that the fear is the discord of her own making. ... In order for healing to occur within this one these matters will need to be addressed.

You will also relate that which will foster a movement within the energy exchange between the ethereal and the material for the cultivation of genius.

This one has a great potential to develop a kind of rapport and a kind of connected movement within the consciousness that would produce a great capacity for creation. There are many experiences which this one has had which include the inner workings of the intuitive abilities and skills and we see that there is acquaintance with these. There needs to be developed a respect for them and therefore a respect for the Self in that manner as being an intuitive being. There also needs to be a corresponding respect developed in the reasoning capacities for this one has the ability for reasoning and the potential to unite the two within the creative endeavors this one might pursue.

It is this one's self-imposed limitations that have created a barrier *that includes ideas, not so much of fear, although this one is the main distraction that this one allows, but more so than that, is the idea that there is drudgery in the command of the Self and mind, that it is hard work, that it is beyond her, that she does not want to put out the effort for it, that it may be a lost cause or not producing what this one hopes.*

This one has great difficulty in being able to respond to disappointment. Therefore, this one constructs ways of thinking to avoid it. What has been described is the sequence of events within this one's thinking that is this kind of protective device. The protective device merely causes this one to shut off the creativity and the potential that is hers. That which this one fears exists within the world that this one lives in. It does not exist within the creative potential that is hers. This one will only know this as this one becomes free of the limitations and is willing to move into the realms of discovery and inspiration that are available to her. This is all.

Very well, relax. (08-12-2000-BGC-1)

This intuitive report shows how powerful visualization can be. As this individual has created fear in her own mind, she can also create inspiration and discovery. It is in her power to choose to fulfill her creative potential and live her personal best.

Reaching for Something Greater Than Yourself

The key to changing self indulgent habits lies in having something greater than yourself to move you forward. I decided to quit smoking when I admitted that I was being a hypocrite with my students. My desire to be a good example motivated me to think beyond my attachment to cigarettes.

The key to changing self indulgent habits lies in having something greater than yourself to move you forward

My student lifted himself out of depression when he realized that other people were counting on him to be a leader. He gave himself to a greater vision which helped him to put into proper perspective the disappointment and self criticism that had previously stimulated him to get stuck.

There are universal laws that guide us to create a fulfilled and wholesome existence. These universal principles work for anyone, anywhere, at any time. Knowing these universal laws gives us security because we can draw upon them in any endeavor in life. One of these universal laws is called the Law of Abundance. It states that when you aid others to abundance, you will have abundance yourself.

What is abundance? Having more than enough, an everflowing and overflowing plenty. This can be material wealth or more ephemeral qualities of love, creativity, knowledge, or wisdom. Simply stated, when we are helping other people to grow, we grow ourselves. If we are feeling lost or stuck or helpless or hopeless, reaching out to aid others brings us love, contentment, self value, and greater recognition of the inner wealth we possess.

This is why imaging something greater than ourselves produces change. As we reach to fulfill something greater, we become greater. This helps us to heal whatever is troubling us or whatever is out of harmony in our environment. The Creative Mind report just quoted describes this:

> There is the capacity to use creative energy toward that which would make something whole, which is the essence of healing. In order for this to transpire there must be the willingness to envision the whole and to cause the energies to move toward that kind of arrangement. This is universally true. Therefore, in regards to this one, there would need to be the capacity cultivated to envision that which is complete and is sustaining and is in harmony.

Another Creative Mind intuitive report gives a very clear picture of what happens within us when we reach to embrace humanity or spirituality to motivate us. The person receiving the intuitive report often held onto familiar habit patterns when feeling insecure. She asked,

"How can I begin movement as far as breaking the pattern that seems to be so ingrained in regards to false security?"

*This would be by this one immersing the mind in that which is valuable concerning the greatest reaches to which this one's mind can go. The concept of God is within this one, the concept of humanity is within this one. Would suggest that these concepts become the focal point for this one's thinking. This then will tend to elevate the thinking, the quality of the thinking, which then will enable this one or empower her to be able to have a new point of security to let go of the old, to move forward in the consciousness that is being immersed. It will in effect, of its own volition, and its own nature, by its own nature replace the older more self-consumptive patterns of thinking that have tended to rule and therefore cause this one distracting elements in the thinking. **It is through the constant giving of the self to that which is beyond the self that the change will occur.** It is through the interaction with like-minded individuals that will help keep this one's creativity level elevated and this would be an essential helpful element in the present time period. This is all. (08-14-1999-BGC-5)*

This is a counsel that has universal applications. How simple it can be for us to change habits that seem to control us. All we need is something beyond ourselves to reach for, and then the change seems to occur "of its own volition." We benefit personally and everyone else benefits, too.

Self Image

"We become as we think." You have probably heard this statement, but have you understood its implications?

Several years ago I worked as an assistant editor for a medical publisher in St. Louis. This publisher specialized in plastic surgery textbooks, and I had the opportunity to work on a book about rhinoplasty, plastic surgery of the nose. One of the plastic surgeons who contributed to this book did a study and found that the best patients for plastic surgery were those with a good self image and objectively severe deformities. The worst patients where those with a low self image and relatively minor deformities. The surgeon had discovered that an unfortunate number of patients came to a doctor expecting that he would "fix" their nose and thus "fix" their life. They found, after the surgery, that with a different nose they still had the same difficulties finding a job, creating healthy relationships, being happy and wealthy. The physical change did not cause an inner change. On the contrary, oftentimes they were even more depressed after the surgery because that was their hope which soon gave way to despair.

One chapter in the book that was especially distressing to me was the one on "ethnic" noses. The book illustrated before and after photographs of people who had rhinoplasty in an attempt to makeover their racial or ethnic heritage. In one case, a beautiful woman with a classic "Jewish" nose had hers changed, the rounded edge taken off and replaced with a ski-lift curve. After the surgery she would not leave her house, because she couldn't bear to look in the mirror with the artificial nose facing her. Her difficulty was not the nose, it was her image of herself. She had learned to hate her Jewish heritage because she felt victimized by anti-Semitic remarks. Never having resolved the core issue — her own sense of worthlessness and powerlessness — changing her physical body only heightened the conflict. She had destroyed a part of herself physically to match the self-hatred she already experienced.

Your physical features may be plain or pretty, but beauty does not come from physical causes. We have all seen women who pile on makeup and get their hair done, yet they still appear unattractive. And we have seen people who, with little adornment, radiate an inner beauty that makes them irresistibly appealing. What causes this inner light to shine? What causes this beauty? Philosophers have debated this question through the ages. The poet John Keats, in his "Ode on a Grecian Urn" wrote,

Beauty is truth, truth beauty, — that is all
Ye know on earth, and all ye need to know.

Beauty is an expression of truth and love. We can see this in the word *lovely,* a synonym for *beauty* which means *full of love.* We look at nature's simplicity and think it is beautiful — a sunrise, a rainbow, a delicate flower, a crested wave. We consider someone beautiful when they are giving completely and sincerely. When people radiate love, when they know who they are and are willing to share themselves with others, they are very beautiful. This is why we think a woman who has just given birth is beautiful — she has offered a precious gift to the world. When one has completed a project, is involved in a creative endeavor, or gives a speech and shares clear insights and deep feelings, he or she is beautiful.

Creative Mind Research

A Creative Mind intuitive report describes how an individual uses his or her mind to create. This intuitive research shows how creative genius can flourish and how it can be restricted, entirely dependent on the individual's thinking. The following Creative Mind report illustrates how attachment to appearances can inhibit the flow of creative thinking:

You will have immediately before you the essence of the entity referred to as ***. You will examine this one's consciousness relating the present state of the Creative Mind and relate this.

This one is consumed by this one's attachment to beauty. We see that because of this attachment the creativity within the Self can both flourish and disappear. We see that the moments in which this one does call upon the creative abilities within the Self become like rivers of consciousness for this one. We see that they are small and gently flowing. We see that it is the manifestation at once of this one's concept of ease and beauty and this one's tendency toward distraction and laziness.

We see that much of how this one utilizes the creativity within the Self is dependent upon the environment. It is dependent more upon how this one believes that others see who this one is and what she does rather than how this one envisions the Self and who this one wants to become. *Therefore, the creative mind in this* *one at this time is very much restricted by the perception of the environment. In some cases this is inaccurate where it is really her own limitations placed upon her Self and they actually have nothing to do with the environment. This one will believe that the environment is judging her a certain way when it is merely a figment of her own imagination and is not rooted in others' ideas or concepts or opinions at all. We see that this one needs to realize this in order to free her consciousness to begin to create in ways that this one is capable of.*

We see that there is a secondary way in which this one does restrict the creative abilities and it is through the attachment to the past. This one holds on very firmly to memories, particular memories from the past and replays them again and again and again in her mind. We see that this occupies her energy and her time where more creative endeavors that would be pertinent to the present and the future could be being created. The degree to which this one is held in the past is the degree to which this one is failing to utilize the creative mind that she possesses.

*We see that it is this one's fleeting conception of that which is transcendent that can aid this one greatly, for we see that **the attachment to beauty is actually this one's desire for love, order, and discipline.** Once this one ascends to recognize this, this one will begin to have something more productive to direct the creative abilities toward and to utilize to bring them to fruition. This is all.*

You will also relate that which will foster movement of the energy exchange between the ethereal and the material for the cultivation of genius.

The release of the past by directing this one's consciousness into present-day endeavors that will lead this one forward toward what this one envisions. The development of discipline as has been related is very important to this one. This one rejects or rebels against discipline because there is not the understanding of the nature of order and the amount of control that it brings.

Would you clarify what was meant by the statement, "That which is transcendent."

This is in regards to glimpses of truth that this one experiences. We see that this one has a great capacity for receptivity and can receive into her Self great manifestations of beauty. We see that this can be experienced by this one when experiencing a piece of music or art or interaction with children. We see that this one tends to link them to what this one is physically experiencing rather than to pursue the consummate joy within the consciousness that it produces within her.

Is this all?

This is all.

Very well, relax. (08-09-1997-BGC-02)

Like the woman who received this intuitive report, some people are more concerned with what they imagine other people think about them than they are about their own self concept. These people easily become tired because it consumes a huge amount of energy to second-guess other people, always thinking about what they think other people are thinking of them.

People who deny their worth and focus on their faults appear old and unattractive. They take from their environment, trying to get attention from other people rather than giving to them to enrich their lives. They become defensive, depressed, and sullen. Their self-centeredness drains other people. They can be demanding. The fear of being left alone becomes a self-fulfilling prophecy.

How we envision ourselves is a powerful determinant of how we experience our lives. When we focus on our talents, skills, and wisdom, giving freely and generously, we develop self value. We become attractive and beautiful. We improve our world because anywhere we go we bring light. We are happy, because we know that our presence makes a positive difference. We touch people with love.

> How we envision ourselves determines how we experience our lives

You can practice this with a simple affirmation: "I make the world a better place because of my presence." Say this out loud ten times a day. Picture yourself improving your environment. Then, look for ways to make a positive difference. Start with simple physical things, like picking up a piece of trash you see lying on the ground and throwing it away. Smile at each person you meet. Be attentive to other people and their needs. If you are on a bus, offer your seat to someone else. Hold the door for another person as they walk into a store. Say "hello" to strangers and ask them how they are doing. You will find that no one is really a stranger. We are all human beings and you can brighten another person's day by showing genuine interest in them. This will help you to know that you are valuable and worthwhile.

Self Image Inventory

To discover how you think of yourself, you can make a Self Image Inventory. On a sheet of paper, write your full name, then write "I am" and finish the sentence with a word or phrase that describes you. Don't stop to think, let your mind go, and write the first thought that comes to mind. You may have a physical description, such as "I am tall," "I am skinny," "I am white"; you may have a phrase that describes your attitude, like, "I am lonely," "I am honest." You may have a statement that describe your skills and abilities: "I am creative," "I am a good writer," etc. Now, write "I am" again, completing with another descriptive phrase. Do this several times until you have a clear image of how you identify yourself.

Once you have finished your list, look it over and determine which qualities and attributes are productive. These are the talents that you have available to use to create your Ideal Self. Then look at the unproductive or negative items on the list. Decide how you want to change those handicaps. For example, if you put "I am depressed," you could change that to "I am energetic with goals that inspire me," or something to that effect. This Self Image Inventory will help you to discover how you think of yourself and will provide a direction for you to create desirable changes.

The next step is to practice being who you want to be. Once you have decided what you want to change, visualize or image the Ideal Self you want to become. For many people, this is the most difficult aspect of visualization. They can easily create images of physical objects or circumstances, but their self image is so ingrained it is hard for them to imagine something different. If this is true for you, look for role models. You may want to research people whom you admire. Read autobiographies to learn how they think, what motivates them, how they have accomplished what they have in their life. If the person is alive, see if you can interview them to ask questions about how they have become the person they are. Draw a picture of your Ideal Self.

Then use your imagination to act as if you are that person. Ask yourself, "What if I were that person? How would I think about this? How would I respond? What would I do?" This will transport you out of your imagined limitation and you will transcend into a new, creative reality. You may even want to choose several people who demonstrate the qualities you want to build and combine these people into a composite role model.

For example, when I first started practicing metaphysics I was very shy. I had been shy ever since I was a child and it was a strongly embedded thought-form image. All my life people had told me I was shy, my teachers in school commented on it, my parents praised me for being quiet, and I identified strongly with this idea. On a number of occasions I forced myself to attend parties and other social gatherings where there would be a crowd of people, but I was very uncomfortable and awkward. I thought of myself as a social misfit. Friends often urged me to go out more, but I insisted that I preferred staying home with a book. Changing this shyness was not really something I *wanted* to change, it was something I thought I *should* change.

Finally, I started to think that this shyness had disadvantages. As I learned more about metaphysics I wanted to share my discoveries with other people, and it was a handicap to be so afraid of people. At first, I didn't have a positive desire image, but I did have motivation — I was tired of being uncomfortable around people. I had also been told from a Past Life Profile that it was selfish of me to hold myself back from communicating because there were other people around me who wanted to know the things I knew. I didn't much like the idea I was selfish! Still, I had so strongly identified with being shy it was hard for me to imagine being anything else.

I had a couple of friends who were outgoing, gregarious, funny, talkative people. Although I envied their ability to befriend anyone, I would think to myself, "I'm just not like that." So I used this thought to my advantage. I observed my outgoing friends Margie and Jennifer, to see what they did, how they interacted, how they put other people at ease. Then when I went to a lecture or to a party or some other event where there were a lot of unfamiliar people, I would pretend to be Margie or Jennifer. I'd act as if I were they. It was amazing how easy it was to find myself laughing, smiling, talking, and initiating conversations with strangers.

In the beginning, I didn't imagine *myself* being like that, but I did imagine what they would be like in a social setting. I imagined that they would very easily go up to anyone whether they knew them or not, they would be interested in the other person, ask them questions, initiate conversation. When I was in that environment I would pretend I was one of them. I visualized what they would do, and imagined how they would think. Then I followed through with the actual practice. Gradually, I found that I was becoming like Margie and Jennifer. I was becoming friendly, outgoing, talkative. It helped me to be much more flexible with my ego, practicing qualities I didn't previously image myself having.

Productive Pretending

This method of "acting as if" will get you started practicing any productive quality you desire. You can "act as if" you are confident while you are building a belief in yourself; you can "act as if" you are a leader while you are learning to develop leadership skills; you can "act as if" you are a good singer while you are educating yourself on the use of your voice. It is important that in this process you *visualize* the desired quality and action, *image* yourself being the way you desire to be as you practice the new behavior. If you habitually think the old way, the physical activity will not produce the results you desire. You will be forcing yourself into activity (or you'll put off practicing anything) rather than causing change by practicing a new image.

For example, there was a young man named Lou whose father was a successful business owner. When Lou graduated from business college, he was hired as the manager of a department in his father's business. Lou was intelligent, capable, and bright and his father believed he could use this position to gain the experience to become an excellent leader.

Lou, however, was very insecure. He imaged himself as a child always seeking his father's approval. He was convinced that he was hired for the job only because he was the boss's son — it never occurred to him that he had any worthwhile qualifications. Because he wanted to please his father, Lou accepted the job but was constantly defensive, on guard in case anyone should ridicule him for being the boss's spoiled son. He imitated other department managers by giving orders, but in his mind and in his imagination he was still a kid. As a result, his fear came to pass. He was faced with rebellious employees who asked, "Why should we listen to you? Just because your old man got you this job?"

Lou had difficulty because he pretended to be a leader by imitating behavior without imagining how those managers thought or made decisions. He never asked any questions to learn how they had achieved the responsibility and authority they had. Pretending alone is imitating behavior without changing the way of thinking. Lou imaged himself as inadequate, inferior, inexperienced, and begging for approval. He was bossy without any foundation based on experience or purposeful thinking.

Had he used creative imagery, Lou could have imagined himself making wise judgments. When difficult situations arose with the employees, Lou could have imagined the outcome of various choices on his part and could have discussed these options with his supervisor. In this way, he would have gained experience in learning how to think as a manager, how to make judgments that would keep everyone's best interest in mind. Then he could have acted on these choices with the intent of gaining further understanding and experience. By turning to his supervisor for guidance and feedback rather than approval, Lou would have grown into a true understanding of authority built on his own knowledge and experience. Lou needed to image himself being an adult, thinking as a leader, and drawing upon his own inner resources to cause a change inwardly and outwardly.

Imitation and Individuality

I have known people who resist the idea of using other people as role models. They say, "I am my own person. There is no one else who has what I want or who is the kind of person I want to be." These are the same people who have difficulty changing. They have a fixed image of themselves that stays much the same.

Using other people as a stimulus for growth is one of the marks of a mental creator. We can purposefully look to other people in our environment to identify qualities that we want to build within ourselves. By imitating people who have already developed what we have yet to build, we are imagining ourselves becoming greater than we are at present.

There was a woman who received a Creative Mind report describing this process. She thought she should be able to cause change and use creativity without needing an outer stimulus. The report showed her that it was actually productive for her to allow her ego to motivate her. She just needed to choose role models whose standards and accomplishments were higher than her own in order to produce growth within herself.

You will examine this one's consciousness relating the present state of Creative Mind for this one.

We see that this one does have a capacity for creating which is linked to the experience of the environment. We see this one is quite capable of reproducing what this one sees or hears or experiences with the senses and we see that this one is also capable of doing more than reproducing a replica of the original. This one places her own individuality, her own stamp, her own uniqueness upon what this one creates.

We see the degree, however, to which this one is dependent upon the environment to supply this one with stimulus is the degree to which this one limits the exercising of her own creative skills. We see that the imagination is employed in what this one creates, for it is the imagination that makes it somewhat different than what this one is imitating.

We see that it would be of benefit in regards to using this tendency for this one to begin to raise the standards of whom it is this one is imitating. This would be one way to cause her to stretch beyond the boundaries that she has set for herself, to transcending limitations that she has in exercising her creative skills. We see that by choosing those who are beyond what she believes her capacity to be would supply this one with the motivation, with the pattern, with the appropriate stimulus to utilize her creativity to a greater extent.

Once this is done, then there could be the delving into the nature of creation itself, the actual mechanics of what is occurring when this one is creating. And we see that this would be an entirely new realm of discovery for this one. We see however at the present time period that which has been stated would be of the greatest benefit to this one in being able to draw upon the understandings that this one does possess, to draw upon the experiences in the present lifetime that have brought this one some deepening of awareness, and to put them to use in ways that astound herself. This is all.

You will also relate that which will foster a movement in the energy exchange between the ethereal and the material for the cultivation of genius.

We see that in some ways this would be enacted by this one heightening her standards. By this one choosing individuals who, for instance, exhibit genius in areas that this one wants to explore and develop. We see that by becoming more discriminative in regards to her stimuli, this one would find that likewise, her creative skills would become far more discriminative. And this one would become acutely aware of the steps that it requires to foster that type of genius merely through imitating the work of those whom this one admires. This in itself would elevate this one's awareness and consciousness of creativity and in that way, begin to introduce this one to spiritual concepts that do manifest themselves in physical means.

It is a simple way to cause a great upheaval in this one's capacity for creation. For in many ways, this one is functioning far below what this one is capable of. It need not be known that this one is using the suggestions that have been given. In fact, it would be better if it is not within the people that are around this one, because in the manifestation of what this one will do with the ideas given, the kind of feedback that this one will receive will be quite astounding to her as well as the creation itself. This is all.

This one says, "How can I learn to draw from within more and the outer less?"

*In the way that has been described. This one is not ready to make the transition that she is asking about, because it is not in a linear fashion as this one thinks of it. **We see that by elevating this one's standards, by cooperating with the natural action of her own ego** to be stimulated and motivated by what is around herself, by introducing* *the element of choosing what, who, and when this one will be stimulated, **this will give this one the experience that will prepare her to be more cognizant of what is within her, rather than dependent upon what is without her.***

Any further suggestions for this entity's soul growth and spiritual development?

*In order for this one to progress in that regard, **this one will need to extend beyond the limits that she has set for herself,** and this has been addressed in what has been given.* (08-09-1997-BGC-8)

Extending Beyond Limits

Any time we cause change, we encounter some resistance. This is normal, because it requires energy to move in new directions. Sometimes it is apparent that the resistance comes from within the self. Other times, we may not even know it's there until we encounter other people who mirror our own limitations.

The resistance, as described in the previous Creative Mind report, is that we set limits as we form our sense of self. Changing means going beyond those limits. When we have a clear image of the Self we are aspiring to become, the resistance can actually be energizing. It can produce a kind of inner thrill or enthusiasm. When we view change as eliminating something unwanted, when we think that change means there is something wrong with us, it is very difficult to be motivated.

The key to causing productive change is to appreciate where we have come from and to imagine a future that is brighter, more expansive, or greater in some way. We can build upon what we have already done and who we already are rather than getting rid of it.

One woman discovered from her Creative Mind report that she was very attached to the past. When she received the intuitive report she was in her late 50's. She believed she had paid her dues in life, having raised four children and worked as a single mother much of the time. She wanted to do what was comfortable and familiar. In doing so, she was keeping herself from discovering a deeper, more expansive Self. She was limiting herself. It was producing great frustration.

Her intuitive report described the process, which she could clearly see. When she needed to change not just her circumstances but herself, she became afraid and stubborn.

There is a tendency for this one to become settled and to become comfortable with certain situations or people and yet we see the greatest spur for this one's creativity occurs as this one engages new people, new places, and new things. Therefore it is important for this one to become more conscious of this ability, this need, and to begin to respond to it in an intelligent fashion. This one has a great capacity to draw to the self what is needed, and the manifestation of this one's desires comes very quickly once this one becomes unencumbered by the self imposed limitations that have been described.

We see that this one can receive ideas very easily and we see that this one often feels insecure in regards to her ability to generate them. We see that if they are related to something that has already occurred this one is very quick to put pieces of information together and to be able to respond. However when it requires a new point of view or a new frame of reference, this one has difficulty with this. We see that this one does have the ability to use resources and this is the quality that this one possesses that enables this one to compensate for the insecurities here. We see that there could be a greater use of her own resources in this one building the imagination as this one would attend to what has been given.

We see that this one at times resists expansiveness of the thoughts and we see in doing so this one relegates the self to doing the same thing again and again. *We see that it causes resistance and it causes a kind of stubbornness in this one that does retard this one's growth and learning, because it does limit greatly the imagination. We see that it would be helpful for this one to recognize that when she is being stubborn that there is a need for the imagination to be employed, for this one to see things in new and different and exciting ways and to begin to cause this to occur purposefully. (05-10-2003-BGC-01)*

She learned from this intuitive report that she needed to use imagination to go beyond previous limitations, to envision herself in new ways. It also counseled her to recognize that when she was stuck in the past her creative mind plummeted, and she became somewhat dull minded. This was amazing to her; she had attributed the fogginess of mind to menopause. She hadn't considered that her thought processes were creating it. Receiving this knowledge fueled her desire to create a new self image. She started forming new ideas about herself as a mother, a grandmother, a teacher, and most important to her, being a healing presence to other people.

The key to causing productive change
is to appreciate
where we have come from
and to imagine a future that is brighter,
more expansive, or greater

Another person who received a Creative Mind report found out that the greatest impediment to him being fully creative was the way he viewed himself. The report described him as having a physical self image. He needed to create a new identity, to change his sense of importance. He strongly identified with the experiences he had had, from being a peace activist to a fabric designer to a geologist. He was so attached to past experience that oftentimes in the present moment he was distant and aloof, missing out on fulfilling relationships and new learning.

The report suggested that he needed to value the wisdom gained from experience more so than the experience itself. He knew what it was talking about. At the time he was a graduate student at a university, concerned about grades and intellectual knowledge. He had returned to school when he was 40-something years old. He had an image of himself as intelligent, hardworking, and studious. While these qualities were admirable, his attachment to his physical accomplishments and image kept him from becoming more soul centered.

We see that there is still a struggle within this one between that which is material and that which is spiritual, that which is temporary and that which is permanent. We see that as long as there is this shifting, from one to the other, there will not be the peace that this one desires, nor will there be the fruition or flourishing of this one's creative capacities. **We see that as this one would become centered in a more transcendent ideal of the Self, and of being, then there could be a point of focus as well as origin for this one's creative endeavors.** *We see that often this origin is missing and this is what then sets into motion what has been described.*

We see that there is a need for this one to become much more committed to the development of being or consciousness. In doing so, there would be the expression *of energies from that new point of reference which would empower this one to be able to direct the senses, to direct the physical experiences through a much more expanded perception of Self and of life. **It will require a transformation of this one's sense of identity, a release of the identity being physically defined, and an embracing of the identity of what has existed, what does exist, and what will exist through eternity.** This is all.*

This one asks, "What is meant by the origin of the creative abilities?"

This would be defined as spirit.

You will also relate that which will foster a movement in the energy exchange between the ethereal and the material for the cultivation of genius.

This would be in what has been given in terms, primarily, of the transformation of the sense of identity within this one. We see that the untangling of the Self from the physical accouterments and entrapments of the physical attention would greatly free this one to be able to enter into the realms that this one has in an intellectual manner entertained.

We see that there is much that this one has brought to the Self in terms of experience. Yet, the accompanying wisdom that is potentially there for this one has not been tapped due to the enslaving of the creative mind in matters that are of the physical.

We see that this one is capable of much more in consciousness than what he has been willing to give. We see that it is only through the allowing to fall away of distrust, or insecurity, or hurt, that this one will be free to explore the creative capacities fully.

By redefining this one's center, by becoming unified with it through meditation, through employing this as a focal point for this one's outer consciousness, this one can begin to envision which will be an elevated drawing upon the creative mind that exists within this one. This is all.

This one asks, "Is it through meditation that I can withdraw the distrust and insecurities that exist"?

Meditation will afford this one visions of what is creation. It is the active transformation of the identity that will free the Self from the physical limitations. (08-08-1998-BGC-1)

When using creative mind, it is necessary to have a flexible ego. To be able to learn from anyone, in any situation, is an art. Some people think they can only learn from certain teachers, or only be happy living in a particular city. Or they will only express themselves in the way they feel is comfortable. These attachments keep them from experiencing the great depth and richness of the whole Self.

How you understand yourself determines what you receive into yourself. If you think of yourself in physical terms, then you experience your life in physical, limited ways. If you view yourself as spirit, as the previous Creative Mind report suggests, then you can understand what is permanent and lasting. This brings fulfillment and joy.

> It is an art to learn from anyone, in any situation

Your Image Creates Your Reality

In creating a new self image, listen to the words you use to describe yourself. Do you say, "I'm only a sophomore," "I've only had two years of experience," or do you say, "I'm already a sophomore," "I've had a full two years' experience"? The difference is assessing what you do have. When you take yourself for granted you forget to appreciate how you have come to be who you are today.

Respect where you are in your development, the steps you have taken and the ones you are currently taking to achieve your ideals. You can have what you envision, and this includes the highest ideals you image for yourself. Describe yourself with honest self respect and pride, practice living the ideals you espouse, be the moral character you desire to be, and you will find that others will treat you as you treat yourself.

You can have what you envision, including the highest ideals you image for yourself

The image you hold of yourself will affect your demeanor, your posture, even your physical appearance. I know a woman who illustrates this fact. When she is productive, creative, and happy, she has a beautiful and warm smile that radiates throughout her whole being. She is strikingly attractive in person and in photographs. But when she is selfish or lazy, she becomes very angry. She blames other people or conditions for her plight, and her face registers the hatred she holds for her life at these times. You can hardly tell that she is the same person! Her face becomes hard and ugly. You may know people like this. When a person is depressed, he hunches his shoulders and walks with a slow, shuffling gait. One who is interested in life walks tall with a spring in her step.

You can observe yourself to see how your self image affects your choices and understanding of creation. When you are budgeting your money to make the greatest use of your resources, do you think of yourself as wise by using the physical world to its fullest, or do you think of yourself as "broke"? Do you shop at second-hand stores because you enjoy creating interesting outfits from recycled energy, being imaginative as you respect the environment? Or do you shop at second-hand stores because you think you can't afford anything else? The same action produces different results according to your intention.

When you create a strong, positive, productive self image you emanate pride, integrity, and excellence. If you create a defeated, victimized, "poor" self image, you will show that, too. You will think the world is against you and that you never get your due. In either case, your own thoughts determine the outcome. It is your choice.

This is why two similarly qualified people have different results when they go job hunting. The person with confidence, who stands tall and dresses respectfully, will speak clearly and definitively about his or her strengths and capabilities. The person who doubts himself will probably slouch. He might swallow his words or she might speak in a high-pitched tentative voice. They may even wear wrinkled clothes displaying their self-effacement.

The confident person with a secure self image is much more likely to be offered a job. She will probably reason and respond in the ways needed to do good work. The doubtful person, even though skilled, may be too hesitant to make decisions and act.

Hold your head high, displaying confidence, growth, intelligence and creativity. You will find that people flock to you. You will find that you have the "Midas touch" — everything will turn to gold in your hands. You will create your fondest dreams and greatest aspirations because you are identifying with the creative intelligence that is the *real you*.

Exploring
Your Talents

Did you ever watch a dancer on television, admiring their grace, poise and fluidity, and think to yourself, "What would I give to dance like that!" Or perhaps you envied a great musician, or sportscaster, or basketball player. Did you think, "I'll do it!" or did you breathe a sigh and say, "I could never do that. I'm such a klutz."

Either way, you are activating the formative power of your mind. Henry Ford said, "Think you can, think you can't. Either way you're right!" When you form an image in your mind, all the forces of the universe follow your command. You are the director of your life. Your thoughts determine the quality of your existence, so doesn't it make sense to image what you want?

Anyone who is successful will tell you that they create a strong thought-form image of how they want to be and then practice, practice, practice. Norman Vincent Peale, author of the famous book *The Power of Positive Thinking*, was a minister who visualized how he wanted to speak and how he wanted to reach his congregation. He described himself as a retiring kind of person, quiet and soft-spoken, so it required a directed use of creative imagination for him to become charismatic. He practiced over and over until his voice sounded like the one he'd imagined.

Arnold Schwarzenegger was at one time a world champion body builder. He has said that the most important element of shaping the body is forming a detailed image in the mind. He visualizes the muscles becoming the size and shape he desires as he "pumps iron" and creates a clear mental image of strength and endurance as he exercises. His life is a great example of the power of visualization; he envisioned himself excelling in many different areas of life. Learning to speak clear English, becoming an actor, playing different roles in motion pictures, moving into the realm of politics to become governor of the state of California, were all manifestations of his mental images.

How can visualization help you bring forth your talent? Dancers watch other dancers, musicians listen to performances of music over and over to hear every nuance of the piece they will be playing. They include in their mental imagery what the music will sound like as well as how they will manipulate the instrument. Basketball, baseball, and football players visualize themselves performing on the field. First they create a strong mental image, and next they practice the physical activity. With the combination of mental imagery and physical practice, these people accelerate their progress.

When you visualize yourself performing as you desire, whether on stage, the sports field, or in the corporate boardroom, you are prepared. This mental preparation is just as important as the physical preparations you make. By visualizing yourself being as you desire, you will perfect *in your mind* the steps you need to take, so that you actually need less physical practice time. This causes you to become much more efficient and directed in your life.

It All Starts in Your Mind

One of the benefits of this mental imagery is that it helps to alleviate nervousness. Anyone who desires to excel experiences "butterflies in the stomach" prior to an important performance. Some people interpret this as anxiety, nervousness, or agitation. Other people interpret it as excitement. This is emotion moving a thought-form from the inner mind outward into manifestation.

Any time a visualized thought form is ready to be birthed into physical existence, there is an accompanying expression of emotion. The purpose of the emotional level of consciousness is to push thoughts out of the inner, subconscious mind into the conscious, physical level of existence. One can either react to this emotion by fighting it, trying to stuff the emotion back and pretending to be "cool" (thus creating even more anxiety which will explode!) or cooperate with it. Cooperating with the emotion means using the enthusiasm, excitement, and thrill of anticipation. You can turn stage fright into a powerful expression of emotional energy.

The following excerpt from a Creative Mind intuitive report describes how emotion can become a distraction rather than a means for facilitating creativity. The young man who received this report is a creative genius, with many different talents that he expresses through music, science, art, parenting, athletics, and storytelling.

When he is focusing on being creative, he is thrilled. When he becomes immersed in the emotions that arise, he gets lost and distracted from the creative process. The solution is for him to realize that emotion is the movement of energy. It can help him manifest his creativity but how he feels about a creation should not dictate what or how he creates:

> *This one has many understandings that are at his command that this one does have the capability of setting into action. We see therefore this one has many different uses for the creative mind in terms of physical*

expressions of it, and we see that this one derives great enjoyment and a sense of thrill from the utilization of these.

We see that this one has difficulty when the emotions become involved in this one's creative endeavors. We see that the degree to which this one moves the focus away from the creation at hand and directs it toward the emotional activity of the creation is the degree to which this one loses sight of the use of the understandings he possesses, the gaining of more understandings to add to the Self to become more complete, and the postponement of the manifestation of what it is that this one desires to produce.

We see that this is true in all aspects of this one's life for we see that it is the emotions which are this one's major distraction at the present time, and we see that this has been a repeated pattern throughout this one's life. We see that there are times that the emotions are used in a conscious manner with awareness, but we see that more often this one expects the emotions to perform whatever function they need to and this one re-acts to the creation in the emotions rather than acting.

We see that this would be changed by this one learning how to gain a perspective deeper than the emotions themselves. We see that this would begin by this one beginning to identify thoughts or concepts in regards to their creative potential rather than the feeling that they have, or bring, or stimulate. Would suggest that this one purposefully define experiences with all the senses. For in this way this one will become more cognizant of direct perception which is what this one desires.

We see that there is some difficulty in regards to the creative process. When this one initiates something new there is an inertia that this one seems to again and again need to overcome. We see that this inertia is the manifestation of the lack of direction being given to what this one would understand as emotions.

Would suggest to this one to begin to consider that the emotions are much more than what this one has given them credit for and they are much less powerful than what this one has given them credit for. They are merely one part of the expression of thought and as this one would begin to develop this kind of perception, there would be a great freedom that this one would have in not only using his creative abilities, but in also manifesting what this one images. This is all.

This Creative Mind report provided valuable insight. It helped this young man understand why he often experienced creative surges and then at other times his creativity seemed to lie fallow. He had not realized how reactive he was. The intuitive report described how much he invested his sense of himself as a creative being in the things he created. The report gave him another place to focus his attention, to create for the purpose of developing qualities in himself. This change helped him to visualize more completely, not only what he wanted to make or do, but who he wanted to become.

You will also relate that which will foster a movement in the energy exchange between the ethereal and the material for the cultivation of genius.

Since the major disruption in the flow of creative energy within this one has to do with his emotional reactions to his creations, it would be of the greatest benefit in pursuing the fruition of creative potential and this one being able to become more cognizant of how this one utilizes the other creative parts of mind. We see that this one has a great capacity for expansive thinking and also to become very specific in identification. We see that the mastery of movement would aid this one greatly in being able to utilize more of the potential, to ease the experience of creation itself and to foster a deriving of deeper meaning to what it is that this one creates.

*We see that this one very much uses the physical manifestation as a gauge for this one's creative ability. This is an inaccurate perception upon this one's part, for **it is what this one has understood, what this one has added to the Self in regards to, not physical things, but in regards to more spiritual things such as compassion, security, courage or autonomy that is the reason why the creative process is even valuable to this one.** It is in these four areas where this one can grow the most. This is all. (08-09-1997-BGC-1)*

It is important in your mental practice time to create a clearly defined ideal which involves your whole being. Image not only how you desire to present yourself outwardly, but also image how you want to give of yourself, the qualities you want to exude, how you want to feel, the thoughts you want to be thinking and creating. This complete image of yourself, from the inside out, will cause success. Visualize *who you want to be* as well as visualizing how you want to appear.

This is the difference between using imagination and pretending. Most children are expert pretenders. They will dress up in Mom's shoes or Dad's hat and pretend to be an adult. But they still think like children. When they start learning how to be responsible, making decisions for themselves, thinking in an adult way how to be productive, they begin to become adults.

You can put on the air of being confident while inside you are quaking. You can image how other people will see you and still feel unprepared. Image yourself being how you want to be in your mind and thoughts and intentions. This will cause your outer expression to be that way.

Here is an example. When I was seventeen years old I was changing my thoughts about myself and my personality. As a child, I had imaged myself as a shy wallflower. As an adolescent, I began to associate with a different group of peers and started seeing myself in a new light. I joined the drama society and learned to express myself in different ways, even singing on stage in a children's musical. As I gained some experience being on stage, I had more confidence and became a little more outgoing.

At the time of completing high school, I found out that I was the valedictorian of my

In your mental practice time, create a clearly defined ideal which involves your whole being

class. In earlier years, I would have fully expected that, having always been a straight "A" student. But in the last two years of high school I had become somewhat lazy with my schoolwork. I had learned to take the courses that were easy for me, like English, humanities, and languages, rather than stretching myself to take the ones that required more concentration and discipline, like math and science. I did expand myself to learn in new areas, learning to be more expressive by participating in drama society and helping to write some plays we performed for elementary school kids. But I had purposely forgone taking calculus and physics since that would have meant studying and memorizing formulas. I was surprised that I was still at the top of my class. I attended a large school of 3000 students, so my graduating class had 750 students.

I had mixed feelings about giving a speech at graduation. Having had some experience on stage, I believed I could speak in public. At the same time, I felt a little hypocritical giving a speech when I knew I had not done my best. The old Laurel, studious, intellectual, responsible, shy, "egghead," obedient, was proud of being valedictorian and wanted to please her mother and teachers by giving the speech. The new, more popular Laurel, trying to gain approval from a peer group and striving to develop independence, wanted to say, "Forget this establishment stuff. I won't even give a speech." I became aware of a choice, "Whom do I please?" I was caught in the middle of my own ego battle.

When I gave it more serious thought, I decided that the purpose for giving a valedictory address was to offer what I knew and had learned. There was a higher purpose for giving a speech than pleasing the people in my life whose approval I sought. The purpose was for me to be influential, to perhaps change someone's life by stimulating them to think in a new way. I knew that my experience was not unique. It was too late for me to change the past laziness, but perhaps I could help other students learn from my mistakes. I wanted to offer something that could improve education for students who came after me.

Part of me was intelligent enough to realize that my rebellion was destructive. I was aware that I had gotten away with settling for less than I was capable in the last two years of my high school education. I had learned how to play the game, to choose classes that were easy for me so that I could still excel academically without challenging myself. Deep down, I was disappointed in myself for following the line of least resistance. I was aware that I had missed opportunities to find out just how talented and versatile I could be. I wanted to change this in myself. I thought that I might stimulate other students to change similar attitudes before it was too late for them. Perhaps some teacher might hear me and realize how important their influence could be to other students like me. None of my teachers had ever questioned my behavior, none had ever counseled me about drugs nor had any ever noticed that in the last two years I challenged myself less than the previous years. A part of me wished they had.

I decided to give the speech. I carefully formulated the main ideas I wanted to get across. I had heard other graduation speeches that seemed bland and I wanted this one to really *say* something. I thought about what education meant, what its value was, how it could aid students. I knew that school was for learning and that grades were not always an evaluation of how much had been learned. Some grades were indicators of how well the students were able to please their teachers. I knew this from my own experience. I wanted to let people know that although I was valedictorian I had not lived up to my capabilities, and the grades which evaluated who ranked at the top did not necessarily reflect the quality of education. Admittedly the "rebellious Laurel" had a part in writing the speech. I knew that there would be some shock value in saying that grades weren't everything!

Since I completed my coursework in January and the graduation ceremony was in June, I had six months to write and practice this speech. Every day I read the speech and imagined myself giving it to a huge audience. With a graduating class of that size, the commencement ceremony was held in the football stadium. I drove by the stadium to see what it looked like and where the stage would be. As I imaged myself delivering the speech, I memorized the words and created clear thought-form images of what I wanted to say

I had included in my speech an anecdote about a math teacher who taught imitation rather than reasoning. She would teach trigonometry by giving us sample problems and categorizing the problems. Then we were to copy the way the problem was done with other similar problems. One day, an enterprising student figured out a different way to arrive at the solution. She was eager to share it with the class, but the teacher would not let her. She was afraid that Karen would confuse the class. I remember being infuriated because I wanted to know the new way, and I could tell that the teacher was threatened by this inventive and curious student. Although I did not use the teacher's name in telling the story in the speech, I expected that this story would shock some of the audience, so I practiced telling it and pausing at the right moment for impact to hit home.

All of this practice was done mentally. I never practiced the speech out loud, but I practiced it over and over in my mind. The words became a vehicle for my expression. Rather than woodenly repeating words I'd memorized, I had clear mental images that the words described. I wanted to tell the story so that other people could "see" my images. I had a clear idea of the main point I wanted to make: school is for education. Students and teachers should focus on learning. Grades should be for evaluating a student's individual progress, not how one student compares to another. The more I visualized myself creating this idea and giving it to the audience, the stronger it became, and the more desirous I became of giving it freely.

The day of the graduation, the stadium was filled with close to two thousand people. As I walked up to the microphone, I was filled with the immensity of the place and the desire to give, to change people's lives. I wasn't even nervous! I was excited, thrilled, and could feel the anticipation. Because I had visualized this scene over and over it seemed very familiar, like I had been there before. And I had — in my imagination! When I started speaking, I was a little startled because I had never heard my voice over a microphone before. This added to the ability to use my emotions, for in hearing my voice come over the public address system, it lent a kind of objectivity. I could hear myself as if it were another person speaking.

One of the benefits of visualizing and practicing this speech was the freedom it gave me to place all of my attention on giving to the audience. I had no attention on what they were thinking of me, how I appeared or sounded or what I looked like, whether I would "mess up." I simply gave what I wanted to give, and offered it freely. It was surprisingly easy.

The Mind-Body Connection

Visualization can work for anyone in any endeavor. Musicians use it -- they image themselves artfully playing the keys or plucking the strings, then practice the notes of a piece over and over. When the time comes for the performance, they need not give any attention to the mechanics of the instrument. Their attention is free to allow the energy to move through them, playing the music "by heart."

When you visualize a new activity, it is important to believe in yourself. If you have always thought that you were not athletic, you might find yourself visualizing throwing a ball into a basketball hoop and having it bounce off the rim. Or throwing a bowling ball into the gutter, or missing the ball every time you come up to bat. In these cases, you are also using visualization! If you have not experienced success at the task you are attempting, watch those who are successful so that you can receive images in your brain of effective shooting, batting, or whatever you want to do. Then image yourself in the place of that person who is successful. Image yourself over and over performing the action with grace, speed, expertise, or the qualities you desire. You'll find that in your physical practice, your actions will be directed by these productive, positive thoughts.

Using visualization, you will find that you can be good at a task from the beginning. You don't have to be mediocre just because you are a beginner. When you have practiced in your mind before you ever set your hand to a task, it will be familiar and easy for you to accomplish.

I know a woman who has been studying the art of karate for several years. When she practices *katas* which are a series of movements, she concentrates on her form, on using her mental and physical energy most efficiently, on the precision and grace and scientific principles with which her body functions. As she repeatedly practices these dance-like motions, she gives full attention to what she is doing. When she cannot go to the *dojo*, she practices in her mind. Riding a bus, waiting for a friend, in her spare moments, she moves through these motions in her mind. When called upon to act in self defense, or in sparring with a karate partner, she moves swiftly, surely, and exactly. Through the use of mental imagery and physical practice, she is becoming a karate expert.

Visualization does not take the place of physical practice and preparation. You cannot give an effective speech by visualizing yourself on a stage if you have not written or prepared or researched a speech to give! This is pretense. When you pretend without any intention to change, you actually increase your anxiety because you are always afraid of being found out. You cannot play excellent music by picking up an instrument without learning the notes, unless you are going to improvise. Even then, you need to develop skill learning how the instrument functions through practice.

The mental imagery directs your body's actions. When you put your mind into directive action, you can be purposeful with your self expression. Many adults have little awareness of the importance of using the mind to direct the body. Sometimes a physical injury forces you to give attention to this relationship. I knew a man named Leonard who suffered severe nerve damage in a motorcycle accident. As a result, his motor functions were impaired and he was temporarily paralyzed. Leonard was a very active person who hated being handicapped. He had goals: he wanted to teach children, to build a house, to educate people about saving the environment from pollution. He was also very proud and didn't like other people pitying him. He was highly motivated and gave great attention to the physical therapy he received. For several hours a day, Leonard exercised in a whirlpool, regaining some muscle tone and re-learning how to cause his muscles to move.

The most important part of Leonard's therapy was a daily visualization in which he imaged himself walking, moving freely and easily. Leonard discovered that when he was angry about being paralyzed it was easier to cause some motion in his legs, because his *desire to move* was so strong! He would think "I *will* walk! No one's going to stop me!" He would think about what he wanted to accomplish with his life and the need to have a fully functioning body for these purposes. This strong desire-thought-image propelled energy through his body. When he was tired, or when he got distracted from his goals, Leonard would think, "Why bother? I have so far to go... what's the use?" At those times, Leonard's muscles simply didn't respond. After awhile, Leonard began to see that his *thoughts* were the most important factor in pulling energy into his body and causing it to move. This realization spurred his excitement and with practice and time, he learned to walk again.

The Law of Believing and Knowing

Visualization activates a universal law known as the Law of Believing and Knowing. Universal laws govern the mental world. All existence has structure, order, and form. This is true in the realm of the mind and creativity. Guidelines which describe the order and structure of creation are called universal laws, universal because they apply to anyone, any time, any place.

This is why successful people in all walks of life express similar ideas when they describe the secrets to their success. The same principles work whether applied in business, personal relationships, art, music, science, religion, or communication. When you know about universal law, you will be able to transfer the skill you have in one area of life to any other endeavor. You will become more efficient and expansive. You will discover the secret of creative geniuses like Leonardo da Vinci or Benjamin Franklin who excelled in many different realms.

The Law of Believing and Knowing has been described by notable people throughout history. Nobel prize physicist Arthur H. Compton said it very well,

"Every discovery I ever made, I gambled that the truth was there, and then I acted on it in faith until I could prove its existence."

Believing and knowing encapsulates the essence of creative imagery. A belief is an idea you accept into yourself. It is *real* and all it requires is your physical activity to cause it to become manifest in the physical world. Acting on that belief is faith. The knowing comes about through physical activity, for once your thought is physical you *know* it through experience. To cooperate with the Law of Believing and Knowing, create a complete, detailed thought-form image and act upon it until your desire manifests.

In order to activate visualization in your life, start with learning how to *create* belief. When you want to cause a change, or develop a new skill or talent, listen to your thoughts. Do you expect to be successful? Do you think you can? Or do you doubt that it is possible? Creating belief means forming a clear, complete thought-form image in your mind, incorporating your senses in the creation of the image. You can imagine how you will look and feel, how you will think and express your emotions, how you will act, what you will sound like when you speak or sing. You also imagine how you will transform through the experience.

When the thought form is complete, you have created a belief. It will be easy for you to believe in the reality of your thought when you have formed it in detail. **The difficulty most people have in believing is that they never create a complete image of the desired result.** Because their desire is vague, it remains "wishful thinking" rather than a strong, firm belief that inspires action.

When you use Believing and Knowing the physical activity you put forth is worthwhile. Do you find yourself at times becoming lazy, procrastinating, or having difficulty motivating yourself to act on your desires? It is probably because you do not believe your actions will pay off. You think, "Why bother?"

because you haven't imagined yourself fulfilling your desires. You may even imagine yourself being rejected or disappointed.

You can replace these self-defeating thoughts with clearly defined thought-form images of what you want. When you initiate creation in this way, your time and activity is an investment that will be productive because it is directed toward fulfilling your visualized desire. Believe in the power of your mind. The more you practice imagining first and following through with physical activity, the more you will know how to produce success in your life.

The following story illustrates how visualization can help to conquer doubt. This was sent in by a woman who is a psychologist. She is very skilled with people in a one-on-one setting but had not had much experience in large venues. She got promoted to a directorship of a counseling center. Part of the job involved going to groups to speak about the counseling center and its services. Oftentimes these were large groups, and she was very nervous about having to speak in this kind of setting. She said,

> "I have always been afraid of public speaking. When I got a job that required me to give brief talks about the agency, I would get so nervous before a talk I didn't sleep for several days. All I could imagine was being anxious and becoming tongue-tied. I decided to start teaching some classes to help me overcome my fear.
>
> I worked hard at visualizing myself as confident, competent, interesting, and clear. I got through it and with practice I've gotten better and better at it. I still use that visualization before every class and every talk I give. With more speaking successes behind me, the image has become clearer and more convincing." — C.F.

If you have difficulty believing in yourself, consider this. Some people seem to live a charmed life. They always get the job they want, the man or woman of their dreams, they succeed at their goals. What is the difference between that person and yourself? Do you think that you are unlucky? That perhaps some unknown forces are keeping you from achieving your desires?

The universal laws are universal; therefore, if they work for the fortunate person, they work for you, too. Even if you doubt yourself, you can believe in the efficacy of the laws. The laws work whether you are up or down, excited or depressed, feeling good about yourself or not. Fluctuating emotional states do not alter the immutable activity of the laws. They function equally for people of all ages, races, cultures, and religions. What security! Anyone can rely on the universal laws through all the changes of temporary physical existence. If you are humble enough to recognize that there are powers greater than your individual ego, you can draw upon this power.

To cooperate with the Law of Believing and Knowing, create a complete, detailed thought-form image and act upon it until your desire manifests

Cooperating with universal law does necessitate putting forth effort. Imagine what you want and use will power to make choices that move you in the direction of your desire. Will power means making continuous choices in a determined fashion, acting until you accomplish what you want.

The great thinker Thomas Alva Edison knew that "Genius is 1% inspiration and 99% perspiration." Keep this in mind if you are tempted to give up, thinking you don't have time, are not good enough, or smart enough or resourceful enough to fulfill your fondest dreams. The truth is, you probably stop short because you are insecure with your ability to create. The effort you put forth to manifest your desire prepares your mind with the attitude of worthiness to receive it. Put these universal principles into action and you will build security and confidence in yourself as a creator.

I know a man who is accomplished in many areas. A dentist by profession, he engages his creative mind by imagining inventions to make people's lives easier and more simple. One of his inventions is revolutionizing the dental industry. His story shows how persistence and commitment to an idea enabled him to bring it to fruition. Now dental labs around the world can take advantage of his creative genius:

> "I had a clear vision that I wanted to be a dentist from the age of eight years of age. I am thankful for that vision as it made my life very directed and I cannot imagine having found a profession that I could have enjoyed more.
>
> Along with my love of dentistry has been a strong passion for the dental laboratory field. A dental technician is an individual who is responsible for making the crowns, veneers and bridges that the dentist then places in the patient's mouth. For many years I worked as both the dentist and my own technician, which is extremely rare in the dental profession. It was more like a hobby for me, as I felt there was so much to learn from this side of dentistry that it allowed me to become a better dentist.
>
> As I was working two jobs now, over 100+ hours a week for about two years without a day off, I was no longer a well-rounded individual. I was always looking to make my time more efficient and one of the most common ways for making

veneers was one of the most tedious, inefficient and time-consuming processes encountered in the dental laboratory. It amazed me that technicians around the globe continued using techniques that were plagued with inaccuracy and inefficiency. I saw a real need in the industry that could free up the attention of others. There had to be a better way and I was determined to figure this out.

I began by looking at every system currently available for making veneers and decided what worked and what didn't. What would an ideal system look like? The answers to this and a clearer vision of what this would look like began to take shape.

I pitched my first ideas to one of the largest dental companies in the world, a company out of Germany. My prototypes at that time were rather rudimentary and still had some minor glitches, all of which I felt could be overcome. I met with the president and many of the executives of this company, but after they considered it for 24 hours they told me that what I was attempting to do was theoretically impossible to achieve and showed me the door. I just saw that this was the wrong company. I never wavered in my belief that this system would not only work, but would prove to be far and away the most efficient system yet devised.

With a clear vision of developing such a system, I was amazed at all the people who came into my life over the next couple of years who provided me with the technical solutions that were needed to make the current system known as Uni-Pin a reality. I have extreme gratitude that the Law of Attraction brought so many wonderful people into my life.

This product has since launched an entire company with numerous products that adheres to the vision of improving the efficiency of technicians around the globe." —J.P.

You can have success like this when you create strong mental images and act upon them. As you practice visualization, you will come to know the truth that *thoughts are things.* Your thoughts about yourself and your capabilities dictate the kind of life you live. You can develop any talent you desire — whether becoming an inventor, learning to sing or dance, mastering photography, becoming a writer, developing athletic skill, or cultivating leadership. With practice, you will discover that you can wield the universal laws and in so doing build a greater sense of self respect and self worth.

Positive Thinking

The nineteenth-century philosopher and scholar James Allen wrote a classic book on the power of thought entitled *As a Man Thinketh*.

"Of all the beautiful truths pertaining to the soul which have been restored and brought to light in this age," he wrote, "none is more gladdening or fruitful of divine promise and confidence as this — that man is the master of thought, the molder of character, and the maker and shaper of condition, environment, and destiny... All that a man achieves and all that he fails to achieve is the result of his own thoughts."

Allen's statement illustrates a universal law of creation called the Law of Cause and Effect. Simply stated, this law is **"thought is cause, and effect is its manifest likeness."**

With this in mind, can you see the importance of creating purposely cultivated positive thoughts? When life is beautiful and things are going your way, do you appreciate it, or do you think compulsively, "This can't last"? When you are happy in a good relationship, do you create ways to become more loving and attentive, or do you worry, "This is too good to be true"?

When a "disaster" occurs, such as having your car break down a week before payday, do you approach the situation with creative thinking, looking for your resources and examining all alternatives, or do you wallow in self pity, thinking, "This *always* happens to me"? The choice is yours to create a healthy, productive, positive life or to create one of limitation, victimization, and fear.

You always have the choice to look for the good in any situation. You can also choose to criticize or look for what's wrong. Situations are neutral. Your attitude determines whether it is a blessing or a curse, if it will feel good or bad. For example, one day I was having a hard time getting out of the house at the time I had originally intended. The phone kept ringing, it was taking me longer to pack than I had anticipated, and I was getting anxious about being late for a meeting. I was thinking that my day had gotten off to a bad start. To make matters worse, it was raining and I had to load my car in the rain. When I got on the highway, I found that my delayed departure had actually been to my benefit. The rush hour traffic had died down and I made better time than I would have if I had left earlier. After I had traveled a few miles, I came upon a scene by the side of the road that got my attention. A huge truck had been in a wreck. Several mangled cars were by the side of the road. I realized that had I left earlier, I might have been right in the midst of this. As it was, I had missed it completely. As I viewed the wreck, I was humbled, realizing that being late was a blessing in disguise. It may even have saved my life.

Looking for the good in the situation, I saw that I needed to relax and be in the present moment. I needed to plan extra time to allow for unexpected phone calls. I also needed to be grateful for the here and now rather than rushing around and living in the future. It turned out to be fortunate that I left when I did.

This illustrates how adjusting our attitude helps us to have greater equanimity in a situation that might otherwise seem negative. This is one way of having control. Self control is knowing our own mind and choosing our own thoughts. We can also have greater control in life by making changes in our circumstances.

Many people have difficulty believing that their thoughts have the power to control inanimate objects or external conditions. You may have felt stymied at times when you thought that something was standing in your way of fulfilling a desire. Any circumstance in your life is yours, and the more you learn about the mechanics of creative imagery, the more control you will have in any situation. This begins to make sense when you consider how mutable the physical world is. The nature of physical existence is *change*. Every form of physical life is in motion. The mountain is little by little wearing away, the chair you sitting in is in a process of deterioration, the weather changes daily, every cell in your body regenerates every seven years. Because the physical world is so transitory, we can easily mold it and shape it with our thoughts and actions.

It is relatively simple to change conditions and circumstances in our lives once we accept the creative power of thought. The beauty of visualization is that it enables us to see beyond the present; it gives us the power to determine the course of our life. When we are not happy, we can imagine something better, and that is the first step to having it! For example, suppose you are working in a dead-end job that doesn't provide you with enough money for your needs and which involves routine tasks that do not challenge you to use your highest skills. You can sit there and complain, you can wear yourself out with negative thoughts about the boring job, the long hours, the low pay, or you can imagine something different.

What would you prefer to be doing? Imagine the skills you would like to use. Image yourself in a different, more challenging position. Cause your image to be complete, including the understandings and talents you will draw forth from within yourself. Now, picture yourself in the position you currently have, using it more fully. How can you give more of yourself than you have been giving? How can you give your attention more fully to the mundane tasks that face you?

Imagine "going the extra mile" rather than doing just enough to get by. As you learn to appreciate your present situation you will discover the secret to abundance. The more fully you give yourself to what you have *now*, the more you will receive from your present conditions, and the wealthier you will become spiritually.

By imagining beyond your current conditions, you are causing evolution to occur. The next step is to begin looking for a more desirable job (while you are giving yourself fully to the one you have). Create a clear mental image of the conditions you want. Do you want more responsibility? Greater freedom with your time? Do you want to use skills that are lying dormant? Are you interested in writing, organizing, leading?

Realize that the key to being successful in a new position is a new *you*. If you want more freedom, you need to be more responsible. If you want more authority, you need to be willing to be accountable. If you want leadership, you need to be attentive to the people in your charge. Image yourself in these expanded ways to be able to respond to changed conditions.

By imaging more than what you have, seeing beyond the physical conditions that face you, you will cause change. I have heard people say, "I can't imagine that because I've never experienced it." They really mean they need to imitate something they have already seen.

> Imagination gives us the power to create something above and beyond what we have experienced

Imagination gives us the power to create something above and beyond what we have experienced.

Animals function from memory, or past experience. Man, the thinker or reasoner, can imagine a higher and more elevated existence than what he has already experienced. The light bulb,

automobile, and computer were all invented by people who thought to themselves, "What if..." The desire to improve and enhance life fuels our creative imagination.

If you have difficulty with this, draw upon memory images and put them together in a new way. For example, suppose you have an ideal to be a teacher and you want to teach one hundred people in class, but all you have experienced is teaching a class of twenty. All you need to do is to draw upon the memory images you have of teaching classes of twenty people and put them together. In your imagination, combine five classes of twenty students and put them in the same room. Voilà! You have imagined a class of one hundred. Another way to do this is to draw from your memory the image of the class of twenty people, see them in your mind in one classroom, and then image each person multiplying into five people. Once again, you have imagined what one hundred people in a room looks like and feels like.

One image I like to use when combining memory images together is to see people "beaming up," as in the Star Trek show, being transported from whatever situation I have experienced, and "beaming down" into the new situation I am imagining. You can use whatever images work for you. Experiment and you will find the methods that are easiest for you. Visualization is fun; it can be a great joy to experiment with the many different ways to create the thoughts and experiences you desire.

Expecting the Best

The highest and best use of visualization is to create in response to a need for something better, rather than waiting for a crisis to stimulate us into action.

The following intuitive report describes how one can mobilize the mind through crisis. The report, known as a Meditation Evaluation, describes how an individual produces harmony between the inner subconscious mind and the outer conscious mind. In this man's case, he is moved to act when he sees some kind of crisis or problem that needs immediate attention:

You have immediately before you the essence of the entity referred to as ***. You will examine this essence for the state of harmony existing between the inner, subconscious mind and the outer, conscious mind and relate what is perceived.

> *There is a means by which this one does focus the attention that is quite powerful and we see that it is the crux of how the inner and outer minds are harmonized within this one. We see that it is often stimulated by disparaging energies outwardly, what could be termed crisis, where **there is a very strong underlying impulse within this one to right, to make things right, to aright, to actively move toward the resolve. It is in these kinds of states of consciousness that the greatest harmony is experienced within this one.** It has been fostered for a long period of time and it is very pronounced within him to the point that this one has difficulty imagining other ways of being. There is a very strong need for this one to be needed and it has been this underlying need that*

has produced within this one the kind of configuration of attitudes that have pushed this one in the directions that he has moved. It has also in that way furthered this one's growth and development in terms of soul progression and in terms of willingness to serve others.

The intuitive report suggested to this man that the capacity he has to respond swiftly and determinedly in a crisis can be transferred to other experiences. He told him that he needs to envision how he wants things to be and how to produce it with foresight.

There has come a point, however, where this one no longer wants to continue in the same vein that he has become accustomed to and there is a desire for a very different way of experiencing this same sense, inner sense. There is some reticence concerning this for there is not the imagining of the way and therefore there is some anxiety attached to making a change where there is not direction. This is wisdom within this one and should not be seen as a problem.

*There is a great capacity within this one to transfer the alignment of the Self that he has built into any endeavor. First, he must recognize that this is true that the capacities within the Self are not limited to the means by which they have been used previously. Once this is realized then there can be the opening of the imagination to realize that the motivations that previously served this one well no longer will suffice and **this one needs to pursue a different motivation that would be more directed toward a vision or an expected outcome** not based upon something being wrong or disharmonious or ill, diseased in some way, but rather **based upon the wisdom that this one has accumulated in terms of what can be and***

> ***ought to be according to this one's determination.*** *It is by making this kind of addition to this one's thinking that there can be a greater harmonization of the inner minds and greater awareness of what this harmony brings. This is all. (10-09-1999-BGC-3)*

In addition to using visualization for creating new, changed conditions in your life, you can also visualize particular attitudes you want to have. Your attitude is how you look at life. When you think thoughts like, "I am unlucky, disasters always happen to me," you are creating a victim consciousness which will manifest as disasters in your life. You can just as easily (in fact, *more* easily) create a positive attitude about life: "I have the ability to create what I want. I am a valuable being and the power to create is in my hands. I am learning how to be a better creator every day."

It is easier to think positive thoughts than negative thoughts, because the mind naturally moves forward toward productive ends. Therefore, when you create positive thoughts you are harmonizing with your mind. You have more energy. Negative thinking fights with the natural motion of your mind, and it causes fatigue. When you decide what you want and create the *how-to* attitude, that is, when you think in terms of *how* to create your desire, you will be flooded with energy and inspiration!

> It is easier to think positive thoughts than negative thoughts, because the mind naturally moves forward toward productive ends

For example, a child who is eagerly anticipating Christmas will stay up late and still jump out of bed early in the morning, animated with excitement. Even though the child may have only slept a few hours, his or her passionate desire fuels the body with limitless energy. Adults experience this, too. When a person has something positive to expect, his mind and body prepare for the best with zest and vigor. On the other hand, an adult who hates his job may go to bed early but find himself exhausted in the morning when he needs to arise. Although he has had plenty of sleep, dread and lack of enthusiasm leave him fatigued.

If you have been a negative thinker for a long time, it will require practice to learn to think in positive ways. A little bit of practice will reap tremendous results. A good way to create a positive attitude is to listen to the words you say. Listen particularly for the word "if." Do you say, "*If* I get this job I will be happy"? Or do you say, "*When* I get this job I will be happy"? Do you say, "I wonder *if* I will find the right dress for the wedding"? Or do you say, "I wonder *where* I will find my perfect dress"?

In small or large creations, the power of your expectation is crucial. Change the "if" to "when." Ask, *when? where? how? what?* to define what you want. This will create an attitude of positive expectation, one which indicates that you are the commander and ruler of your thoughts and your life.

Ask, when? where? how? what? to define what you want

Listen also for words like "can't," "I don't know," "maybe," "I'll see." These words indicate doubt and indecision. Every thought you think is like a seed that you plant in the fertile soil of your own mind. When you plant seed-thoughts of doubt and indecision, you reap like manifestations. Plant seed thoughts of security, authority, and definition! Say, and think, "I will," "I know," or "I will find out," or "I will commit myself to it," "I'll plan on it."

I know a woman who is afraid to commit herself to anything that she has not previously experienced, because she doubts the power of her imagination. Recently, this woman Lisa was talking about her desire to be married. Lisa's previous marriage ended in a divorce which left her somewhat cynical about relationships with men. Lisa is still afraid that if she marries she will find herself trapped in an unpleasant liaison, so she avoids relationships. I asked Lisa what kind of marriage she wants, and her response was, "Oh, there's no such thing as a good marriage. Men are all alike." Lisa's negative expectation keeps her from experiencing anything different!

Joyce, on the other hand, has also been divorced and wants to be married. When Joyce's marriage ended, she examined what was unsatisfying in the relationship. Then she started asking herself, "*What if* I had said this instead of ignoring the problem?" "*What if* I had gone after the job I wanted rather than thinking it would interfere with being a mother?" "*What if* I had been more affectionate?" "*What if* I had voiced my desires instead of denying their importance?"

With each question, Joyce imagined herself being different. She began to perceive how she could experience marriage in a more productive way. When Joyce met a man who seemed like a potential husband, she was scared that the relationship might turn sour. She practiced the *what if's* that she had imaged and because *she* was different, she started to see that this relationship could be better than her failed marriage.

 Then Joyce found a ring that she decided to wear on the ring finger of her left hand. She imagined what it would be like if she were married to Joe, her new beau. When problems arose in their association, instead of dropping the relationship she asked herself, "*What if* we were married, how would we handle this?"

Over time, Joyce discovered that she could commit herself to change and to causing the kind of union she desired. Wearing the ring was a physical prop that helped her to imagine being happily married. When she and Joe finally decided to tie the knot, they were on their way to a fulfilling marriage, for which they had prepared using creative imagery.

Trusting Yourself

Some people doubt their ability to commit themselves to a project or goal which has not yet manifested. They say, "I'll say yes, but I don't know if I can do it." This difficulty in self trust can be easily cured by practicing reliability, making your word good. When you do what you say you will do, with no excuses, no procrastination, you develop confidence and security.

This requires faith, the energizing factor in producing success. Faith comes from acting on belief. When you imagine what you want, believe it will happen, and act on it, you will produce success.

Imagination and will are the magic twins. They are powerful mental tools you can use to create anything you desire. To commit yourself to a goal or project means that you imagine the completed results and then exercise your will. The will is your ability to choose.

When you imagine what you want, believe it will happen, and act on it, you will produce success

When you choose to move your mind and body in the direction of your ideals, you are using will power. The power is in your attitude. Do you have a "can-do" attitude? Are you thinking, "I will do it no matter what" or "Although I've never done this before I can figure it out"? Then you are making choices that will produce the success you desire.

When you think, "I don't know if I can do it, because I've never done it before" you are relying upon memory alone. You have the ability and tools to go beyond your previous experience. It requires imagining yourself being who you want to be and having what you want. Then choose to move in that direction with thought and action. By imagining the end results you desire, you can anticipate the activity which will produce your desired outcome. With a vague or fuzzy image of the end result, you may not know which direction to turn or what action to take.

For example, let's say you want to go from Missouri to New York but you have never been there before. If you hop in your car with a vague idea of going east, you may arrive somewhere in the vicinity but most likely you will get lost! Now, suppose you look at a map and image precisely where you want to go. You can observe the various routes which lead to your destination, and choose the ones which best suit your purpose -- the most direct and shortest highways, the scenic roads that will take you past lakes or mountains, the routes that go by cities where relatives live who you want to visit. With a clear image in mind, you are better able to choose.

If you have trouble making decisions or if you doubt your ability to do something you've never tried before, the solution is to strengthen your thought-form images. Visualize being different and practice the new way, and you will become different. Your actions produce the changes you desire when you direct the physical activity with creative thought.

The following story is inspiring. It shows the power of positive expectation and belief. It was written by Karen who was directing a School of Metaphysics branch center in Des Moines, Iowa. The school needed to pave the backyard parking area, a requirement of the zoning board. Karen received estimates and discovered the cost of paving the yard would be $9500, a daunting amount in her mind. Karen wrote,

"I want to update you on what I am learning with the paving of the parking lot in Des Moines. We have been very consistently earning the money for this project. My personal goal is to include others in the creation of the project. My purpose is to learn to trust the Universal Laws and to practice the steps of manifestation.

I have to admit that the idea of raising $9500 seemed to be a difficult problem. Once I finally decided that I needed to harmonize with the idea of paving our back yard, I realized what a great benefit it would be to the school. We would not have to push people out of the mud during the spring thaw here in Des Moines and it would be a lot easier to clear off snow. It would also allow us to harmonize with the people at the Zoning Board. I shared this idea with others in the school so that we would all see the benefit of paving.

The students have been amazing. They really do want to help. I also found that people in the community will respond to needs if we just let them know. I have learned not to place limitations on where we will receive money. People who I thought for sure would give donations didn't. Many donations came from unexpected sources.

Unexpectedly for me, my sister gave a very generous donation of $1000 for the parking lot. We also received a generous donation from the sister of a student in response to a mailing we sent out talking about our need for financial support. She sent a check for $1000 and a note that said she was happy to help the school with the parking lot. Just like that.

A former student of the school requested Health Analyses for all the members in her family as a way to support our efforts to raise money. From generous donations from students and teachers and the community, to garage sales, to making and selling cheesecakes, we have made great progress in going from believing to knowing that we can create and receive what we desire. We have held this goal as our candle flame (point of focus) for understanding.

This last week we were still short $200 for the parking lot. I wondered who would donate the money. Would it be in intuitive reports, or from someone purchasing our books, or in donations? On the way to teachers' meeting I received a call on my cell phone. I am a nurse and it was from a doctor at work. I have never received a personal phone call from a doctor before, and I was really surprised.

We talked for a few minutes and then I asked him what he needed. He reminded me of my request for the parking lot fund. I remembered talking to him about ordering a cheesecake to help support the parking lot fund, telling him we still needed $200 more to reach our goal. So I asked him if he wanted a cheesecake. He said no, that he had talked with his wife and they wanted to donate $200 so we could reach our goal. I was at a loss for words. I was filled with such relief and such gratitude that I couldn't say anything for a few minutes. Thank you seemed so inadequate. I told him I would see him Monday. It happened! We had received what we desired. I can hardly wait to tell the students when I see them Monday.

It has been an incredible journey for me as developing my willingness to believe that it could be done, developing purpose that aligned with the highest good for all concerned, holding the goal holy even in those moments when doubts would creep in and recognizing the benefits for everyone in the community and the school. I now understand how important being a director and directing this project has been for my own soul growth and spiritual development.

I am extremely grateful for this opportunity for learning." — K.M.

The Greatest Power

Thought directed with intelligence is the greatest power in the universe. Understand this truth and it will change your life! With intelligently directed thought, you draw upon universal laws of creation. When you do not change your thought images and try to act in new ways, you find yourself forcing activity that results in fatigue, depression, and eventually giving up. Why go out and look for a new job when you are imaging yourself being rejected by every employer you talk to? Why spend your energy cleaning the house when you are visualizing how tired you're going to be rather than the improved, clean condition?

View your time as an investment. It makes sense to expect your energy to produce the results you desire. Make wise investments by putting forth activity toward a desired result which you have visualized. When you are "trying" to make a change, in most cases, you are visualizing a point at which you will fail! Why waste your time and energy for failure? Learn to expect to succeed by creating the image of the desired change. Then view the choices you make and actions you take in that direction as an investment of time and energy which will produce what you want.

Thought directed with intelligence
is the greatest power
in the universe

I know a young man who often battles with self doubt. Recently he had an opportunity to learn the importance of investing himself in expecting the best. We had planned a seminar months in advance. In the beginning, he visualized having 100 people attend. He made appointments to talk to executives in some local companies, inviting them to attend and explaining how it would help them improve their skills in concentration, listening, and communication. He also sent out a large mailing to people who were friends of the School of

Metaphysics. At first, he was very positive and received positive responses from the people he contacted.

Then he got involved in other activities, became less disciplined about talking to new people every day about the seminar, and began to doubt whether anyone would register. He was afraid that he would fail, and afraid to admit the doubts so he didn't talk about it. The fear and doubt grew in his mind. He imagined giving up, talking about the seminar as if it were over even though it was still several weeks away.

While he was engrossed in these doubts, there were other people who were willing to help, to travel from other cities to assist with teaching, to host participants, even to contribute money for scholarships for people who couldn't afford the fee. He ignored their help because his own fear of failing was so huge it blinded him.

I was planning to give the seminar no matter how many people attended, whether ten or a hundred. I was not afraid of being disappointed because I knew it would be a good experience for learning in any case. Another teacher talked to him and said that the seminar was going to happen, even if only the two of us were there! So giving up was not an option.

He realized that he could not throw in the towel. The seminar was not going to go away even if he wanted to avoid it. He decided that if we were going to spend the time to set up the room, order food, organize the teaching materials, host volunteers coming in to assist, and make all the other preparations, it made sense to visualize success. He imagined having the room full of people. He imagined their interactions with each other, the learning and exchange of energy that would occur.

When he changed his thoughts from those of doubt to imagining the seminar as a desirable, attractive event, a couple of people registered. This sparked his enthusiasm, and a few more registrations came in. There was a student who wanted to attend but didn't think she could afford it. She applied for the scholarship money, but it was given to someone else. As she was talking about her desire to attend, her husband heard her and offered to pay the rest of her way.

There was another woman who wanted to attend but she had a series of business meetings on the same day. She asked if she could attend for part of the day. We told her that it would interfere with her experience and the experience of the other participants and invited her to attend the seminar in another city on a day when she could attend the whole thing. In a couple of days, she rearranged all of her appointments so that she could make the seminar for the entire day.

These changes occurred because the young man changed his thoughts of doubt to those of desire. When he envisioned the seminar as desirable and attractive and when he was willing to commit himself to its fruition, his thought form became an attractive force, drawing to it people of like mind.

As he talked to people about the seminar, he learned to be a better listener. He became more open and friendly. He helped people to consider other options so that they could find ways to attend when at first they didn't think they could. In this way, the experience was worthwhile because he grew through it, even though forty-five people attended the seminar rather than the one hundred he originally wanted. He discovered that he needed to develop greater openness to all kinds of people in order to be ready to interact with a hundred. Making that change in himself is the step he needs to take to accomplish the greater goal.

The same thought energy can be directed positively or negatively. The results you produce are directly related to the thoughts you create.

Visualization will aid you in conquering the old, negative ways of thinking you have had in the past. Many people have been taught in some way to fear new experiences. Sometimes parents teach this to their children: when the child is climbing on the back of a sofa, the parent says, "Don't! You'll get hurt!" The parents mean well; they are trying to keep the child safe. They don't realize that they can teach safety without instilling fear. Many adults have forgotten the messages our parents taught us, but our fears surface in subtle ways when we approach unfamiliar or uncomfortable experiences. Some fears can be instilled by the media, seeing pictures on television or hearing reports of danger, disaster, and terror. Some people try to "overcome" a fear. The image of "overcoming fear" is like having a huge boulder (the fear) that is in your way. You try to shove it aside, or climb over it, or get around it. Perhaps the fear is like a stone wall blocking your path and you try to blast it with dynamite. Whatever image you have, "overcoming fear" carries the connotation of hard work.

There is an easier way, one which is pleasant and exciting. Forget about overcoming your fears! It is okay if you have fears; they are not your enemies and you need not demolish them or blast them to smithereens. Learn instead to cultivate the attitude of *curiosity*. Curiosity will conquer more fears than bravery ever did. Think about this: it is late at night, the room is dark, the closet door is open a crack, and some strange noise is coming from the closet. Alone, in the dark, you are afraid because you do not know what is causing the noise. You can try to be brave and overcome your fear to see what's there, but, trembling and frightened, you will have to force yourself to get out of bed.

Now, suppose you are curious to find out what is making the noise. You don't even think about fear, because your drive to discover, to explore or to investigate takes the upper hand. You go over to the closet and open the door because you are curious to find out what is going on. You find out that something fell off a shelf, making the noise that troubled you. Now that you know what made the noise, you can be secure in the knowledge that you are safe.

The same action will work for any fear. Suppose you are shy and afraid to talk to people you don't know. Quit trying to overcome your shyness. Practice instead being curious about the new people you can meet, to discover the interesting individuals you can encounter. Learn how to be intrigued by the new ideas and perspectives you hear in a conversation with a stranger. You will find it easier to be curious and interested in other people than to focus attention on yourself and your insecurities as you force yourself to overcome what you see as a disability.

Replacing Fear with Love

The following excerpt from a Creative Mind report gives a beautiful description of how to move beyond fear by replacing it with love. It's all in the attitude. As we look at life as an opportunity to transform and become more loving, fear no longer restricts us.

> *... this one holds onto, very tightly, a persona that she has built. It is in essence her armor. It is the way that this one tries to protect the self from imagined hurt. We see that it is based upon memories where this one was hurt, therefore it does have some foundation. However, **the perpetuation of it has merely been a means by which this one has caused her own pain, not that others have stimulated the pain, but that this one has caused her own pain.** And we see that it is time for this one to become cognizant of this for it is hampering this one's ability to move forward, to transform herself, to learn and grow to the degree to which this one is capable...*

> *We see that this one can be highly intuitive but we see that the intuition often becomes confused with this one's fears whether real or imagined. As a result, the capability of using the creative mind is diminished. We see that as this one would use the will to keep the attention where*

this one desires it to be and would cultivate the sense of love that this one very much wants, there would be a great freeing in the creative mind. This one would find that these two concepts fill her time, give her a means to use her energies and do unfold her creative abilities. This would be replacing that which holds this one back and down, that which keeps this one tied to the past and to the old concept of the self....

Any suggestions for deepening the learning in the activities, in what this one does?

Would suggest this one release the concept of learning and embrace the concept of transforming herself. **Would suggest that this one fall in love with the idea that in any experience in her life at the end of the day or at the end of the experience this one will have been touched in some way that she will be transformed, that she will be different than she was before.** *For it is in this difference that the benefit, the joy, the growth, the progression is measured. (08-09-1997-BGC-5)*

This counsel is the key to living a purposeful life. It is always worth it to put forth effort when we expect to be transformed through the experience.

Positive thinking can be applied to any situation which you fear. I have had people ask me how to protect themselves from evil influence. They fear the negative influence of people with whom they work, of "bad vibes" in a house, of a former spouse who is bothering them. You do not need to protect yourself from anyone or anything when you develop inner strength and awareness. When you create strong, clear, positive thought-form images of love, you are a very powerful, dynamic force. Negative thoughts will not penetrate the aura of your love and light. This is not a shield or protective barrier, it is a warm and nourishing vibration. Think of love and light, or awareness, as having a healing, harmonizing influence. Positive thoughts are always stronger than negative thoughts. Thinking positive thoughts will center you so that you do not need to be concerned about the negative thoughts of people around you.

I used to work in an office of twelve people. **Think of love** When I started working there, I noted how **and light** negative the other people's thoughts were. It was **as having** a popular topic of conversation to complain -- **a healing,** about the boss, the weather, the long hours, the **harmonizing** world situation, the company, their teenagers, **influence** anything! I noticed that oftentimes one person would start to grumble, then another would jump on the bandwagon and complain about something else, then another would chime in. Getting involved in these gripe sessions was a way to be popular and one of the crowd.

I decided to try an experiment. Instead of preaching about positive thinking, I would go into the office in the morning and smile, saying something pleasant. When another person started complaining, I would think, "I love you" and say a kind word. Then I simply gave it no further attention. Gradually, as I practiced saying positive statements and thinking loving thoughts, one of my co-workers noticed. She started telling me how much she enjoyed having me work there because I was always so serene and calm. She repeatedly told me I was always so positive. She started complaining less often, and over a period of time even began to speak of the good things that were occurring in the office.

Then another person started complimenting her co-workers. One by one the people at work were influenced by my positive thoughts and words. In a few months the whole atmosphere and vibration of the office had changed. Although complaints were not completely eliminated, they were dramatically reduced. This showed me how much influence one person can have, and how strong a positive way of thinking can be.

DESIRE Graph

To practice positive thinking, here is a simple practice that will help you create and fulfill your most heart-felt desires. It is called a *DESIRE Graph*. **D**ecide what you want, be **E**nthusiastic about it, be **S**pecific when you create it in your **I**magination, shine **R**adiant light upon it, and **E**xpect to receive it.

Have you ever seen a pie chart or graph? Your *DESIRE Graph* is like that. Draw a circle and divide it into sections or wedges. In each section you will write down something that you want. Make the sections different sizes according to the degree of importance you place upon the desire.

Give some deep consideration to what you want. What is most important to you? Include physical desires and mental or spiritual qualities. Write these down in the circle, with the most important one occupying the largest wedge, the least important one with the smallest section. Describe the items in detail. Then look at the graph every day. As you read what you have written in each section, visualize yourself having these objects and using them (if they are physical) or exhibiting and expressing the qualities (if they are mental or spiritual). Create your images with love and enthusiasm. Get into the spirit of your picture.

Practice being Decisive, Enthusiastic, Specific, Imaginative, Radiant, and Expectant. Writing down what you want helps you to be committed to your desires. As you write down each desire, include in your image how you will use it to change. Image who you will become in the process of accomplishing it. Then invest your time in activity which will produce the expected results. **You will find that by visualizing what you want, you will not need to invest as much physical activity as you would if you had no mental direction.** You will also find that instead of creating approximately what you desire or settling for less than what you want, you will be able to create exactly what you image.

A *DESIRE Graph* is a useful tool to help you practice proper perspective. It will help you communicate to yourself what you want and how important each desire is in relationship to the rest. When you make the sections, you will be able to see what needs the most attention. You may learn that you need to change your priorities. For example, let's say that you have on your chart "a new job, a car, deeper meditation, good communication with family members, confidence, and a new business suit." Perhaps you have divided these desires into sections with deeper meditation occupying one-fourth of the graph, good communication with family another fourth, a new car with one-sixth of the graph, and the other desires filling the rest of the space in equal amounts.

Suppose that you have been unhappy in your current job for awhile. It is grating on your confidence because you think that you are qualified for a job with greater responsibility and more income. This affects your communication with your family, as you are often irritable and short-tempered. Perhaps you spend most of your workday thinking about how much you dislike your current job and wish you had something better, but you aren't spending very much time looking for another job. As you look at your *DESIRE Graph*, you will be able to see that "a new job" needs to occupy much more space than you have given it. Putting more importance on a new job will help you to make the other changes you see as important, such as good communication with your family and greater confidence. As you work with your graph, you will find that some desires you thought were important may not be such a priority in relationship to the other things you want.

One benefit of putting physical objects on your graph is that it gives you a gauge to evaluate your progress. Physical objects are easier to manifest than the mental and spiritual qualities, as the spiritual ideals require time and practice to make a permanent part of yourself. Because physical objects are tangible, you can perceive them with your physical senses, and it is therefore simple to know when you have accomplished your results.

I have heard people say, "This seems kind of silly. I can just go out and buy what I want. Why do I need a *DESIRE Graph*?" There are several reasons. First, you can create exactly what you want for the price you want to pay. You may find with practice that you don't even have to spend money for some of the desired objects. When you communicate, sometimes people will give you what you want, or you will find them for a less expensive price than you might otherwise pay. You may discover that you can trade goods or services for what you want to receive.

Second, the purpose for living is to learn how to create. All the physical possessions in the world will not bring you happiness! Your joy comes from learning *how to create*, producing understanding within yourself of your creative nature and ability. The more you discover about your own creativity the more peace, contentment, and security you experience. Physical possessions do not last; sooner or later they deteriorate. If you build your happiness around these changeable things you will find yourself becoming depressed and disappointed. When you focus on learning about your talents, skills, abilities and creativity, you will be fulfilled. These understandings become a permanent part of yourself; they go with you anywhere you go and you can apply them to any situation in life. This is real security, solid and dependable.

Third, you build confidence as you practice fulfilling desires with your graph, for you come to know that your thoughts are creative and powerful. You will build the ability to cause what you desire at will. You will be able to create bigger, more expansive desires. Then you can progress to teaching others and aiding them to higher creativity also.

Here are some examples showing how a *DESIRE Graph* has worked for me and others. The first item I knew I created from the graph was a pair of shoes. I wrote down "a pair of shoes that are very comfortable, good for walking, feel as if they are made for my feet, and cost under $10." At that time I didn't have a car and I walked to most places. I have wide feet which are sometimes difficult to fit, so the comfort of the shoes was of primary importance. I looked in shoe stores, asked people who wore shoes I liked where they had obtained them. I tried on several pairs. None of these activities produced the shoes I desired.

Then one day I went to a special sale that was being held downtown. Many stores in town had special displays at this fair. There was an athletic store that had many shoes for sale. As I looked through them, I saw that there were about twenty pairs of most styles on display. There was one pair of shoes, however, that was the only pair of its style. I tried them on, and they felt as though they were made for my feet. Unlike most new shoes that need to be broken in, these were soft and very comfortable. I walked around, and could tell that they had excellent support and would be good for walking. Then I looked at the price: $9.95. This was when I knew that these were the shoes I had been visualizing, because they felt exactly like the shoes I had imagined when I read my graph every day, and they were just under $10.00. So I bought them, because I knew they were mine. The only problem was, they were suede tennis shoes. What I wanted was something a little dressier that would be appropriate for me to wear to work. Although these shoes were marvelously comfortable and great for walking, they were too sporty for business wear. But as soon as I saw them, I realized that in all the time I was visualizing, I had never imagined what I wanted the shoes to *look* like! I had concentrated on how I wanted them to *feel*, and when I put the shoes on my feet I could tell that they *felt* like the ones I had imagined.

This experience was very productive, because it helped me to adjust my visualizations to include the use of all the senses. It wasn't until I had the actual shoes in my hands that I realized I was missing an important element — the sense of sight. Because all the other conditions matched exactly what I had imaged I knew these shoes were my creation, and I was proud of my work. It helped me to recognize how I was visualizing and what to add for even more exact results.

I have used visualization to imagine what I want for many years. As you try it out, you will discover how powerful and resourceful you can be. Remember earlier I said that you can fulfill material desires without having to spend money for them? Here are a couple of examples. Terry decided he wanted a guitar and wrote it on his graph. He played the piano and loved music, knowing that music could be used to bring people together. As a boy scout leader, he wanted to use music as a form of creative expression and to provide a link between parents and their children at social gatherings. Terry had found that when people got together to sing, they could transcend their differences. He traveled quite a bit and decided that a guitar was a more practical instrument than a piano which had to stay in one place and could not be hauled to a sing-along around a campfire.

Terry imaged himself playing the guitar, surrounded by happy families, emanating love and joy. He looked at the guitars he saw other people play, asked questions about them, bought music books and started to teach himself the guitar chords. One of his friends who was a guitar player showed him some basic fingering. Then he started talking about the guitar he had written on his *DESIRE Graph*. The second person with whom he spoke asked him what kind of guitar he wanted. Terry did not know much about guitars but he had formed a clear image of his purpose and described it. The friend said, "I have an extra classical guitar that is just sitting in a closet. You can have it." He brought it over the next day, a beautiful guitar in excellent condition. He had even bought new strings for it. This was a simple, easy, and inexpensive desire to fulfill!

Another example is Marie who decided she wanted a bicycle. Bicycle riding was one of her favorite forms of exercise, and when she moved across the country she had given away the bicycle she previously owned. She did not want to pay a lot of money for a bicycle, but she did want one to ride in beautiful Colorado, her place of residence. She wrote on her graph, "a ten-speed bicycle for less than $50," imaging herself riding in the wind and sun, enjoying scenery and becoming physically fit. Marie talked about this desire. She asked questions to find out about different kinds of bicycles so she could determine what would best suit her needs. She was teaching adult education classes at the time and knew that one of her students was a bicycle enthusiast who raced bikes and belonged to a bicycle club. She was aware that he owned two bicycles which he used for different purposes. One evening he was talking about a meeting of his bicycle club, and

Marie asked him if he knew anyone who wanted to sell a used bicycle for a good price. He said he didn't know, but he would ask.

There was another student in the room at the time who asked what kind of bike Marie wanted. Marie responded, "a ten-speed for under $50." The student said, "That's so funny. I just bought my husband a new mountain bicycle for his birthday and we've been trying to figure out what to do with his old one. It's an old ten-speed but it works fine. Do you want it?" Marie asked her how much they wanted for it. She said, "Oh, we'd give it to you. We were trying to find someone to give it to, but everyone we know already has a bicycle." This student brought it over the next day and Marie had her ten-speed bicycle for well under $50 — no charge at all!

Several years later, Marie moved again. Once again, when she moved she gave the ten-speed to someone else, knowing 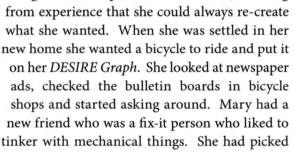 from experience that she could always re-create what she wanted. When she was settled in her new home she wanted a bicycle to ride and put it on her *DESIRE Graph*. She looked at newspaper ads, checked the bulletin boards in bicycle shops and started asking around. Mary had a new friend who was a fix-it person who liked to tinker with mechanical things. She had picked up a couple of used bicycles to repair. Marie's friend Jody found these bikes at her apartment complex, ones tenants left as trash when they moved out. Jody fixed up one bicycle and kept it for herself. She was working on the other one which needed a major overhaul. She had no use for a second bicycle, but she enjoyed the mechanics. When Jody heard that Marie was looking for a bicycle, she asked her if she wanted the one currently being repaired. Marie said, "Sure!" and when Jody was finished with her work she gave it to Marie at no cost.

People often think that the *DESIRE Graph* is magic. It does, indeed, seem like magic because the more you use it the more you discover how easy it is to fulfill desires. It helps you to become a positive thinker because you gain experience learning how to expect what you want and receive it. Sometimes the creation of a desire comes about from discovering a resource you never knew you had.

For example, a friend of mine named Frank was planning to move to attend college. He had prepared to move, arranged to pay for his tuition at college, was expecting his final check from his job including overtime and vacation pay, and was all set to go. At the last minute he discovered that he had less money than he thought he would to cover his daily expenses for the coming semester. Frank had some spending money, but he wanted about $500 more to cover incidental expenses. He wrote down on his *DESIRE Graph* the desire for $500 to pay for minor expenses at school. He thought about ways to earn the extra money before he moved, but he was very busy and did not think he had time to work an extra job. Frank thought about borrowing the money, but decided he did not want to add that burden to himself. He visualized having the money and using it, and then released the thought.

Frank continued preparing for his move and started to pack his belongings. As he was packing, he saw the jar of coins standing on the floor of his bedroom. He had been throwing his extra change in this jar for years, and he remembered his father telling him long ago that one day he would be glad that he had saved his change instead of wasting it. "Maybe, just maybe, this is what I've been looking for," Frank thought. He stopped packing, poured the coins out of the jar and started to count. Pennies, nickels, dimes, quarters, a few Susan B. Anthony dollars. The stacks of coins grew and Frank's excitement grew as he wrapped the coins into rolls. When he had rolled all the coins he totalled the amount, which came to $521.50! Another example of the power of positive expectation.

A student of mine told me that she doubted the efficacy of this tool because it was hard for her to believe that she could just think of something and it would appear. I replied that it was important for her to create an image of exactly what she wanted and then to act upon it, even if the activity was simply communicating the desire to others. Linda decided she would give it a try. She graphed the most significant desires first, and then was stumped for a final, material desire to include. She remembered that when her daughter recently moved away from home, Linda had given her their DVD player. Although Linda did not watch DVDs as much as her daughter, after she gave the player away she realized there were times she would like to have one. So she decided to put a DVD player on her graph, occupying a very small section. She talked to her friends about it, telling them that if they ever saw a used one for a good price she would be interested in buying it.

One Friday night, Linda was at home reading a book and doing some homework assignments for her metaphysics class. There was a knock on the door, and standing there in front of her was a friend who had recently gotten married. In her arms was a DVD player. Linda's friend said, "I was moving in and realized that we now have two DVD players and certainly don't need both of them. I remembered you saying you were looking for one, so here, you can have this!" Linda was astounded, but a part of her was not surprised, for when she put the DVD player on her graph she released it and said to herself, "When I receive the DVD player it will prove to me that this stuff works." She had her proof, her own experience.

Modern Creation Stories

A *DESIRE Graph* can be used for collective goals. It is a wonderful tool to use in a business or family, or group operation. Many marriages would grow and change in creative ways if husband and wife sat down together to create a *DESIRE Graph* for their mutual desires and family experience.

When I was first opening a School of Metaphysics a number of years ago, the students created a *DESIRE Graph* for our metaphysical center. We had a building, students, and a few chairs. We needed everything else to furnish the place. As we are a non-profit organization and the staff is all volunteer, we often rely on donations to take care of our needs. The students and I created a list of priorities. One of the first items was a desk. I drew a line drawing of the kind of desk we wanted, with three drawers on one side, a file drawer, very large surface area, a pull-out surface for a typewriter. We put the drawing on the wall in the place where the desk would sit when we received it. 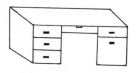 Every time anyone was in the school, they saw the drawing and imagined the desk being there. With each student's visualization the thought form grew stronger, more solid, and real.

One of the students was in the process of using applied metaphysics and visualization to create a business she had dreamed about for fifteen years. In establishing her business, Jewell was furnishing an office. One day, she was talking to the office supply place on the phone and asked them if they ever donated furniture to non-profit organizations. The man on the phone said they couldn't donate anything, but he did have an old desk he would sell and deliver for twenty dollars. She said fine. Jewell had never seen the desk, had no idea what it was like, but she figured that twenty dollars for a desk and delivery was worth it. The next day the store came and delivered the desk. It was heavy wood, beautifully finished oak, with a huge surface area, drawers exactly like the ones on the drawing on the wall, with all the features we desired. When she and I looked at the picture I had drawn and looked at the desk, we stared in amazement. The actual desk was a perfect replica of the drawing, except in reverse. The drawers I had drawn on the left side were on the right side of the desk. An example of the power of many minds working together!

The following story illustrates how Tina used a *DESIRE Graph* to create the job of her dreams:

"I knew I had to find another job because savings don't last forever without cash inflow (not to mention that it is good for me to have a job to feel like a valuable human being). So I looked in the newspaper, called people, and went to interviews. But to start out with I didn't have much of a vision of the kind of job I wanted.

Then I thought about jobs I had before and what I liked and didn't like. I know I like working with computers and I had figured out that one of the most important things to me is the work environment — good quality people to work with, enough space and light, and moderate stress level. So I wrote down these conditions and started visualizing myself going to work and being cared about and supported by the people around me, being calm and happy throughout the day and using a computer.

I attended some workshops sponsored by the University of Missouri career center in developing interviewing skills. These helped me see where my skills and interests fit into the world of work.

I also attended a creativity class at the College of Metaphysics. The teachers inspired me with talk about how the great geniuses of history achieved the things they did, also to be actively looking for things that I want to be part of my picture for creating the conditions I desire.

After that, every interview I went to I used to identify desirable characteristics for a job. I also learned about my own self value and that I have valuable skills and abilities. My intelligence, ability to focus and pay attention to detail, my college background, my typing ability and knowledge of computers could all be used to obtain and do well at a job.

I decided I would like to work in an agency dealing with education, health, or natural resources. I had several interviews with the Division of Natural Resources and wanted to work for that agency. As time went on, I thought about all the interviews I'd had and wondered, "Why don't I have a job yet?"

I checked on my thoughts and attitudes and reminded myself of the purpose for getting a job — to free myself from financial worries. I made sure that I truly desired a job and started to affirm the belief that I deserved a job and would get one.

Every day I visualized a person offering me the job that was right for me. I very clearly saw myself picking up the phone and conversing with this person who would offer me a job. I sent this very strongly and insistently to my subconscious and the universe using will power.

Finally, I had done all I could do. I decided the next day I would go and see if I could get assistance from the Division of Family Services. I had been holding off on doing that because I thought, "any day now I'll get a job." I also looked for opportunities such as living with an elderly person and taking care of them in exchange for room and board.

It was at this point I finally released my desire to the universe. I thought I had done that a while back, but actually it wasn't until then that I released it. The next day I got a call from the Division of Natural Resources while I was out. The answering machine message said they wanted to talk to me about a position I had just interviewed for. The next day they called back just as I was getting ready to call them and offered me a job, which I accepted." — T.M.

All of these stories are true. I could fill an entire book with manifestation stories from my own life and lives of people I have known who visualize specifically what they want. To experience the wonder and splendor of creation, try it for yourself. I encourage you to put some small physical items on the graph (like my pair of shoes) because in the beginning it is easier to believe in your ability to create these. You will therefore be calling upon the powerful drawing factor of belief or faith. By giving yourself a tangible way to see results that match your formulated thought, you will gain confidence. As you have more practice learning how your thoughts cause definite effects, you will be inspired to create in greater ways.

When you use the graph be sure to communicate what you want to others. Every time you write down the desires, you are communicating to your own subconscious mind. For other people to aid you to fulfill your desires (and people truly do want to help one another) you need to communicate verbally as well. Linda would never have received her DVD player had she not told her friends what she wanted. As you say out loud the words, "I want..." you will add power, substance, and energy to your desired thought form. The verbal communication will help you to affirm the desirability of your ideals.

Use words that describe your expectation and desire. Say, "*When* I receive my new job, I *will* go out to lunch with you," rather than, "*If* I receive that new job I *could* go to lunch with you." The words you use describe your thoughts, so practice listening to yourself when you speak. When you hear the words that come out of your mouth, become aware of the thoughts and images you hold in your mind. When they are productive, creative and positive, know that you are on the right track. Continue that kind of thinking. When your words are negative or limited or despairing, change them. The beauty of free will is that we can always cause change.

Decision Making and Planning

In today's society, one of the most common complaints is that people don't have enough time to do what they want to do. People run around, busy and hurried, but often at the end of the day they wonder where the time went. Since everyone has the same 24 hours in a day, what is the difference between a person like this and one who accomplishes their goals? The difference is the way one uses his or her creative mind to visualize.

Recently I watched a television program that featured a young woman who was afraid to take her driving test. Having failed several tests previously, she feared repeating the same mistakes. Her downfall was parallel parking. In the scene in which she approached the markers for the parking test, the young woman began to sweat and the terror mounted. Her instructor, a kind Oriental woman, wisely told her to visualize the car like a snake, slithering into the space. "See it slithering into the space and image yourself in control of it." The young woman followed her advice and parked the car correctly. This is an example of how visualization can be used to accomplish a task that seemed impossible. Visualizing the end results gives the mind direction.

Planning Produces Success

People often find themselves so busy running around doing different activities, they do not complete what they start. With many different desires, how do you determine what you can fit into a day? How do you know what you can realistically expect to accomplish, when you are wasting time and when it is well spent? How do you organize your life to include all that you desire? With visualization you can begin to plan your life much more effectively.

By imagining your goals and activities, you will begin to form an idea of all that you need to complete your desired objective. You will have some idea of the length of time you need to invest to produce your desire. You will be able to use proper perspective to determine what you need to do first, and what comes later. You will become more adept at foreseeing potential problems so that you can correct them in advance.

For example, let's say that you are going to host a dinner party but are not sure what steps to take. Sit down and imagine the night of the party. Visualize the whole scene, from beginning to end. "Zoom in" on your picture so that you imagine every detail. This complete visualization will aid you to determine what steps to take to create the event you desire. Who will be there? How many guests do you want to invite? This tells you how much food to prepare and how many chairs you will need. What kind of personalities and interests do these people have? This may determine what kind of entertainment to provide — music for dancing, board games, charades, group singing, and so forth. You may also use your imagination to decide what food to make — as you picture your intended guests you may remember that Mary is a vegetarian, Joe loves spicy food, Harold told you last time that your stir-fry was the best he'd ever tasted.

Imagine what you want to wear, what beverages to serve, what kind of decorations you will have. These factors may be related to the activities you visualize at the party. You may decide upon an Oriental theme because of your guests' love for such food; in this case, you may visualize yourself wearing a kimono and decorating the room with fans and lanterns. Perhaps you visualize your guests eating fondue, and you know that you do not own a fondue pot. In that case, you will need to buy or borrow one. How will your guests know about the party? Imagine the time required to mail out invitations or to make phone calls and decide accordingly which method of communication to use.

If you have children, where are they? Do you imagine including them in the party? Are you inviting your guests' children? Or do you intend to include adults only? By visualizing the conditions, you will be able to determine how the party will change with or without children. If you decide you want the party to be for adults, you will need to include in your plans someone to care for your children, or arranging for your kids to stay at someone else's house for the evening.

In your image you may see your living room clean, with soft lighting and candles. But today your living room is messy and the lighting is harsh. Some of your preparation, therefore, will be cleaning the room and obtaining softer lights.

This kind of visualization improves with practice. In the beginning, you may imagine it takes very little time to do a task. Once you have the experience, you discover you underestimated the required time. The next time you plan a similar event you can adjust, planning more time to do what is needed.

You will find that the more you exercise your imagination, the better you become at including details and therefore anticipating the many different elements that make up a particular project. The more completely you visualize the event as you want it to occur, the more details you will imagine and the more prepared you will be.

If you have difficulty organizing your thoughts, you will find that the imagery will help you. By imaging what you desire, you foresee the various components of the final scene. Then you can separate out which elements need to come first, second, third, and so on. Using our party example, you may have difficulty determining what kind of food you want to serve, but after you have imaged the guests you intend to invite, you can choose the most appropriate meal based on their tastes.

Organization as a Creative Endeavor

Creative imagery can help you learn how to be organized. I have used imagination to set up office spaces, to organize kitchen cabinets and workplaces, to file papers and to pack suitcases. The key is to imagine how you will use the objects you are putting in order. For example, in arranging cabinet space, visualize what appliances and tools will be used more often. There are the ones you want to be most easily accessible. Who will be using the space? How tall are they? You can visualize what height will be within easy range for the person who needs to use it. If this is an area that will serve many people's needs, imagine who else will be there. When you put things in a particular place, will it be easy for someone else to find? Will they have to move something out of the way to see the item they want to use? These questions can be easily answered by imagining the scenes, who will be in them, what they will be doing, how they will use the objects you are organizing.

When you completely picture an event in your mind, it helps you to relax. You don't have to worry, wondering if you have taken care of everything. You will know what you have prepared because you will have imagined it. When you do worry, it is usually because you haven't visualized the upcoming event, or your visualization has been vague. When it is vague, with little detail, oftentimes you have left out important items. You may be late for an appointment because you forgot to include in your image the time to iron your clothes, since you neglected to visualize what you were going to wear ahead of time. Or you may have ignored the need to plan time to find a parking space if you haven't visualized where you are going.

Worry comes from letting your imagination run wild. Using the discipline of concentration you can be more productive with what you imagine. When you find yourself worrying, spend a few moments visualizing the event from beginning to end in detail. Look into the picture to see the details so that you can determine what else you need to do to create the desired outcome.

I have known people who think that organization is boring and that being creative means doing whatever they want to do, however they want to do it. They view planning ahead as being restrictive. They prefer the freedom (as they see it) of responding in the moment, "flying by the seat of their pants." It is valuable to be flexible and to respond. **The greatest freedom comes from setting the mind into directive action by visualizing and then being flexible enough to make adjustments as needed.**

The following excerpt from a Creative Mind intuitive report describes the creative nature of organizing and planning:

> *This one is very linear in the way this one approaches creativity. It makes this one capable of producing many things in the life. This one is quite talented in many areas, some of which this one is aware of, some she is not.*
>
> **We see that this one would benefit greatly by expanding her idea of what creativity is.** *Of being able to recognize that* **it is the capacity to set into motion the imaging ability in the consciousness and to utilize the energies and substance within the universe to create forms desired.** *We see that this one has a great capacity*

for this in the life in regards to people, in regards to things such as the household. We see that until this one will realize that the creative nature of the Self transcends artistic or musical or endeavors that would be described as fine arts, this one will continue to deny the creative ability that this one uses.

This one has a great capacity to organize and to bring together, whether it is substance or people or ideas. This one needs to purposefully place the Self in positions where this one would be actively bringing together so that this one can begin to pay attention to the creative abilities of the mind. ... This one will find that her creativity will flourish in positions of leadership, particularly with people. (08-09-1997-BGC-3)

A Crystal Ball

Visualization may also be used for making decisions. You can develop the sight to perceive probabilities. When you practice imaging the probable outcomes of different choices you become clairvoyant. The word clairvoyant is French, meaning "clear seeing." When you imagine what will probably occur as a result of a particular choice, you do see clearly. Suppose you are faced with a decision that seems difficult. You have several options, and all seem feasible. What to do? Which one to make? What direction to take? Sit down, relax, and visualize step-by-step what will probably occur with each choice. Imagine not only short term future, but as far into the future as you can image.

This will aid you to determine which course of action will be the most satisfying. It will keep you from impulsively jumping in and out of conditions with little contentment. This use of creative imagery is important for major decisions with long term effects, such as marriage, career, and education. It can help in small decisions like what food to eat. Will it taste good temporarily and then later leave you feeling bloated? Will it feed your body the nutrition it needs and satisfy your hunger?

There was a young woman named Chris who used her imagination to help her make a significant life choice. As a sophomore in college she was considering transferring to another school. She had received a good education so far, but decided that she wanted to go to a larger university. Although she still had not chosen a major, she had a good idea of her interests and the subjects she wanted to pursue. After applying to several schools she narrowed her choices to two: a private university on the East Coast and a state school in the Midwest. Both were high caliber schools offering similar quality education. There were several personal factors that entered into the decision as well. Chris was already attending college on the East Coast, had grown up in that area, and had family who lived close by. She had a boyfriend who was to be attending law school near the eastern university she was considering. The midwestern university was halfway across the country in an area in which she knew no one.

Chris visited both places, and received the impression that the students at the private eastern university were somewhat snobbish. The people she met at the midwestern university were more friendly and exhibited a welcoming attitude she was not accustomed to on the East Coast. Both campuses were lovely, but something about the midwestern college struck her fancy — the area was surrounded by trees, the buildings were stately and architecturally intriguing, the extra-curricular activities included many concerts, museums and cultural events. There was an excellent architecture school and law school and these were both fields Chris had considered for graduate study.

Chris wished she had a crystal ball, for she believed that her choice of college would greatly influence the rest of her adult life. She made a list of pros and cons about attending each school, and found that the lists balanced each other. She then imagined herself at each school, picturing the people she had met, visualizing herself walking around, sitting in the classrooms, attending the cultural events on campus.

She also imagined herself being separated from her boyfriend and family at the midwestern school. Although she could foresee being homesick, she also visualized far enough into the future to imagine that she would make new friends. She figured that if her relationship with her boyfriend was solid it could survive a physical separation. If her only reason for choosing the eastern school was to be near him, she would end up resenting him in the long run.

After getting into the spirit of each image, it became clear to Chris that she could imagine being happy and stimulated at the midwestern university much more readily than the eastern one. She knew that she could survive at either place and that both would offer an excellent education. With those factors being equal. the atmosphere and attitude of the midwestern school suited her temperament more. She was ready for a change, and having always lived on the East Coast she imagined the different outlook in the Midwest as very appealing. As a result, she chose the midwestern school and was very pleased with her decision. The attitudes of the people there were as she had imagined and she appreciated the change.

Life is a continual process of learning, discovery, and exploration

As you use visualization to anticipate the future, you will want to understand that you can never know the exact outcome of an event that has not yet happened. People make choices and thereby change the course of events. Conditions and circumstances change. Some people want to know for sure what will happen before they make a move, afraid to make a mistake or afraid of the unknown. Life is a continual process of learning, discovery, and exploration. We would miss out on delightful surprises if we knew everything before it happened! Visualization does help you to have greater control because it increases your awareness of options. When you passively wait for what will be and let other people make decisions for you, you may feel like a victim afraid of forces beyond your control. Instead, you can give direction to your life by making decisions and learning through the process.

Sometimes people who are not fully conscious of their clairvoyance live in fear because they do not understand the source of their feelings. They may worry that a particular choice will not turn out well, but be in the dark as to why they have a bad feeling. With directed visualization you can bring such fears to light. Using concentration, you can still your mind to see or perceive what is unsettled in yourself. Disciplining your imagination is the key to turning worry into planning. You can change apprehension to facing facts.

For example, I used to live in Colorado and discovered that in the wintertime the news media often broadcast the weather

Disciplining your imagination is the key to turning worry into planning

report with great emotion. When there was the potential for snow, the weather reporters spoke of it as if it could be a potential disaster. Some of the people who lived there were afraid to go out if there was even a chance of snow. I knew this because I was teaching evening classes in the School of Metaphysics, and we'd receive phone calls at the school from students who did not want to leave their homes because they'd heard it might storm.

Every once in awhile there was a storm that closed down highways, but about 80% of the time I received these phone calls there was only a slight dusting of snow flurries. Sometimes there was no snow at all. I learned how powerful mass emotion could be. Even people who were good drivers got caught up in a kind of mass hysteria worrying about snowstorms. At the time, at least once a month I had to drive from Colorado to Missouri, a full day's drive. Sometimes I found myself worrying and fearful about snow when I heard other people panicking about it.

I learned that instead of worrying, I could watch the weather patterns. One of the students was studying meteorology and he showed me what to look for in the weather reports to have some idea of the timing of storms. Seeing for myself what was predicted, I could change my driving plans if I needed to, leaving earlier to have more time to drive across the country or choosing roads that would be more likely to be plowed. I also learned that doing concentration exercises to still my conscious mind helped me to discern when I was absorbing fear from other people. I did not have to get caught up in their fear. It gave me the awareness to know when I needed to make different choices in my own thinking.

Positive thinking does not mean that you put on blinders and pretend that everything will be fine when, in fact, there are changes that need to be made. It means that you determine which way to go and what choices to make to lead you to your destination. When you visualize you can see clearly in what direction you are headed. With creative imagery you move toward your desires and can tell when you are getting distracted. You thus become the commander of your life.

Step-by-Step Process

Understanding the step-by-step process of visualization will help you to have more control of the events in your life. You will become more effective at planning and decision-making when you understand the science of setting your mind into directive action.

There is a 5-step formula for creating your future:

1. Stimulus
2. Desire
3. Decision
4. Plan
5. Activity

The first step in creating something new is a **stimulus** that comes from the completion of a goal. In other words, the time to begin to visualize a new endeavor is when you are nearing the completion of the one you are currently pursuing. You don't wait until after graduating from high school to decide what college to attend. This preparation starts when you are a sophomore or junior. If you are a building contractor, you start looking for new projects before you complete the one you're on.

The stimulus brings your attention to a need for change, expansion, or growth. Life is always moving forward. There is an everpresent flow of energy moving toward awareness. You can see this in the way a plant reaches toward the light, the way a baby reaches out to explore the environment. When you have completed a goal, the energy of life doesn't stop -- it continues to move. You may experience this as a feeling of restlessness, anticipation, or being "high." When you are finishing a project, you are stimulated to imagine what to work on next. When you are close to completing the novel you're writing, new ideas are stimulated for your next novel. This stimulus is a glimpse into the next step of your evolution.

To illustrate, Susan is an actress who has been making her living acting in commercials and modeling. Recently, she filmed a series of commercials, receiving much praise from the people running the project. Susan became very anxious and restless as the project was nearing completion, finding herself irritable for no known reason. A friend asked Susan what was bothering her and Susan answered tearfully that she didn't know. As she talked about her emotional state, she blurted out, "I just feel like I'm wasting my talent! I should be in New York!"

It surprised her to hear the words tumble out of her mouth. She realized that she had spent several weeks listening to the people on the film crew talk about their dreams to go to the Big Apple and pursue a career in television. This stimulated her to imagine herself as a Broadway actress starring in plays, the original dream that had inspired her to become an actress. Since

Susan was nearing the end of her job filming the commercials, she was ready to pursue her next creative endeavor. Before her friend asked her what was going on, Susan hadn't set a goal beyond what she was currently doing, thus, the emotional build-up.

If you exercise your creative mind, you can fulfill many desires in a lifetime. If you think in limited ways, like "there's only so much one person can do," you may try to clamp down on this inner stimulus to grow and change and expand. In that case, you interpret this movement of energy as pressure. People talk about feeling pressured by others, when in truth, it is an inner pressure to change. By stilling your mind and learning to listen to this inner stimulus, you can activate the next step in the creative process, which is desire.

The **desire** for more is a natural element within us. Creative desire is inherently ours. The thought, "I want" urges us to decide what to create next. When people are listless or passive, when they think they don't want anything, they are denying their most basic urge — the desire to create. What can you do to re-awaken or recognize the powerful drive to create when it seems to be lost or forgotten? Look for needs, either in yourself, in other people, or in your environment. You may see a need for improvement. You may identify things that seem wrong. Understand that your awareness of need will stimulate your desire to change, to be helpful, or to bring improvement to situations around you.

Even so-called problems
can be a stimulus
for the creative mind

Even so-called problems can be a stimulus for the creative mind. They bring our attention to needs. John, for example, was the leader of his church youth group. He had the remarkable ability to inspire the teenagers in the group with his charisma, encouraging them to become involved in community service projects. The congregation admired John because many of these young people had been rebellious troublemakers before coming under John's wing.

John didn't understand their admiration; he downplayed his ability to motivate the teenagers.

One day the roof of the room in which the youth group held meetings sprung a leak. John was concerned about the problem because the church was not financially prosperous. He decided to have the members of the youth group raise the funds and donate their time to repair the roof. At first he met with doubt from the congregation. "These kids won't even pick up their rooms or take out the trash at home. You expect them to raise money *and* spend their time to work when they're not even getting paid?"

John said yes. He spoke with the kids, painting a vision of the beautiful new roof they could build, how it would last for further generations, and how each person in the group could make their mark. He inspired them to believe in themselves, to see how important they were to many, many people. The teenagers were enthused. They generated lots of ideas about how to raise money, and even solicited help from their friends who were not members of the church. The experience prodded John to bring forth the understanding he possessed of how to inspire through communicating a clear vision, how to nurture belief, how to produce group consciousness. John stimulated a desire in the young people by clearly communicating how they were needed.

The problem of the leaky roof became an opportunity for John and the youth group to create, to expand their awareness of their capabilities, to go beyond their previous limitations. You can practice this yourself. When you think there is something wrong in your life, see what you want to be different. Don't kill your motivation by defending yourself with excuses. Admit that you could improve. If you think there is nothing you can do about it, imagine, "If I *could* do something about it, what would it be?"

Then, develop respect for your ability to create by learning to see what you do well. It may take some practice to look for what you have done well if you are used to taking this for granted. At the end of each day, review your accomplishments. List what you have completed and how you have made a positive difference in people's lives. Write down even the smallest actions: "I smiled at the lonely-looking woman on the bus. I cleaned my room. I organized the files at work. I told my mother I love her when we spoke on the phone. I went to exercise class. I practiced the piano." Anything you have accomplished, completed, or produced counts. With daily practice, you will begin to recognize your value and worth. This will help you to believe that your desires are important and that you can make them happen.

Desire is a very powerful force. Some people are taught that desires are sinful or bad or selfish. A parent may teach an older sibling to sacrifice his or her own desires so that a younger sibling can have what they want. A mother may learn that her desires are less important than those of her young children who need her. In the Buddhist tradition, desirelessness is considered to be a virtue. How can this be reconciled?

The word desire means "of the Lord." Desire is essentially divine, for it urges us to create and in so doing to fulfill our destiny. The desire to improve life is the fuel for great inventors, leaders, statesmen, teachers, and writers. The desire to make the world a better place stimulates people to be responsible. The desire for happiness motivates people to change. The key is to use discrimination with desire. Is your desire for soul growth or for temporary sense gratification? Will it produce understanding? Will you use it wisely? Does the desire benefit the whole, is it for the goodness of all concerned? Is it self centered? Will it interfere with someone else? These questions will help you discern which desires to create.

There is a difference between desires that are purely physical and desires that produce growth and awareness within the Self.

Physical matter deteriorates, so desires that are purely physical will be temporary. Soul growth, awareness, or understanding are permanent. Desires to ful-fill the self with understanding will return energy to the mind. They will produce greater wholeness within our individual self and will bring to our awareness truth with universal applications.

Illumined thoughts, thoughts that are comprehensive and multidimensional will also be universal thoughts

Following is an excerpt from an intuitive report for a young man who thought in physical ways. He was actually depleting his mind because he was creating for physical purposes only, with no thought of feeding his whole Self with understanding:

Much of the harmonization of this one is pressed into service for physical desires and needs. We see this one tends to be very focused in the physical world, upon what this one wants and what this one believes he should accomplish and therefore the mind is called upon to fulfill that which this one creates physically.

We see that there is a great ability when this one employs reasoning and particularly his will to fashion and to create what this one desires, and the subconscious mind readily responds to this in bringing it to this one. We see that it is not always perceived by the conscious mind that what this one has wanted has been produced; however, it is a perfect mechanism in that it only reproduces what this one imagines. We see that this then causes the working together of the two minds; however, there is not necessarily a harmony.

This difficulty arises because the conscious mind is not invested equally in returning something back to the inner mind; therefore, there is a slow depletion that is beginning to occur in the mind energies itself and its substance. We see that there is a need for this one, in order to continue to experience the kind of harmonization that this one has become accustomed to, to begin to expand this one's thinking to realizing a greater obligation within the mind. That the obligation goes beyond merely caring for or receiving what this one wants out in the physical material world, but that the obligation extends beyond the physicality of the self.

There is some awareness of this however there is not the integration of it in the consciousness; therefore, it does not move itself within the life. And we see that although this one is able to pull upon the mind's energy and substance to produce what is desired there is the slow depletion of both because of it.

In that regard it would be helpful for this one to begin to develop a stronger sense of purposes. This is not to say reasons for what this one wants, but more where what this one wants will lead this one, **the kind of person that it will aid this one to become, how it will build qualities and virtues and characteristics in the self that extend beyond merely the physical life and the materiality of the self.**

It is through the cultivation of this kind of thinking into the consciousness so that it becomes a part of the self that will aid this one in expanding and elevating the sense of harmony and will aid this one then to begin to return the used energy back into the mind for the elevation of consciousness. This is all.

How can this one learn to discern a thought that comes from the highest or inner self or High Self from one that comes from the conscious mind?

Illumined thoughts, thoughts that are comprehensive and multidimensional will also be universal thoughts. They will apply to anyone, any time, anywhere, any place within the known universe.

What suggestions will be given for attuning the conscious and subconscious minds to the superconscious mind for greater enlightenment and self awareness?

This one must be willing to turn the attention inward to be invested in the whole self and the willingness to give back to the self. It is very easy for this one to be tempted to give to the physical only and that is its own reward. In order for there to be attunement to superconsciousness the attention must be redirected inward. There is no alternative; this is the means by which superconsciousness becomes known. (10-13-2001-BGC-3)

Once our desires have been stimulated, the next step in learning how to visualize is making a **decision** about what specific desires to fulfill. Here is where you become a specialist. You decide that not only do you want a car, you want a particular color, model, price, with particular features. If you want a job, you decide how many hours you want to work, what kind of skills you want to use, how much travel time you want to spend, and how much money you want to make. This process of creating a specific, detailed object of desire insures that you will have exactly what you want. You are responsible for your decisions, so choose wisely those desires that will aid your soul growth.

Oftentimes, people who are indecisive say, "I guess it wasn't meant to be" when an opportunity passes them by. Sometimes the indecision is a way to avoid facing insecurity. Eva, for example, was working as a nurse's aide, but her true heart's desire was to be an artist. She had drawn and sketched ever since she was a little girl, had taken a few art classes, and was quite talented artistically. Secretly Eva wanted to believe that she could become a professional artist, but she was also insecure. When she found out that the local newspaper was looking for an illustrator she thought about applying for the job. But she had no professional experience, only twenty-five years of sketching in private notebooks and journals!

Eva collected all her drawings together and called the newspaper to find out about the job. The receptionist told her that they were having interviews that week, and to come in. Eva mustered her courage and made plans to go in for an interview. As she was ready to leave, she found that her car wouldn't start. Frustrated, but also a little relieved, Eva contacted the auto repair shop. They promised to work on the car and have it back the next day. The next day, Eva called the repair shop and was told that they didn't have the part needed for the repair, so the car wouldn't be ready until the following day. Eva figured that was all right, since there was still another day left for interviewing. The next time she called to check on her car, she discovered the part still hadn't arrived and her car would not be available until the following week. By this time it was late Friday afternoon, the week was practically gone and Eva decided not to attempt the interview. Sighing to herself about the aborted attempts she said, "I guess it wasn't meant to be."

In truth, Eva's insecurity made her hesitant to interview for the job because she feared she might be rejected. When the problems arose with her car, had she been determined to go to the interview she could have explored other options: the bus, borrowing a friend's car, a taxicab. Instead, she rationalized defeat by pretending that circumstances beyond her control were a "sign" that she shouldn't go to the interview.

The daily decisions of your life are yours to control. They

are not dictated by forces outside of you. The creative power of your mind resides within you when you form clear, specific, detailed images and choose to take action on them. Deciding what you want focuses your mind and creative energies in one place. This is how you direct your life.

Some people have difficulty with this step of deciding and being specific. For example, one young man believed that if he were definite it would limit his freedom. He received a Creative Mind intuitive report which shed some light on the need for him to understand the purpose for decisiveness:

> We see that it is when this one needs to become specific that there is ... resistance to the creative process. **We see that this one enjoys the expansiveness and the movement; however, we see that there is the need for this one to equally enjoy the commitment, devotion, dedication, and single-pointedness.** Previously this one did see this as losing something. And we see that in reality this one was afraid that this capacity would not be present in the self. There are understandings in this regard and there is some cause for the fear and anxiety. We see that this is from what has yet to be brought to the conscious mind in the learning of how to become definitive, specific, decisive. There are many associated memory thoughts to these qualities that have previously gotten in this one's way.

> We see that it is important for this one to become open minded once again in regards to the importance of limitation. This will then aid this one in the emotional expression as well. It will cause this one to move beyond the passivity or indifference that this one has practiced and begin to open the self to the learning in ways that are needed in order for this one to accomplish the picture that this one holds.

> *...We see that this one has a very strong urge toward*
> *people. And we see that this is the means by which this*
> *one learns. We see that it is also a means by which this*
> *one is learning how to create. We see that the building*
> *of this will cause there to be the catalyst in regards to*
> *this one's creative mind. We see that in interacting with*
> *others this one will be in a position to be definitive and*
> *to be stable in ways that have not always been present.*
> *We see that this one has been seeking to understand the*
> *stability as a moving force for sometime. And we see that*
> *this one has the capacity to do so. It will require this one*
> *understanding previously held attitudes that stability is*
> *stagnation and burdensome.* **In order for this one to**
> **evolve as a creator this one will need to understand**
> **the value of sustainability, the need for inertia, and**
> **the place that limitation holds in the creative process.**
> *(2-28-2004-BGC-3)*

When one has difficulty being decisive, it will help to understand that being definite produces stability. **To move thought from the mind out into physical manifestation, one must be decisive and definite.** This produces security. It provides a clear direction and forges experiences so that learning can occur.

Once you decide what you want, the next step is to **plan** how to go about fulfilling it. A plan is like a map, a visualized image of the exact route you'll take to get where you want to go. If you want to go on a trip, you need to know your destination before you can choose whether to go by boat or plane or train or car. The same is true with your life experiences. Deciding what you want comes before making a plan.

In making a plan, it is helpful to ask questions like *who, what, where, and when?* For example, once a year my sisters and I make plans to spend a weekend together. We live in three different states and it requires advance planning to make sure we can all be together. A few years ago we decided that we wanted to have a "sisters weekend" with just the three of us (that's the *who* in the plan.) Next, we decide *what* kind of weekend we want — a hiking trip in the woods, a city expedition to see plays and museums, a historical sight-seeing adventure? Once we decide what we want to do, then we can explore options to determine *where* we will go. If it's a city, will we go to New York? Chicago? Atlanta? And then, we check our calendars to choose a time *when* we are available. We each have very full lives, so sometimes it requires planning eight months in advance to find a weekend that will work for all three of us.

Once we've made these plans, then we can proceed with the rest — where to stay, what kind of transportation we'll need, how much money to bring, what kind of clothing to pack. Some of the details of the plan need to be made far in advance (like hotel and plane reservations). Others can be determined as the time for the weekend draws near.

The last step is the **activity**, carrying out the plan. Some people stop short of fulfilling their desires because they never complete the necessary activity. Often called follow-through, the activity can be likened to the water needed to nurture a plant once a seed is planted. When there is hesitation in following through with activity, it is beneficial to cultivate love for your creations. You can view physical activity as a way to nurture and care for ideas so they can manifest, as described in this excerpt from a Creative Mind report:

> *We see that within the creative mind this one can produce ideas very easily and very quickly. It is in the nurturing, the caring for the idea which will enable it to expand and to grow and to take on physical substance where this one becomes lax. This one has some difficulty in what this one would describe as following through or completing projects. (08-09-1997-BGC-5)*

You might consider this physical world we live in as a schoolroom for us to grow and mature, to learn how to become creative and loving. The physical activity needed to bring ideas into manifestation can change us. When we view every opportunity as an avenue for transformation, we have a deeper motivation for following through with activity. Practice applying the steps of stimulus, desire, decision, plan, and activity, and you will gain proficiency in creating the life you want. You will be directed, motivated, and fulfilled.

Relationships

We associate with other people in a variety of ways. Early in life, we learn love through relating with our parents and other family members. As we grow older, we learn how to give and receive, how to share, and how to communicate through association with friends. In adolescence we begin to explore the realm of romantic love and discover new forms of expression. We have co-workers, bosses, teachers, students, teammates apprentices — people with whom we share ourselves, learn and grow. In all of these relationships, we have opportunities to discover our uniqueness. We can learn of our influence.

Visualization can help us to be happier and more fulfilled in all our relationships. We can develop patience, generosity, compassion, and many other qualities which help us to be closer with others. We can become more loving. If another person is not being the way we wish they would be, we can imagine ourselves being different. It's kind of amazing; when we change, the relationship changes!

When our visualization includes other people, it is important to respect their choices. Some people want to create for other people. Mothers often want to visualize their children doing well in school. Lovers imagine how much happier they'd be if their partners were more attentive and loving. Coaches visualize their protegés excelling in sports. These well-meaning attempts to help our loved ones improve often meet with frustration, because each individual needs to create his or her own life. We can use visualization to aid one another to grow, not to do it for them.

Visualization can also be helpful in resolving conflict. When we stop trying to get other people to change and start looking inward to change ourselves, we become much more powerful and effective. Some people are always in conflict with their associates, whether spouse, business partner, parent, boss, offspring, or friend.

I knew a woman named Alice who was always complaining about someone. She was angry with her husband for his inattentiveness, annoyed with her children for their irresponsibility, irritated with her preacher for his self-righteousness, upset with the clerk at the supermarket for being slow. She never seemed to be content with anyone, and certainly would not admit that she was causing some of these problems. Alice wanted the other people to change, convinced that if only her husband paid her more attention she would be happy, if her kids would straighten up she could be proud of them. If her preacher had a little more compassion she might listen to him and if the supermarket hired someone intelligent she would get better service.

Alice was rather unpleasant to be around since she was continually finding fault with other people. One day her ten-year-old daughter said to her, "Mom, I love you even when you're crabby. Do you love me when I'm sloppy?"

This took her by surprise, and she said, "Crabby? Me?"

"Oh, yeah," the child said, "Everyone at school calls you 'the crab' but I just tell them you're moody."

The child's innocence was so sincere her mother listened

and started paying attention to herself. "I guess I am kind of irritated most of the time. I'll try to be more pleasant."

Alice imagined what it would be like to smile and enjoy her husband's company instead of barking at him. Lo and behold, she found that he gave her much more attention when she was pleasant to be around! She started to praise her children when they had done a good job, and while continuing to give them the discipline they needed, she made sure to verbalize her love for them. She gave them more hugs.

Alice discovered that as she practiced being more loving and compassionate she started to like people more. She was willing to listen to them. She started to develop respect for their thinking and expression. In a relatively short period of time Alice changed from a negative, complaining nag to an optimistic, loving, caring person.

You Can Be the Change

Mahatma Gandhi was a great spiritual and political leader. He said, "You must be the change you want to see in the world." In a similar vein, the philosopher Aristotle wrote, "Let him who would move the world, first move himself."

These truths reveal that the secret to creating desirable relationships is to image *yourself* as you desire to be. You cannot change another person. You can influence others, you can touch them with your love. You can give to and receive from them, you can communicate with them and create with them. You can cause change in yourself. As you change, it changes how you relate with the other person. The dynamics between you become different.

One of the greatest joys in life is to associate with other people who are different from ourselves, for through knowing them we can learn to expand our own thinking. When we listen to a person with a different point of view we have opportunities to see another perspective. As we share our thoughts with them, we can influence them and arrive at a greater understanding of our own thinking. Together, we can arrive at a more complete picture of truth. We become more well-rounded. If we *did* succeed in making someone be how we wanted them to be, we would rob ourselves of the benefit of receiving what they have to offer us.

Let us use for example the desire for a "perfect" relationship with a member of the opposite sex. A lot of people think that they will be happy if they can find Mr. or Ms. Right. They visualize what they want: someone tall, dark, and handsome, with money, a good family person, sports-minded, etc. These people think that the other person will cause them to be happy. Many of us have been raised on fairy tales to believe that all we need to find is the perfect mate, the prince charming or lovely princess, and we will be fulfilled and whole and complete.

Some husbands refer to their wives as their "better half." The idea that you are a half-being until you have a spouse is a physical interpretation of a universal truth. Plato described this mythological idea that in the beginning the soul was split in half, and each of us is a half-being wandering around looking for a mate to make us whole.

In his dialogue *Symposium* he wrote,

"... Each of us when separated, having one side only... is always looking for his other half... human nature was originally one and we were a whole, and the desire and pursuit of the whole is called love."

What is this soul mate that people seek? It is a desire for fulfillment. It is a desire to love or be loved. It can be a desire for meaning and purpose. Oftentimes it is a desire to share ourselves completely with another. Another person cannot fill up an emptiness within us. We find this fulfillment in our own soul, our own inner self. When we feel empty it is because we lack experience and understanding of how to create. We need to learn how to love.

The truth is that we are essentially whole. We are spiritual beings with physical experiences. These experiences are for our learning and growth. When we think that we are physical beings only, that the material world is all there is, we experience a kind of separation from our true nature. Every physical thing we own is temporary, so if we live life only to accomplish physical goals, after awhile it becomes empty. The meaning or fulfillment in these experiences comes from what we learn, who we become. The physical world is our schoolroom for learning. When we use our physical experiences to learn, to grow, to develop ourselves and to become better human beings, we feel content. The missing half we seek is to live life with a purpose.

Ever present within us is an urge to grow, to create, to express, to give and receive. Have you ever seen a plant reach toward the light? We are somewhat like that, reaching out to something greater than ourselves, reaching up for growth and higher *The missing half we seek is to live life with a purpose* awareness. Associating with other people provides avenues for self expression. It gives us a place to discover more fully who we are and what we have to give.

When we are actively creating and developing self awareness, we are whole and happy. Think about times when you are doing something you love to do, when you are being creative. You feel fulfilled. When you are engaged in creative projects with other people you are inspired and energized. The feeling of being in love with another person is a manifestation of the natural urge within each of us to love and to share our love. In giving to another individual and receiving from them, in sharing love, we learn who we are. We experience the dynamic, creative power of love.

In an intimate relationship with one partner we can discover more deeply who we are because we are committed to completely giving and receiving. We need to draw upon qualities we may not have known we had. We discover understandings within ourselves. We have opportunities to learn karmic lessons. **The willingness to respond to all the changes of physical life as we share mentally, emotionally, and physically brings us self revelation.**

Finding Your Soul Mate

To develop this wholeness and draw to yourself a compatible partner, decide what qualities *in you* you desire to give, to share, to explore and experience with another person. Who do *you* want to be in the relationship?

Image yourself as you desire to be, the ideal person you want to become and express. Image yourself being affectionate, warm, loving, sincere, attentive, or whatever qualities you want to develop and practice. Picture yourself sharing these beautiful attributes with another person, leaving the face off the image of the other person. (The idea is for you to imagine your Ideal Self, not to imagine your ideal partner.)

If you have difficulty with this, start by identifying what you want in a partner. Then, practice the Golden Rule: do unto others as you would have them do unto you. In other words, if you want a loving partner, you be more loving. If you want someone who is responsible, you be responsible. If you want someone who is strong and charismatic, then practice these qualities yourself. By imaging and practicing to become the ideal *you*, you become an attractive, magnetic center of vibrant thought. A person with compatible desires will be attracted to the thought-form image you create.

If you feel good in the presence of another person, identify what it is about him that you like. List the qualities you find pleasing. Describe what he stimulates within you. Perhaps you find him funny, warm, affectionate, friendly, and compassionate. Look to see how many of these qualities you practice yourself. When you are actively building these attributes within your own being you will be at ease with the other person. You will be free to speak your mind and to be yourself. If you do not make these a part of you, most likely you will become dependent on that other person to fill in these missing qualities in yourself. You may find yourself irresistibly drawn to him or her. You may drop other important activities in your life to be in the presence of your beloved. You might attempt to build your life around him or her. This produces an unhealthy dependency.

You cannot make another person your reason for living. This breeds resentment, either within you or in the other person. People change. People have the freedom to choose. Healthy relationships involve individuals who are strong and have a clear sense of their own identity with their own goals. The mutual ideals they share form the basis of the relationship. When you do not have this as a point of reference, you find yourself feeling controlled by the other person, or reacting to the other person because you see them as the cause for your happiness or unhappiness. While you may depend on them to make decisions for you, you will also resent it when their choices determine the course of your life. This leads to the eventual destruction of the relationship.

> Healthy relationships involve strong individuals who have a clear sense of their own identity with their own goals

Decide who *you* want to be and practice being that. Create yourself as the ideal mate, partner, or friend that you want to be. Bring to the relationship your best Self so that you are contributing rather than trying to take something from your partner. Visualize how you want to communicate, to be intimate, to express the qualities you desire. Image the conditions you want in your association. Visualize yourself being open, loving, compassionate, generous, strong-willed or however else you want to be. Then, become what you have imagined. Live your ideals.

One person received a Creative Mind intuitive report that described the value of interacting with other people as a way for him to know himself. He had a tendency to initiate thought processes and then project his ideas onto others, that is, to attribute to them what he was thinking. He never claimed his own thoughts. This made it difficult for him to identify his values or what standards to use to govern his life.

The Creative Mind report helped him to see how relationships could help him transform:

> *Would suggest it would be most helpful for this one to define the ideals that this one intends to live by, not that this one just wants to, but that this one intends to live by, to become very specific with these, to become very self revelatory in regards to how this one lives and what it says about his values. Becoming more cognizant of this will aid greatly in this one's capacity to more fully express and use the Creative Mind, for much of this operates in an unconscious fashion within this one rather than in a fully aware one.*

> *...The tendency for this one to project his thoughts onto other people is the point at which this one ceases to be responsive to his own creation and in effect sacrifices it or gives it up. This then leads to a host of emotional reactions within this one that does shut this one down...*

> ***Giving and receiving with other individuals is an essential part of this one being able to grow and to learn*** *that which has been given, for it is in how this one interacts with others that what has been given is reflected. As this one would be willing to still the mind, to entertain the ideas of another, whether they are like this one's or not, is the point to which this one can experience the fulfillment of Creative Mind or the shutting down of it... (08-14-1999-BGC-06)*

Common Ideals

How do you create a satisfying relationship without trying to mold another person in your image? The key is to first decide what your ideals are in life. If you are wanting a business partner, determine your ideals for the business and then look for someone with compatible ideals. If you want to locate a roommate to share your home, identify what you desire in an ideal living situation and then find out if your prospective roommate has similar ideals. If you desire to be married, write out what you want in a marriage — friendship, spiritual development, communication, and so forth. Then consider if the person who sparks your interest values the same things.

Once you know what is most important to you in life, ask yourself, "Does this person's ideal align with mine?" Too often people fall in and out of love because all they look for in a romantic partner is someone they find sexy, or someone who makes them feel good. It is difficult to form a lasting, creative and satisfying union if you have very different values. Create your individual ideals first, then determine if your individual ideals are compatible with one another. If they match, you can probably create a productive relationship. If they are widely divergent, you are setting yourself up for unhappiness.

You cannot make another person your goal. People move, they change, they die. When you build your life around another person it keeps you from knowing yourself. Build your life around your ideals, and then cooperate with other people in the creation of those ideals.

For example, suppose that friendship is very important in your life. Communication is very important to you. Perhaps other essential elements to your happiness are spiritual development, travel, music, and teaching. When you associate with another person who shares these ideals, you can create a dynamic life together. Suppose you meet someone who values material success above all else, who likes to spend most of his time alone and prefers to keep his thoughts to himself, who does not believe in a Supreme Being, and who would rather stay at home than venture into unknown places. As attractive as you may find this person, it is likely that in a short time you will be bored or he will try to keep you from your travels. Either one or both of you may begin to pull the other down. This is not necessary! It does not mean that one person's goals are right and another one's are wrong, it is not a case of better or worse; it is simply a matter of different choices and interests. When you share ideals with another person, you move together in the same direction. It is like holding hands while walking along the same path.

When you cooperate with another person, you learn to consider their needs

These same principles work for forming any kind of association. There were a couple of women who wanted to create a local organization to raise money for civic projects. Jill's idea was to create large fund-raising projects in order to support local projects like renovating buildings and beautifying the downtown area. Sally wanted a group that would share creative ideas and projects together. Her primary focus was getting to know other women in town and developing friendships; the money raised was secondary. For Jill the primary objective was to raise money and the friendship was a fringe benefit. When Jill and Sally started the women's guild they briefly discussed their ideas but did not clearly verbalize their ideals. Each had her own idea of what she wanted, firmly pictured in her own mind, but neither one communicated.

When they initiated projects they ran into conflicts because neither one knew what the other's priorities were. Jill came up with projects that could raise large sums of money, like selling raffle tickets, but Sally rejected those ideas because they did not bring the women together for communication and artistic expression. Sally suggested projects like quiltmaking that would serve her purposes, but Jill vetoed them because she didn't see how they would raise the funds she desired. Finally the two women talked about their ideals and purposes, and in an enlightening blend they learned how to add to their own interests through cooperation. They decided to get together a group of women to make a quilt, fulfilling Sally's desire, and then to raffle the quilt to raise the money Jill wanted to give to the community. This is an example of how to use a relationship to give as well as receive, and how a little communication about ideals can go a long way to resolve conflict.

Remembering that we all make choices helps us to live the kind of life we desire and to respect others. We may not always agree with the choices another person makes but we don't have to agree to understand how someone else thinks. We learn to communicate and cooperate by asking questions and listening. Understanding our differences helps us to understand our own uniqueness and aids us in learning to love others.

Developing Compassion

When you are making decisions that concern other people, you need to consider yourself in relationship to the whole. Do the conditions and circumstances you desire blend with the other people involved, or does one person's desire override everyone else? Cooperating with your desires and the desires of other people may mean that temporary conditions are not always to your liking, but the long term benefits are worth the temporary unpleasantness. Any new parent knows this! They sacrifice sleep and the temporary comfort of their own body to serve the needs of their infant child who awakens at 3:00 a.m. wanting to be fed. The parents want to love and nurture the child and to satisfy his or her needs. They know that their own needs for sleep will be met as the baby grows older. One who has imagined themselves being the kind of parent they want to be can apply this kind of proper perspective.

When you cooperate with another person, you learn to consider their needs. You learn to be generous, compassionate, respectful, and understanding. Oftentimes, idealistic people become disappointed or bitter when they discover "faults" in another person. Human beings are not perfect. Hopefully we are all learning and striving to improve. The more you view relationships as experiences for your own learning and growth, the more willing you are to accept another individual's learning and growth.

An example close to home is the story of my marriage. When I first became a student of metaphysics, I wanted to become involved in a romantic relationship but never seemed to meet the kind of man who was compatible. I asked in an intuitive report for some help in understanding why and received this counsel:

> *"Consider your reasons for desiring this. Consider the individual to whom you have directed your attention, and consider your own nature desirous of true and genuine expression." (07-06-1980-02-GAD)*

Before this time, I had never considered my own nature, I had only looked for what I wanted in someone else. After listening to the advice in this intuitive report, I determined that I wanted someone with whom to share my ideals. I viewed myself as idealistic, strong, committed to my beliefs, goal-oriented, and determined. I wanted someone who would admire and respect these qualities rather than being intimidated by them. I was interested in education, leadership, and creative endeavors and wanted to share these interests with a partner. Through the processes described in this chapter, I imagined being loving, warm, affectionate, gentle and generous. I created an image of sharing my ideals with a man equally committed to being a leader and educator. I wanted to be involved with a man who was self sufficient, mature, willing and desirous of learning, and creative. I broadcast this desire mentally and also communicated it verbally. I kept my mind alert and watched for the individual to enter my life who possessed the qualities I desired.

Some years later, I met John who was creative, assertive, a leader, with strong ideals and values. We were drawn together through our participation in the School of Metaphysics, both teachers and leaders. In the beginning we were friends and as our association developed through creating projects together, we grew closer. I discovered that John shared a desire to be affectionate and warm and to become a close, intimate friend. We wrote down our ideals in life and discovered that we had compatible desires. We shared not only mental and spiritual ideals, but many physical goals as well. It seemed to be a match made in heaven!

There was one major problem in the association, however. John had juvenile diabetes. He had been taking insulin since he was fourteen years old, and John was in his early 30's when we met. The medication and high blood sugar levels had already taken their toll in ways neither one of us fully comprehended. In the beginning I knew little about diabetes. As I became closer to John I saw some of its complications, like wounds that took a long time to heal and insulin shock reactions that produce a comatose state. Although I found John powerfully attractive, I was afraid that diabetes would be an ongoing problem. I had already been to the emergency room with him a couple of times. I had a choice. I could decide not to pursue a relationship with John based on my fear of losing him through disease. I could decide to commit myself to developing an intimate relationship with John, knowing that there was a probability of complications resulting from diabetes. I could also be indecisive, spending time with John while holding back part of myself out of fear of being hurt and abandoned.

I decided that the benefits of committing myself to a relationship with John outweighed the problems. I believed that if I gave myself wholeheartedly to John, I would receive the fullness and depth of love. I didn't think too much about the possibility of an early end to our association, because John was a student of metaphysics and wanted to use what he was learning to heal. I thought I could help him. I decided that I would rather experience the joy and fulfillment of sharing a creative union for as long as it lasted than to cut myself off from love because of fearing loss.

Some people asked me, "Why did you choose a mate with a chronic illness?" When asked this, I realized that I had not chosen an illness. I had chosen John for his loving nature, his playfulness and gentleness, his intelligence, his warmth, his creativity, his desire for soul awareness, his leadership.

I also had a clear commitment to an ideal: to learn how to love the way that God loves. I believed that a committed relationship with a man would offer me an opportunity to give completely and to receive completely, in essence, to bring God's love to earth through loving another soul.

I did not know in the beginning of our association how severe diabetic complications could be. The diabetes proved to be more serious than I had imagined. In the short ten years that John and I were together, his body deteriorated with many complications, including blindness and kidney failure. He died when we were both young. John had some miraculous healing experiences and many medical crises. Although fraught with much emotional pain, the whole experience also was one of great learning and enrichment. My love for John was very deep and I learned a great deal about compassion and respect. I had to admit that I could not learn John's lessons for him or take away his pain. I couldn't make him change. I could learn my own lessons and be a force for good in John's life.

The experience helped me to recognize that this physical world truly is our schoolroom. People are learning human lessons and divine lessons. They have places of misunderstanding along with their virtues, strengths, and understandings. This marriage gave me many opportunities to resolve karmic lessons of my own, lessons I didn't even know I needed to learn. (I have shared this story in the book *Karmic Healing*, published by SOM Publishing.) It also helped me to become more accepting, a lesson which has served me well in my teaching and my relationships in the present.

When you choose to associate with another person, you receive a package deal. Good and bad, pleasant and unpleasant, ups and downs. For better and for worse, in sickness and in health. If the productive qualities outweigh the unproductive ones, you can be reasonably sure you have made a good choice. By the same token, if the detriments overshadow the benefits, you may want to make a different choice. If you choose a person who beats you or who lies to you, who keeps promising to change and then repeats the same destructive thinking and behavior, you are denying your own worth. You cannot claim to be a victim when you are the one who has chosen to be in such a relationship. The choice is always yours to choose how to use the situation to learn. You can use relationships to develop self awareness and to produce understanding.

Using visualization you can image yourself being compassionate, understanding, honest, and helpful with another person. Rather than being annoyed or irritated or angry at another's faults or weaknesses, image how you can aid that person. Image yourself being a positive force for good, for productive change, and for healing. When the other person wants assistance, you can make a remarkable difference in his or her life. You will discover more of your own strength in this way and will challenge yourself to draw forth from within yourself qualities you never knew you had.

> When you commit yourself to learning, you discover new facets of yourself

Commitment

In this process you will discover a secret which will aid you in all of your visualizing work. This secret is called commitment. When you commit yourself to learning, you discover new facets of yourself. In relationships, do not commit yourself to the other person, commit yourself to the fulfillment of your ideals with that person. Commit yourself to expansion, to growth, to change, to learning. When this is a mutual commitment, both people are willing to do whatever it requires to understand, to harmonize, to add to their awareness and understanding.

Commitment is necessary for accomplishing any goal in life. When you commit yourself to the fulfillment of a desire, do not let limitations interfere with achieving your ideal. Use the obstacles as challenges, for each seeming stumbling block gives you a place to reach within yourself for greater understanding. You are called upon to build new qualities, to develop endurance, patience, to exercise a new skill. Committing yourself to learning gives you the motivation to understand the cause for problems, difficulties, rough spots and conflicts. It inspires you to cause creative change. When you respect your choices and strive to make choices that produce learning, you will more easily respect the choices of others.

Commitment means that **you give your whole self to whatever you are doing.** You engage your mind, your spirit, your emotions, your body. You do whatever it takes. You view everything that comes your way as a gift, giving you something new to learn, a way to expand, to bring out of yourself hidden talents or understandings.

In my marriage, for example, I was committed to loving John through the ups and downs of disease. I learned that love endures beyond the body. I discovered that it is always worthwhile to give because giving enriches me. Even after John's withdrawal from physical form (death) the love is with me and within me. I am able to be more loving and generous with other people.

Commitment to an ideal greater than yourself provides the motivation to go beyond limitation and to identify the learning opportunity in so-called problems. The following Creative Mind intuitive report describes how to change from thinking life is a burden to appreciating the creative challenges life holds.

We see a retarding of the mental energies at this time. We see that it arises from an attitude of being burdened. We see that in many ways this one's creative mind is chained. This one is not allowing it to expand, grow, nourish and to respond. We see that much of this one's creativity is engrossed in unconscious patterns of thinking. We see that the imagination is being tossed from one extreme to the other.

We see that there are times when this one is capable of imagining and freeing the consciousness to be stimulated to imagine very complete ideas that affect many, many people. We see that there are other times when this one's imagination becomes bound by this one's own doubts, fears and misconceptions. At those times it does create that which works against this one and keeps this one chained to unpleasantries in the past.

*We see that initially **this one would need to recognize that what this one imagines is totally up to him.** It is not up to someone else, it is not a factor of someone else being in control of this one's emotion. And we see that to the degree to which this one allows the imagination to be trapped in the unconscious part of this one's thinking, the emotions then become the predominant factor in this one's life. This then creates a barrier, for it is the emotional reactions that this one becomes trapped in and it is a barrier to this one being able to utilize the full potential of the mind and the creativity.*

We see that this one has a great capacity for growth, for expansion, for influence. This one is highly charismatic in regards to this one's creativity. This one needs to control the emotions, bring forth what is unconscious into the forefront of this one's awareness so that this one can either use it with intelligence, discard it as not needed, or come to terms with it where there is understanding that needs to be made. It is only this kind of activity that will free this one from the bondage that is presently being experienced. This is all.

You will also relate that which will foster a movement in the energy exchange between the ethereal and the material for the cultivation of genius in this one.

This one does have the capacity to both imagine and remember in a subconscious fashion the experience of surrendering the Self to a greater good, *surrendering the Self to a concept of deity, surrendering the Self to that which is sacred. The degree to which this one allows the Self to be engrossed in the outer mind is the degree to which this one is away from this understanding and these memories. In order for this one to draw upon these understandings, to make them usable in his present existence, this one must release the attachment to physical verification and validation.*

This one is capable of great depths of spirituality and these can be experienced as this one is willing to surrender himself to the concepts that are familiar to him. It is from the surrendering that this one's eyes will be opened to an entirely different way of experiencing, of understanding. It is in this way that the imagination will be stimulated to new heights of creativity that will border upon that of genius but more importantly will serve as a living example of a holy existence. This is all.

This one says, "How do I bring forth that which is unconscious?"

It is not a matter of bringing it forth for it operates within this one daily. It is a matter of this one bringing forth awareness so that it is no longer unconscious. This would be through utilizing and drawing upon the skills that this one has built in utilizing attention, concentration and memory — purposefully. It would be through this one's efforts to find the truth in anything. This would be particularly in regards to interactions with people. To discover both in a direct fashion through physical interaction but also in a direct fashion through intuitive subconscious rapport what the truth is in the thoughts and the ideas and the actions.

Any further suggestions for this one to be able to realize this one's full mission this lifetime?

This would be in this one abandoning the excuses that this one holds on to. This one believes that they provide him with protection or a false sense of security. We see that in actuality these are what hold this one back. They are the burden to his consciousness that has been described. Therefore the release of these would aid this one greatly in utilizing the full potential.

Any suggestions for this entity becoming more honest about what those excuses are?

To become more acutely attentive to listening. This would be listening to the Self for when this one cannot identify his thoughts, this one can hear his own words. Therefore this one would be listening mentally and hearing physically the negations that this one promulgates which in effect destroy what this one most wants, rather than create it. (08-09-1997-BGC-4)

Dealing With Difficult People

Sometimes people in our lives challenge us to bring out our best, when our first reaction is to want to avoid them or banish them. Undoubtedly you have had experiences with people who disagreed with you, people you found unpleasant, who irritated you. Have you ever tried to make those people change? Have you avoided them because you didn't know how to get along? Perhaps you gritted your teeth and tolerated their presence. Or you may have plastered a fake smile on your face while silently resenting them. All of these coping mechanisms do not solve the cause of the conflict.

When you avoid conflict with other people, you keep yourself from producing understanding. You can change this. Start with examining how you look at people. Sometimes people view life as a kind of tennis match, with themselves pitted against an opponent. They view communication as a contest, with one person being right and the other wrong. The one who is more insistent is the one who wins. The problem is that no one wins in this kind of scenario because people tune each other out and don't learn from their interaction.

To change this, imagine a new paradigm. Consider that you are living in a world which is benevolent. We are all in this together, with common ideals. His Holiness the Dalai Lama, a remarkable man who is compassionate even with the people who have destroyed his homeland, describes a worldview that is a foundation for peaceful relationships:

"When I meet people in different parts of the world I am always reminded that we are all basically alike. We are all human beings.

"Maybe we have different clothes, our skin is of a different color, or we speak different languages. That is on the surface but basically we are the same human beings. That is what binds us to each other. That is what makes it possible for us to understand each other and to develop friendship and closeness."

His Holiness the Dalai Lama was awarded a Nobel Peace Prize for exemplifying these values. You can develop compassion by learning to love people as companions in the universe we share. This may seem like an abstract concept. The more you give your undivided attention to each person you meet, believing that he or she is inherently good, the easier it will be for you to perceive them as a soul. Living the Golden Rule, treating others as you would want to be treated, is a simple way to grow in divine love.

Resolving conflict with other people starts with recognizing that these difficult people stimulate something *in you* that you have yet to understand. One of the first steps in harmonizing with such a person is learning to communicate. Communication means "a shared gift." It begins with asking questions and listening. You still your mind to completely receive the other person so that you can see their point of view. When you listen, your mind is like an empty cup, expectantly waiting to be filled. Some people mistakenly believe that listening means being quiet outwardly while they are still thinking their own thoughts. They compare what they think with what the other person is saying. This is not listening, because when you are thinking your mind is aggressive. Listening is receptive.

When you listen and receive another person into yourself, you have the opportunity to grow, to become more well rounded or to develop a more whole perspective. Wanting to understand how the other person thinks and what they feel provides motivation for listening.

When you speak, give the truth as you see it. Give completely, without holding back or judging how you think your gift will be received. Do not be attached to being heard by the other person. More important is for you to hear yourself so that you become more aware of what you understand and know.

Communication involves honesty. It requires having a still mind to be in the present moment. I have heard people give up on others because they hang on to hurts, real or imagined, from the past. I've heard people make broad generalizations like, "you just can't trust people," or, "I've learned never to believe what anyone says," or, "If I want something done I'll have to do it; I can never count on anyone else."

This kind of thinking keeps people separated from one another. The truth is, trust begins within yourself. If you want to trust other people, you need to be honest yourself. You need to believe and imagine that all of your associations with other people will be beneficial, rather than expecting that people are untrustworthy or unreliable. I have found from my own experience that oftentimes misunderstandings arise when one or both people in an interaction have busy minds; therefore, they do not hear what the other person is saying. It's not a matter of trust (or mistrust). It's a matter of needing to be still and listening to hear what the other person has to say.

Recently, I spoke with a young man who refused to talk to his teacher about a lecture he had given. He was disappointed in himself and wished after the fact that he had better organized his thoughts before speaking. His teacher, who had more experience than he did in public speaking, could have helped him to improve. Yet, he thought he should be able to figure it out on his own rather than asking his teacher's advice. He said that his interactions with her in the past had always been dissatisfying because all she did was criticize him. Therefore, he was imagining that this would occur in the future, too.

As he spoke about this, I could hear the tone of his voice becoming more and more defensive, and his thoughts becoming more and more accusatory, expecting that this teacher was going to rake him over the coals for doing a poor lecture. He was imagining this conversation in his mind and it hadn't even happened! When I pointed this out to him, at first he didn't see it. He was convinced that his teacher would treat him this way.

He had to admit that he was the one criticizing. Because he had not prepared and practiced the lecture as he could have, he had a guilty conscience. He was self critical. Rather than imagining change, he projected these thoughts onto his teacher. After listening to my perspective, he decided to do a mental exercise to clear his mind so that he could talk to the teacher with an open mind, expecting that he would receive some beneficial wisdom to help him improve.

To his surprise and relief, the conversation went even better than he had expected. The teacher gave him several ideas which were innovative and different from what he had done. He put them into practice, and it improved his ability to give a good lecture and to draw a bigger audience. The valuable lesson he learned was to discipline his imagination. He needed to have a still mind, expect the best, and then to imagine the kind of giving and receiving he wanted. When he imagined what he wanted, he was able to create this *in his own attitudes.* This then changed his communication and the results were positive.

Resolution happens in the present moment

Resolution always happens in the present moment. Conflict is always self-created and can therefore be self-corrected. Recently I heard an Intuitive Health Analysis that described how a person unconsciously created conflict in associations because it gave her a sense of importance. This might seem odd, but it is not really so unusual. Many people are attached to pain or suffering because it is familiar. They feel important when they are a victim. Or sometimes they pick fights so that they can "kiss and make up" to know they are loved. All of these unproductive reactions stem from past experiences that they bring into the present and re-create over and over. The Intuitive Health Analysis offered counsel to help the woman think differently and therefore produce different experiences within herself and her associations:

It will be helpful for this one to place the past where it belongs, and to begin to recognize its value in terms of who this one has become, rather than as a controlling factor of what this one will think, and how this one will think it.

We see that this one has a tendency to allow the past to intrude into the present, and we see that this is the root of the conflicts that this one experiences. We see that this one needs to learn how to direct the attention and to use the mind more economically and more truthfully. For in doing so this one will be able to see the present moment for what it is, and will be able to bring the inner self forward. Until this occurs this one will continue to push the inner self away and this one will become lost in the conflicts that this one recreates.

This is emotional as well, and we see that this one has attachment to these conflicts for it gives this one a certain sense of familiarity, a certain sense of comfort, and a certain sense of importance. As long as this one's ego is attached to the conflicts, this one will continue to provoke them, and will continue to drag the past into the present, in ways that are not appropriate." (07-26-2005-BGC-1)

The key to resolving conflict is to understand your own mind, your own attitudes, your own expectations. Some people want to control the other person, to get them to change or to stop what they are doing, or to think differently. They imagine how the other person will treat them, what the other person will say. Then they become frustrated because the other person makes their own choices and thinks their own thoughts. They can't control that. They don't have to, they just need self control.

Here is a simple practice that will help you develop this kind of self control. When someone irritates you, write down all the reasons why you don't get along. Record everything, the smallest to the biggest irritations. For example, she pops her gum when you are trying to work, she is noisy, she doesn't listen, she is inconsiderate, she is selfish, etc. List everything that bothers you.

Then, learn to give to that person. Look for ways that you can change. Ask yourself, how can I be different? How can I look at this in a different way? What does this person need? What one thing can I do to make a difference? You might even ask the person, "How can I help you?" This will require honesty. Some people find it difficult to admit what they need to change when they view another person as the problem. They often want to blame the other, or get back at the other person for bothering them. They may think that the only way the relationship will change is if the other person changes.

In truth, when you change, the dynamics of the relationship change. You can create harmony with another person by becoming more gentle, kind, considerate, generous or sincere. When you give, you will receive greater awareness, understanding, patience, and love.

> The key to resolving conflict
> is to understand your own mind,
> your own attitudes,
> your own expectations

Here is an example of how it works. A woman named Nancy irritated her co-worker Sharon for the reasons listed above. They worked in an office that had little cubicles which created the illusion of privacy but had no doors, no ceilings, and no sound insulation. Nancy used to come to Sharon's desk in the morning, plop herself down, pop her gum, and talk about her daughter, her husband, her church activities, everything except the work she or Sharon needed to do. She was not aware that she was bothering Sharon. Sharon never said a word, she just silently fumed about it. She never asked Nancy to leave, nor did she tell her that she was trying to concentrate. Instead, while Nancy jabbered on, Sharon mentally told her to shut up, ignored her, or blamed her for the distraction. Sharon pretended to be polite when in her own mind she was inconsiderate of Nancy's need to have someone to listen to her. Sharon did not verbalize her thoughts out loud, but tuned Nancy out by being engrossed in her own thoughts.

Although Sharon's outward expression was different from Nancy's, the very things that irritated her were the same attitudes she practiced in her own thinking. She never realized it until she wrote down what bothered her about Nancy and examined it in a new light. When she asked herself, "How can I help you?" Sharon recognized that Nancy needed someone to listen to her. Nancy was distressed because her husband worked nights so she rarely spent time with him. Since he was often preoccupied when he came home, he did not give her much attention.

Sharon decided that one change she could make was to give Nancy the listening ear she wanted when she came over to Sharon's cubicle. Do you know what happened? When Nancy received Sharon's undivided attention, she was at peace and did not talk for so long. She left after a short while, prepared to face her day and go about her work. Sharon also started telling Nancy when she wanted to be alone instead of silently berating her for being insensitive. She let Nancy know when her presence was disrupting her work. Sharon had been expecting Nancy to read her mind. This was irresponsible and inconsiderate, because Nancy did not know that she was bothering Sharon when Sharon pretended to enjoy her company.

Within a few weeks, Sharon learned to reconcile her conflict with Nancy. They became good friends as Sharon understood Nancy's needs and practiced greater consideration. She learned how insensitive and uncaring it was for her to be outwardly quiet while inwardly being self-centered, consumed with her own thoughts. By looking for ways that she could give to Nancy, she discovered attitudes that *she* needed to change.

When you are willing to cause change in yourself, you can learn how to be a friend to anyone. When you initiate communication, you can resolve conflict within yourself and your relationships. This gives you a great deal of power because you always have tools for causing change at your command.

Being Heart-Centered

The power of love is at the heart of every living thing. Love is a magnetic drawing power. It is a dynamic interchange of energies. This is the essence of all relationships — giving and receiving, blending and harmonizing. When people practice respect — putting themselves in another's shoes, seeing the other's vantage point, feeling what the other person feels — they can have compassion. Resolving conflict is a process of transformation that produces greater awareness of ourselves and others.

Love is a magnetic drawing power

A Creative Mind report gave a beautiful definition of what it means to be heart-centered. It is wise counsel that anyone can use to deepen their relationships:

> *... it would be of help... for this one to be much more mindful of the will in the present experience, to be much more mindful of what this one's heart says needs to happen in the present moment rather than what this one's head leads him to believe. We see that the heart is linked to the understandings, the head is linked to the pretendings and the imaginings. We see that there is a need for this one to become much more heart-centered, aware of his understood experiences and how these can be brought forth into the present time period in order for this one to manifest the seed of who this one is to be.*

This entity says, "How can I be more heart centered?"

Be willing to receive the truth, the beauty within the self and others, the ability for undivided attention, the ability for wonder and curiosity of what an experience or a person will bring the self, the ability to care, to tend to and to care.... *it needs to be present in every moment.* (08-09-1997-BGC-4)

The heart is our connection with our inner self. When we practice discipline of the outer conscious mind and ego, causing stillness, we can listen to the inner self. We can listen to others. We can then respond with a natural sense of conscience, with truth, with a pure desire to relate to other people for the goodness of all concerned. This is divine friendship.

Becoming Empowered

Within each one of us there resides a spark of life, an inner urge to create, a drive to improve, expand, and multiply. We may perceive this as a desire to make a difference in the world, to leave a mark, to touch people, to influence the environment in a productive way, or simply a desire for self expression.

Every time we create — whether it is a work of art, piece of music, healthy relationship, physical object, business venture — we become more aware of our creative power. We come closer to understanding creation through the creative act. We live in a beautiful world. It is full of resources — people and places and things for us to use, to enjoy, to share, to explore, and to discover. Too many people waste this precious gift of life by struggling to survive. What's the point? Why struggle to feed the body when there is no time left for appreciating a beautiful sunset, for sharing a tender moment with a child, for receiving the awe of a Mozart sonata?

By understanding visualization, you will come to know your creative power. You will learn that visualization is much more than manifesting desires. It is understanding how creation works. It is understanding the whole self, understanding the purpose for existence.

The creative mind includes an outer mind called the conscious mind and an inner mind called the subconscious mind. The conscious mind, which works with the brain and physical body, can reason. When we use imagination effectively, we cause change by reasoning with our experiences to produce understanding and self development. Fulfilling experiences are those which are purposeful. This means that we are producing understanding. We fill the inner mind with understanding and become more self aware. (To learn about the science of how the inner and outer mind work together, read the second volume of the Visualization series, *The Universal Laws of Creative Mind.*)

One Creative Mind intuitive report described the difference between using creativity in a physical manner and employing imagination in a way which develops the whole Self:

> *This one can be highly creative in an external sense in being able to very quickly put people, places and things together in creative ways; however, this misses the meaning of creative mind itself, for creative mind implies that there is action and interaction between the inner and outer Self. It implies that in every experience there is an understanding that produces completion of the soul. This has yet to be the experience that this one has produced in the use of consciousness. (10-19-2002-BGC-4)*

This is an important distinction. When one uses creative mind to produce soul-centered understanding, s/he experiences peace and contentment. Another intuitive report described to one young woman how she could achieve greater harmony within herself and her life by viewing her creative mind as a garden. She was counseled to be attentive to the seed thoughts she was planting in her mind and to water them with love:

It would be of benefit for this one to begin to envision the inner world as a garden that this one must tend, that this one has the privilege of existing within and of taking care of determining what exists there, what thrives there, what blooms there, what lives there, and to create it with the love that this one does have within the Self. Through this kind of inner endeavor, there will be a broadening of the awareness and a quickening of the energies that will aid this one to have a deeper sense of connectedness with her whole Self.

The creative power of love is magnetic and attractive. It draws to us whatever we imagine and nourishes us. As we recognize the potential to love always exists within us, we become more aware of our power to create. M**'s intuitive report illustrates this.

It is through any situation where this one experiences love that this one experiences the greater harmony within the Self. This is for several reasons. We see that it is in these types of situations where there is an object of this one's affection that there is an open channel that is immediately created between the inner and outer Self where there can be the free and full and complete expression of energies that begin to move.

It is as if there is such a power arising from within the self of wanting to express the affection and love that it is immediately given without any reservation on this one's part. *All of the limitations that would otherwise be present are gone. This is most powerful, it is very rare in this one's existence. It has subtle types of expressions on a much less expressive level in this one's existence. However, it is the point at which this one needs to cultivate living. For it is for this one the essence of life. Therefore, to bring love into every moment of the existence is most important for this one to be able to establish the harmony and to draw upon it.*

It would be helpful for this one to realize in the situations in the life where this one cannot imagine how this type of love could be experienced that these are either situations that need to be altered and changed to be let go of, or there is something within herself that needs to be altered and changed and let go of so that this one might bring the love into that area of the life. It is a process of doing both, it is not a process of one or the other. It is a process of this one learning how to bring the life within herself outward and to then return it back into herself so that there is a completion, a wholeness, and a feeding within the Self of knowledge that transcends that which is outward. There is such a craving to love and be loved that this one often tends to deny, that this one needs to accept this urge and to gently receive it and direct it, for it is what ties this one to her inner being.

M*** was not always happy. She did not understand why, especially since the intuitive report described her ability to be creative and loving. M*** learned that just as she has the capacity to create with love, she can also restrict her creative power. The choice is in her hands to determine what kind of life she will live:

What is the source of this one's constant imbalance and stress and being put in situations that this one does not want to be in, and out of this one's choosing?

This is relative to what has been given in terms of the greatest harmony is when this one loves with what this one would outwardly judge as abandon, but it is the rare times when this one has loved completely. Most of this one's life is not like this, and therefore the imbalance, or disharmony exists. The calibre of this one's life is the result of her choices, whether they have been with full awareness or unconsciously made. It is the capacity to understand and to love the Self, the learning, and others that will bring this one the greatest unity within. There are many ways in which this one does hold the Self away from this unity. The degree to which this one remains disharmonious, ill at ease, or miserable in the conditions of her life, refusing to give love to herself and to others, is the degree to which this one erects a barrier between her outer self and inner Self. The barrier is of her own making. The barrier will of necessity be removed by herself as well.

This entity is concerned about a life-mate and has been told that this one would never have a life-mate until she learned to love herself completely. Any information here, any knowledge or wisdom? What is perceived?

This one will have whatever this one imagines. *It is important for this one to become much more attentive to what this one is willing to believe.* *(10-09-1999-BGC-6)*

It is important to realize how powerful imagination is, for we can imagine what we want or what we fear. When we use visualization with control we become the commander of our lives. We free ourselves from entrapping thoughts, negative brain pathways, and limitations.

We each have the ability to imagine and choose. This means that we have freedom when we create responsibly. It is our duty to use this schoolroom called life for learning and understanding. When we create with purpose, when we strive to improve ourselves and to develop our full potential, we can experience a life full of riches and power.

It is our duty to use this schoolroom called life for learning and understanding

When we deny our creative potential and live according to habit or by repeating the past, we experience limitation and stagnation. This produces a struggle for survival. Sometimes it shows in our lives as procrastination, waiting for a crisis to motivate action. When you find yourself "stuck," unhappy, limited, or victimized by conditions in your life, ask yourself, "Who is controlling my life?" To whom are you giving up your power? Nobody can make you think a certain way or make your choices for you. It is always up to you to choose how to think, how to act, how to live. It is in your hands and intelligence to cause and create your own life.

Your Thoughts Give You Power

Your thoughts create your life and reality. Physical conditions do not cause you to be who you are. Listen to your thoughts. Thinking, "I can't help it, I'm only human," "I just didn't have any choice," "I can't do anything about it," entraps you in your own limitations. You are denying the creative power of your mind. When you think that other people make you happy or sad, when your financial situation causes you to miss out on something you want to do, or when you feel trapped by any situation, you stagnate by refusing to imagine and cause change. You think you are a victim of other people, conditions or circumstances when you allow your mind to remain passive.

Some people interpret this to mean that when things are not going well it is their fault. "I'm not to blame for my car breaking down!" Please understand that "cause" and "blame" are not synonymous. I do not believe that anyone intentionally creates disasters in his or her life. I do believe that some people are ignorant of how to effectively use their mind power. Some people are energized by crises, or they view creativity as problem solving, so they set themselves up for crises and problems. Learn to forgive yourself for conditions that displease you and then do something different. Learn to listen to your thoughts so that you can identify ways of thinking that contribute to poverty, or illness, or whatever limitation you face. Then, use visualization to cause change.

If you find that you repeatedly experience conditions in which you are limited or feel like a victim, some form of counseling may help you to discover the cause in your thinking. As a counselor, I have found that people who have difficulty admitting their participation in such situations describe them using the word "you" instead of "I."

For example, I was counseling a woman I will call Carol. She was promiscuous and kept getting involved with men who treated her poorly. She was describing how her mother embarrassed her when she started developing a woman's body in adolescence. Her mother was afraid that Carol would get hurt by boys so she deliberately had Carol wear clothes that were unflattering to ward off any male attention. As Carol described it, she said, "you feel really bad when your mother wants you to look ugly." By speaking this way, Carol removed herself from the situation rather than claiming her own feelings, "*I* felt really bad because my mother wanted me to look ugly."

Gradually, she started admitting how she felt and the choices she made as a result. She had purposely chosen to run around with many men to prove to herself that she was an attractive woman. By admitting her desire for importance, value and worth, she gained some perspective on her reason for making these choices. This was very empowering, because it helped her to realize that she had chosen to defy her mother in an attempt to assert her own worth. She could see that she had in fact perpetuated her thoughts of worthlessness. Carol's actions were similar to those her mother had chosen when she was an adolescent and it was those very actions her mother wanted to protect Carol from experiencing.

Once Carol faced her own desires and admitted how she set up these situations, she was free to cause change. She started imagining different ways to give to develop self value. She became a teacher, helping children learn and grow, and as Carol experienced a positive influence in their lives she found out that she was a good person. She started making different choices in her relationships with men, no longer craving their attention to know that she was worthwhile. Through creative imagery Carol broke a dysfunctional family pattern. She learned to understand her own motives and imagined a different way of living to fulfill her desire.

In most cases, when you think in limited ways, it is because you have learned this. Perhaps, as a child, someone told you, "You will never amount to anything," "The Joneses have always been poor, and you are no exception," or something else that you accepted and believed. Your parents are not to blame. They gave you what they knew, and you responded according to your understanding at the time.

Do not dwell in the past. Counseling can help you look for the cause of unproductive ways of thinking. This means discovering how and when you began forming certain attitudes that have limited you, not pointing the finger at someone else who destroyed your life. *You* accepted the unproductive attitudes, *you* imaged them, and *you* have practiced them. The power to change is therefore in your hands. Whatever you have imagined about yourself is your creation. You have repeated it through habit and practice. Because you have imagined yourself to be a certain way, you can also imagine yourself to be a different way. What freedom! You can choose how to think and what to imagine. Examine your thoughts to decide which ones are productive and useful and which are not. Change the limiting thoughts to those which will produce what you want.

If you have difficulty imagining the prosperity, success, or conditions you desire, use role models. Find people who live the kind of lifestyle you would desire. Look for people who exhibit qualities and traits you want to emulate. Real people, fictional characters, and historical figures all can provide a stimulus for your imagination. Research, read, and meet people. Learn how they think. Craft an image that is appealing to you. Then, image yourself being like the people that you admire. The more you imagine yourself in this way, the more you will become like that.

> When you realize that you can choose your thoughts, you become empowered

When you realize that you always have the ability to choose the thoughts you desire, you become empowered. Will power is a series of continuous and determined efforts and actions focused around a desire, persisting until you have accomplished your goal. Making consistent choices that move you in the direction of your desire produces the change you want.

When you recognize that you have been thinking negatively, appreciate your ability to be aware of your thoughts, and visualize something else. Do not become discouraged. Keep practicing to visualize the way of thinking that will produce success. Practice makes perfect. It is important to remember that "perfection" is not a stagnant state. Often people will put off acting on a desire because they fear they will not be perfect at accomplishing it. Achieving perfection in every activity means doing your best, striving to become better and to improve and grow and learn.

Everything in nature expresses itself naturally. As human beings we need to learn to do this because our conscious minds often become clouded with thoughts of whether we are good enough. Recently I watched an insect called a walking stick climbing over a leaf. It kept falling, then it would turn itself upright and move again. It kept going until it finally got to the top surface of the leaf. As I watched the bug, I noticed that the leaves on the ground were many different shades of green, brown, gold and scarlet. Some were spotted, some irregularly-shaped, some even appeared torn. It became apparent that in nature nothing is perfect. Each leaf or bug or bird in nature is individual — some graceful, some awkward, some straight, some bent, some fast, some slow — each one just is what it is. All are moving toward something and each makes up a part of the whole. Imagine if all human beings developed a self concept like this. We could release thoughts of condemnation and appreciate the beauty of life. We could embrace the changes and stages of learning and growth.

You Are the Cause

Admitting that *you are the cause* for your life will bring to you a great awareness of your power. When you understand that "cause" means command, you will cease blaming yourself for the conditions you don't like. Respect your ability to cause and direct your thinking in a new way to visualize the conditions and circumstances you want. As long as you blame other people or conditions outside of you for the situations in your life, you will feel weak and helpless. You cannot change someone else. You can change yourself.

A simple place to practice this kind of command is in your communication with other people. Many of us have been taught in some way to give other people credit for our own thoughts, feelings, or conditions. "Oh, she makes me feel so good," we say when we're in love. "He drives me crazy," when we're angry. Another person can stimulate you. They can bring to your attention the thoughts or feelings in your mind. When you understand that they trigger what is already within you, you have opportunities for self respect, to see yourself through their eyes. You also have freedom to choose your response.

Clear communication helps you to know yourself. Communicate from the perspective of what *you* want and what *you* think and feel. If something displeases you, do not blame the other person for making you angry, or unhappy. Use "I" statements to describe your experience. This will give you the awareness of how *you* think. It will give you the perspective of how much freedom you have to choose what to do in the situation. You will understand yourself, your motives and your intentions in this way. You will be able to perceive your friend's needs.

For example, let's say you have a mate who wants a lot of attention from you. Perhaps you have avoided communicating with her, and you ignore her needs to fulfill your own. She is jealous, and when you spend time with your friends she pouts to get your attention. Suppose you have lived with this for awhile, you have stewed about it, and now you are angry. Instead of blasting your spouse with accusations like, "You make me so angry! You're such a baby! You have no reason to be jealous," which will only provoke defensiveness, give yourself some credit for what you experience. Admit the mistakes you've made and the needs you have. "I am sorry I have not given you the attention you need. I feel isolated from you and I want to talk with you. I want to be close with you and I get angry with you when I think I can't. I feel pulled in two directions when I want to see my friends and I know you feel neglected. I am unhappy when you are pouting because I want to grow with you."

This is more honest, describes your feelings, and lets the other person know what your perspective is. Then she can respond with what she thinks and feels. Rather than, "You don't care about me. You care more about your friends than me," she can say, "I want your attention and I feel lonely when you are out with your friends." These kinds of statements will open lines of communication that will lead to great discoveries of your thoughts, attitudes and the feelings that result as well as the thoughts and attitudes and feelings of your partner. You will know what you want and what your spouse wants, and vice versa. It will aid you to respect and love one another. You will discover that you can create better ways of relating with one another.

You can practice this kind of communication with anyone — your children, spouse, boss, friends, or parents. You will find tremendous freedom and power as you own your thoughts. You will discover that every thought and reaction is of your own making, and you can shape your thinking as you desire. Living your life will become a creative art. Just as a sculptor molds clay or a painter puts a brush to canvas, you can form the attitudes, actions and responses that express your ideal self. You can alter these at any time to create the *you* that is most fulfilling and desirable. No matter what conditions life brings your way, you are free to respond and change and move your own destiny.

> You will find tremendous freedom and power as you own your thoughts

Being responsible for yourself and your creations means that you respond to your desires with action. When you desire something, whether it is a new pair of shoes or a more honest relationship, the power is in your hands to create it. As long as you think that someone else is pulling your strings, they will be. When you practice creating what you want, causing change with your visualized thought forms and accompanying actions, you will find that your experiences are unlimited. Your ability to change is never ending. Your awareness of yourself and your relationship with all of creation will expand to heights greater than ever before.

Affirmations

As you learn to build confidence in your ability to create, you may encounter doubts and temporary setbacks. Perhaps you are imaging yourself working as a sales representative for a particular company, you interview for the job and believe you are going to attain it, but then you find out that they have hired someone else instead. Don't lose hope! It is likely that there is a better job waiting for you ... all you need to do is find it.

To help you build a strong faith in yourself and your creative power, you may find it beneficial to use simple affirmations. An affirmation is a positive, clear statement of your desire. Just as a road sign along the highway helps you to stay on the correct path, a written or spoken affirmation will aid you to keep thinking in positive ways.

When you affirm something you make it firm, you declare definitively that you are dedicated to the fulfillment of your desire. The more clearly and the more often you affirm your objective, the more solidly it becomes fixed in your own thinking. If you find yourself becoming swayed by the negative thinking of other people around you, silently chant a positive affirmation of your desire. Soon you will find that your own resolve is not so easily disturbed.

Affirmations work when they describe mental images. The language of the mind is one of images or pictures, so your affirmative words must describe mental images that you create and hold in your mind.

The most effective affirmations are those which have meaning for you. If you use someone else's words, be sure that those words describe an image that lives in your own mind. You may use another person's words as a springboard to write words that verbalize your own image in a more personal way. The affirmations you use will change according to your desires. For example, if you are visualizing yourself healing a broken leg, you might affirm, "I am healthy and full of vigor with strong muscles and solid bones." After the injury is healed you may choose to voice a completely different affirmation for a new desire.

Affirmations work
when they describe
mental images

Following are some affirmations you can use to get you started believing in yourself as a creative, mighty, resourceful, happy being. As you practice affirming your desires, you will discover words that empower you when you speak or write them.

I am happy, creative, and fulfilled.
Life is full of unlimited resources.
Wherever I am, good things happen.
I am full of joy.
I am free!
I give thanks for the treasures in my life.
It is a wonderful day!
I love my life.
I give thanks for abundance and prosperity.
I look for the gift in every experience.
I am ready and willing to receive life's abundance.
I love the divinity in each person I meet.
I salute the divinity within you.

I improve the earth plane wherever I go.

I am a fountain of joy.

I give ever-increasing riches from the source
of my abundance.

I am a spark of light.

I am loving and generous.

I am a positive influence on everything
and everyone around me.

I bring light to every situation.

Every person I meet has a gift to offer.

I have integrity, dignity, and strength.

I am a creative, interesting person.

I am secure and at peace.

I love and am loved.

Today is full of hope.

I expect the best.

I expect my efforts to produce wonderful results.

I am intelligent and creative.

I am strong mentally and physically.

I can choose my response.

I easily respond to everything in my life.

I release all limitation and receive all abundance.

I love the people around me.

I am confident and at ease in all situations.

Every situation brings me opportunities to discover
my power, creativity, skill, and talent.

There are sources of support around and within me.

The universe is benevolent.

All things are possible.

You might want to write one or more of these affirmations on an index card to carry with you in your pocket or purse. You could tape it to your mirror or place one on the seat of your car. Experiment to find out what works best for you and share your growing joy with all you meet!

Power Points

The following points will help you to admit your power:

1. Thoughts are things and everything is created with thought.

2. You are a mental-spiritual being and your physical experiences are for your learning.

3. The secret to visualization is creating clear, detailed thought forms using all five senses.

4. The language of mind is in pictures or images.

5. You always have the freedom to choose the thoughts you want to think and create.

6. Other people also have freedom of choice. You can create yourself as you desire but you cannot create someone else.

7. The physical world, your physical body, and physical conditions will respond to the direction of your thoughts.

8. Thought directed with intelligence is the greatest power in the universe.

9. You are endowed with imagination and will; therefore, you have an inherent ability to be a mental creator. Imagination and will are the magic twins that enable you to produce what you desire.

10. Like attracts like. Therefore, create positively and with love.

11. The nature of matter is change. If you don't like something in your life, you can change it to become what you want. Imagining how you want to improve yourself and conditions in your life is the first step in making it so.

12. You have the freedom to choose your response to any person, place, or thing in your life. Love your enemies by creating understanding. When you initiate the response you desire, you have the power of understanding, which produces inner and outer peace.

13. When you feel trapped in any limitation, imagine every alternative you can think of. When you have exhausted the probabilities you can imagine, start imagining possibilities. Remember that you can always add to what you have and what you experience by imagining "what if...?"

I hope that you will use this book to create your life in harmony with universal law. As you come to a greater understanding of your creative power, share your discoveries with others. Use your developing awareness of your power to help other people. When you aid others to abundance, you will have abundance yourself.

Be purposeful about what you create so that you create for the goodness of all concerned. When we are all fulfilling the innermost desires of our souls, the world will be a better place.

I give you my circle of love.

Artists and Illustrators

Aisha Causey (Cover design and photo)
Aisha Causey is a graphic designer by trade. She is currently a student at the College of Metaphysics, learning to apply metaphysical principles in everyday activities. Aisha's Dharma is creativity. Many thanks to her for her teaching and guidance in the layout and graphic design of this book.

Chris Sheehan (p. 11, 85, 90, 98, 102, 105, 107, 117, 140, 167)
Chris Sheehan is an accomplished artist who has recently expanded his repetoire of creative expression by painting large murals and designing entertaining films. He envisions domes to house the School of Metaphysics in every city where SOM has a branch location.

Dr. Pamela Blosser (p. 5, 6, 128)
Dr. Pamela Blosser is a teacher in the School of Metaphysics. She has travelled the world and currently serves as area director in Urbana and Bolingbrook, Illinois. Dr. Pam draws upon her artistic and musical talents through teaching adults and educating children.

Megan Lytle (p. 71)
Megan Lytle is a student at the College of Metaphysics. She explores various media including wood-burning and drawing as vehicles for aligning her conscious and subconscious minds.

About the Author

Dr. Laurel Clark devotes her life to humanitarian service through teaching, writing, interfaith ministry, and counseling. She has been a teacher in the School of Metaphysics since 1979 and currently serves as President.

An accomplished speaker, Laurel lectures throughout the United States to corporations, universities, civic and social organizations, hospices and hospitals on the application of Universal Law for more effective living.

She is writing a book of metaphysical fables for children of all ages.

Additional titles available from SOM Publishing include:

The Emptiness Sutra by Dr. Daniel R. Condron
ISBN: 0-944386-38-5 $10.00

The Secret Code of Revelation by Dr. Daniel R. Condron
ISBN: 0-944386-37-7 $15.00

The Purpose of Life by Dr. Daniel R. Condron
ISBN: 0-944386-35-0 $15.00

Master Living by Dr. Barbara Condron
ISBN: 0-944386-36-9 $18.00

Dharma: Finding Your Soul's Purpose by Dr. Laurel Clark
ISBN: 0-944386-34-2 $10.00

The Wisdom of Solomon by Dr. Barbara Condron
ISBN: 0-94438633-4 $15.00

Every Dream is About the Dreamer
Dr. Barbara Condron
ISBN: 0-944386-27-X $13.00

Peace Making: Nine Lessons for Changing Yourself,
Your Relationships, & the World by Dr. Barbara Condron
ISBN: 0-944386-31-8 $12.00

The Tao Te Ching Interpreted & Explained
Dr. Daniel R. Condron
ISBN: 0-944385-30-x $15.00

How to Raise an Indigo Child by Dr. Barbara Condron
ISBN: 0-944386-29-6 $14.00

Atlantis: The History of the World Vol. 1
Drs. Daniel & Barbara Condron
ISBN: 0-944386-28-8 $15.00

Karmic Healing by Dr. Laurel Clark
ISBN: 0-944386-26-1 $15.00

Spiritual Renaissance: Elevating Your Consciousness for the
Common Good by Dr. Barbara Condron
ISBN: 0-944386-22-9 $15.00

Superconscious Meditation: Kundalini & Understanding the Whole Mind by Dr. Daniel R. Condron
ISBN: 0-944386-21-0 $13.00

First Opinion: Wholistic Health Care in the 21st Century
Dr. Barbara Condron
ISBN: 0-944386-18-0 $15.00

The Dreamer's Dictionary by Dr. Barbara Condron
ISBN: 0-944386-16-4 $15.00

The Work of the Soul by Dr. Barbara Condron, ed.
ISBN: 0-944386-17-2 $13.00

Uncommon Knowledge: Past Life & Health Readings
Dr. Barbara Condron, ed.
ISBN: 0-944386-19-9 $13.00

The Universal Language of Mind: The Book of Matthew Interpreted by Dr. Daniel R. Condron
ISBN: 0-944386-15-6 $13.00

Dreams of the Soul: The Yogi Sutras of Pantanjali
Dr. Daniel R. Condron
ISBN: 0-944386-11-3 $13.00

Kundalini Rising: Mastering Your Creative Energies
Dr. Barbara Condron
ISBN: 0-944386-13-X $13.00

Permanent Healing by Dr. Daniel Condron
ISBN: 0-944386-12-1 $13.00

To order write:
School of Metaphysics World Headquarters
163 Moon Valley Road
Windyville, Missouri 65783 U.S.A.

Enclose a check or money order payable in U.S. funds to SOM with any order. Please include $5.00 for postage and handling of books, $10.00 for international orders.

A complete catalogue of all book titles, audio lectures and courses, and videos is available upon request.

Visit us on the Internet at www.som.org

email: som@som.org

About the School of Metaphysics

We invite you to become a special part of our efforts to aid in enhancing and quickening the process of spiritual growth and mental evolution of the people of the world. The School of Metaphysics, a not-for-profit educational and service organization, has been in existence for three decades. During that time, we have taught tens of thousands directly through our course of study in applied metaphysics. We have elevated the awareness of millions through the many services we offer.

If you would like to pursue the study of mind and the transformation of Self to a higher level of being and consciousness, you are invited to write to us at the School of Metaphysics World Headquarters in Windyville, Missouri 65783.

The heart of the School of Metaphysics is a four-tiered course of study in understanding the mind in order to know the Self. Lessons introduce you to the Universal Laws and Truths which guide spiritual and physical evolution. Consciousness is explored and developed through mental and spiritual disciplines which enhance your physical life and enrich your soul progression. For every concept there is a means to employ it through developing your own potential. Level One includes concentration, visualization (focused imagery), meditation, and control of life force and creative energies, all foundations for exploring the multidimensional Self.

Study centers are located throughout the Midwestern United States. If there is not a center near you, you can receive the first series of lessons through correspondence with a teacher at our headquarters.

As experts in the Universal Language of Mind, we teach how to remember and understand the inner communication received through dreams. We are the sponsors of the National Dream Hotline®, an annual educational service offered the last weekend in April.

For those desiring spiritual renewal, Spiritual Focus weekends at our Moon Valley Ranch on the College of Metaphysics campus in Missouri offer calmness and clarity. Each weekend focuses on intuitive research done specifically for you in your presence.

More than a traditional class or seminar, these gatherings are experiences in multidimensional awareness of who you are, why you are here, where you came from, and where you are going.

The Universal Hour of Peace was initiated by the School of Metaphysics on October 24, 1995 in conjunction with the 50th anniversary of the United Nations. We believe that peace on earth is an idea whose time has come. To realize this dream, we invite you to join with others throughout the world by dedicating your thoughts and actions to peace for one hour beginning at 11:30 p.m. December 31st into the first day of January each year. Living peaceably begins by thinking peacefully. The hour is highlighted with recitation of the Universal Peace Covenant (see next page), a document written by over two dozen spiritual teachers. Each year, we encourage people around the world to read the Covenant as they welcome the new year. During this time, students and faculty at the College of Metaphysics hold a 24 hour peace vigil in the world's Peace Dome. For more information, visit www.peacedome.org .

There is the opportunity to aid in the growth and fulfillment of our work. Donations supporting the expansion of the School of Metaphysics' efforts are a valuable way for you to aid humanity. As a not-for-profit publishing house, SOM Publishing is dedicated to the continuing publication of research that promote peace, understanding and good will for all of Mankind. It is dependent upon the kindness and generosity of sponsors to do so. Authors donate their work and receive no royalties. We have many excellent manuscripts awaiting a benefactor.

One hundred percent of the donations made to the School of Metaphysics are used to expand our services. The world's first Peace Dome located on our college campus was funded entirely by individual contributions. Presently, donations are being received for the Octagon, an international center for multi-dimensional living. Donations to the School of Metaphysics are tax-exempt under 501(c)(3) of the Internal Revenue Code. We appreciate your generosity. With the help of people like you, our dream of a place where anyone desiring Self awareness can receive education in mastering the mind, consciousness, and the Self will become a reality.

The Universal Peace Covenant

Peace is the breath of our spirit. *It wells up from within the depths of our being to refresh, to heal, to inspire.*

Peace is our birthright. *Its eternal presence exists within us as a memory of where we have come from and as a vision of where we yearn to go.*

Our world is in the midst of change. *For millennia, we have contemplated, reasoned, and practiced the idea of peace. Yet the capacity to sustain peace eludes us. To transcend the limits of our own thinking we must acknowledge that peace is more than the cessation of conflict. For peace to move across the face of the earth we must realize, as the great philosophers and leaders before us, that all people desire peace. We hereby acknowledge this truth that is universal. Now humanity must desire those things that make for peace.*

We affirm that peace is an idea whose time has come. *We call upon humanity to stand united, responding to the need for peace. We call upon each individual to create and foster a personal vision for peace. We call upon each family to generate and nurture peace within the home. We call upon each nation to encourage and support peace among its citizens. We call upon each leader, be they in the private home, house of worship or place of labor, to be a living example of peace for only in this way can we expect peace to move across the face of the earth.*

World Peace begins within ourselves. *Arising from the spirit peace seeks expression through the mind, heart, and body of each individual. Government and laws cannot heal the heart. We must transcend whatever separates us. Through giving love and respect, dignity and comfort, we come to know peace. We learn to love our neighbors as we love ourselves bringing peace into the world. We hereby commit ourselves to this noble endeavor.*

Peace is first a state of mind. *Peace affords the greatest opportunity for growth and learning which leads to personal happiness. Self-direction promotes inner peace and therefore leads to outer peace. We vow to heal ourselves through forgiveness, gratitude, and prayer. We commit to causing each and every day to be a fulfillment of our potential, both human and divine.*

Peace is active, the motion of silence, of faith, of accord, of service. *It is not made in documents but in the minds and hearts of men and women. Peace is built through communication. The open exchange of ideas is necessary for discovery, for well-being, for growth, for progress whether within one person or among many. We vow to speak with sagacity, listen with equanimity, both free of prejudice, thus we will come to know that peace is liberty in tranquility.*

Peace is achieved by those who fulfill their part of a greater plan. *Peace and security are attained by those societies where the individuals work closely to serve the common good of the whole. Peaceful coexistence between nations is the reflection of man's inner tranquility magnified. Enlightened service to our fellowman brings peace to the one serving, and to the one receiving. We vow to live in peace by embracing truths that apply to us all.*

Living peaceably begins by thinking peacefully. *We stand on the threshold of peace-filled understanding. We come together, all of humanity, young and old of all cultures from all nations. We vow to stand together as citizens of the Earth, knowing that every question has an answer, every issue a resolution. As we stand, united in common purpose, we hereby commit ourselves in thought and action so we might know the power of peace in our lifetimes.*

Peace be with us all ways. May Peace Prevail On Earth.

created by teachers in the School of Metaphysics 1996-1997

ABOVE AN ABYSS. TWO NOVELLAS

ABOVE AN ABYSS: TWO NOVELLAS

RYAN MASTERS

Radial Books

Also by Ryan Masters
Below the Low-Water Mark

Thanks to my wife Claire and son Jackson; to Eric Sun for giving me a place to write when I needed it; to Ben Kostival for his fine editing and to Tricia Yost for still giving a damn.

Published by Radial Books
radialbooks.com

Above an Abyss: Two Novellas / Ryan Masters, 1st ed.

ISBN 978-0-9984146-6-9

Cover Art: *Girl on a Trampoline*, Steve Mahon, 2008.

Typesetting services by BOOKOW.COM

For my mother,
Kay Lorraine

"The cradle rocks above an abyss, and common sense tells us that our existence is but a brief crack of light between two eternities of darkness."

VLADIMIR NABOKOV, *Speak, Memory*

Contents

Trampoline Games

A trampoline is attractive to nuisances. That is how I met Finn Levy.

My mother and I moved to Sandy, Utah on the first Saturday of summer 1986. The next morning, Finn skulked through the tall, brown grass of our backyard, wearing a white laboratory coat decorated with New Wave buttons. He kept his head down as he went, long red bangs covering his eyes. With each step, a mismatched Converse high top stirred a cloud of crickets—crickets so large I could hear the meat of their bodies pelt the baked earth when they landed. As I watched from the kitchen window, Finn mounted the fence and clambered over, disappearing into the neighbor's yard.

My mother hadn't noticed. She was busy watching a game show with a drink in her hand. She had made it clear from the outset she was unhappy with my father's decision to relocate our family to this Salt Lake City suburb for two years, especially once she discovered he would remain in California until Labor Day to orchestrate a massive round of layoffs "thanks to the Japanese." I didn't like it much either, but whenever I complained, my mother would set her jaw like an animal's and acidly explain my father was at a critical juncture of his career at National Semiconductor and we all had to make sacrifices.

I knew the red-haired kid in the lab coat was a Levy because he was a boy. When the woman from my father's company had let us into the barely furnished house, she mentioned a family with four girls to our left named the Hansons and a family with four boys to the right named the Levys. After the woman had gone, my mother made a joke about Mormons, Catholics, and rabbits.

Inside the kitchen, the microwave was loud, industrial, working hard to rotate macaroni and cheese for breakfast. The plastic wrap gurgled and warped. I held my fork in a fist and stared through the murky portal, waiting for the ding. In the next room, my mother watched *The Price is Right* on TV. A large, black woman was overwrought with the prospect of winning a rotating Buick. A shrill bell clanged. She threw her hands to her mouth, high-stepped in a circle before throwing her big arms around Bob Barker's neck. My mother laughed and swirled the ice in her drink. I removed my breakfast from the microwave with an oven mitt and went into the backyard to eat it. A lazy rhythm of squeaks drifted over the fence from next door.

Behind our new house, a seamless grid of suburbia ran all the way to the Wasatch Front, a jagged wall of Tolkienian mountains. I sat on the back step of the bare patio to eat. A cricket leapt onto the concrete beside me. Crickets plagued this place. They were everywhere. Utah was unlike California in many ways—mountains, Mormons, crickets. And the air was thin and dry. My lips felt like the salt flats we'd driven across to get here.

I finished my macaroni and cheese and left the plastic dish, fork, and oven mitt on the step beside me and snuck across the lawn to the fence that the red-haired boy disappeared over. Peeking through the slats, I saw the green of their grass, but couldn't see what was squeaking, so I climbed the fence as quietly as I could.

Finn jumped on a large, round trampoline in the center of the yard. He bounced from his back to his feet to his stomach to his feet to his back. The tail of his lab coat fluttered like a flag as he sailed through the air. His Converse lay in the grass between the fence and the trampoline where he'd kicked them off. He rebounded gracefully back to his feet from his stomach and then spotted me staring over the fence and paused, bouncing idly.

"Hey!"

He stepped gracefully from the black mesh of the trampoline, lit like Peter Pan upon the skirt of blue padding that ringed it and landed hard in a crouch on the grass, his knees absorbing the impact.

"You just moved in."

"That's right," I answered.

He glanced at the Hansons' house.

"I don't live here. I live on your other side. It's okay, though. These people aren't home."

"Are we allowed?"

"They'll be at church for hours. Come over and jump."

I climbed over and let myself carefully down into the Hansons' yard.

"You're sure it's okay?" I asked, taking off my shoes.

"Sure, I'm sure," he said, climbing back onto the trampoline.

I crawled up onto the padded skirt, stood, and stepped carefully out onto the fabric of the trampoline, immediately losing my balance. Its surface warped and lurched treacherously beneath me. The force of Finn's leaps made the trampoline surface buck like a horse. Off balance, I fell to my hands and knees. My skeleton jarred uncomfortably.

"Jesus," I said. "Hold on. Wait."

I scrambled backwards, my elbows locked up, unready for each new jolt. I felt ridiculous and a little scared. The alien physics of the trampoline paralyzed me. Finn laughed from somewhere above me. His buttons—The Clash, The Cure, No Heroes, Devo—glimmered. Beneath me, the warm, black mesh had a pleasant plastic smell in the sun.

"You swore. You said Jesus."

"Stop for a second, okay?" I asked.

The trampoline's convulsions petered out. I climbed unsteadily to my feet while he waited at the perimeter.

"You've never been on a trampoline before?"

"Uh-uh," I said, cautiously bending my knees to test the force of the springs.

"They're really big here. A lot of kids have them. Put your feet wider apart and bend your knees more. Your center of gravity is important. There."

After some experimentation, I found a rhythm and began leaping higher. It was a giddy sensation. The higher I went, the longer the weightlessness lasted, the deeper the trampoline's black mouth sucked me in, the louder the springs squeaked. Before I knew it, I was laughing, bouncing high into the air. I could see over the fences into a succession of yards, each green and square like the last, in every direction.

"Yeah!" Finn yelled. "That's the ticket."

I smiled down at him as I rose.

"Now I'm coming on. Move back a little."

As I rose again, he jumped on, contrapuntally timing his rhythm with mine. We passed each other in the air, rising and falling, our bodies flying dangerously close as their trajectories varied. We jumped until we panted and sweat, until our rhythms lagged, fell off from the other's. At one point when I landed, the trampoline felt like cement and my knees crumpled. I lolled about on my side, exhausted and cringing beneath Finn as he jumped over me from one side to the other laughing, enjoying the sight of me flopping about beneath him.

Before we climbed back over the fence into my yard, Finn beckoned me to a window of the Hansons' house.

"Look," Finn whispered. "This is their room. They all sleep in the same room. The twins sleep in the same bed. I swear."

He peered through the glass, hands cupped around his eyes. It made me nervous.

"Come on. Come look. Their underpants are on the floor. They wear pink panties. I think that's a bra on the bed."

I took a few steps toward the window, but lost my nerve. Instead, I retreated to the trampoline and examined its muscular springs. There must have been a hundred of them, wide as Susan B. Anthonys and as long as my arm from wrist to elbow. Too tight to stretch by hand.

"Come on. Let's go back to your yard," Finn said, tossing his shoes over the fence and mounting it.

Gratefully, I gathered my shoes and followed.

Finn's family were "Jack Mormons," he explained. His parents had recently quit the church. His father was a judge. Finn told me this like it explained why they'd stopped going to church. He was surprised I'd never in my life stepped inside one.

"You're lucky. I spent four hours of every Sunday of my life in a church. Until this summer."

Finn said everyone else in the neighborhood was Mormon, including the Hansons. No one liked that my father's company owned our house because it kept bringing non-Mormons into the community, he said. The church described non-Mormons as disruptions—unwanted wrinkles in the social fabric of Utah. Finn also said Mormons didn't call themselves Mormons. They called themselves Saints. Only non-Mormons called them Mormons. Finn clearly enjoyed calling Mormons Mormons.

As he talked and talked, I sensed his family's break from the church had freed Finn in some way. He reminded me of a *Wild Kingdom* episode where Marlin Perkins released a grizzly bear into the tundra of Alaska. The bear, which had been raised from a cub by humans, just walked in circles around the camera crew for hours, utterly confused by the vast space of the world surrounding it.

We entered the dark interior of my house through the backdoor and I yelled to my mother to give her a warning. Thankfully, she was up and about. When I introduced Finn, his entire demeanor changed. He stood up straight, brushed his bangs off his forehead, and with a formal air shook my mother's hand.

"It's a pleasure to meet you, Mrs. Lore," he said.

I couldn't tell if my mother bought his act or not, but she cooked some cheese-filled hot dogs in the microwave for us and didn't ask where we were going or when we were coming back.

"Sundays are weird for me now," Finn said as we walked through an empty lot full of weeds. "It's like the aftermath of a nuclear holocaust. I'm the only one walking around. Until you came along, that is."

Excited, Finn ran ahead, down through the weeds, crickets leaping frantically out of his way as he went. And I followed. The back of the empty lot was a convoluted BMX track, its dirt berms built up on each turn. But it was empty. Finn ran up the face of a berm and down its other side, the tail of his lab coats whipping behind him. I followed, and we ran around the track once, kicking off the tops of the berms as we went. In California, a track like this would've been packed on a Sunday with a hundred screaming, pedaling kids.

"Come on. I'll show you the creek," Finn said.

Finn veered off the track and disappeared down a slope of tall, yellow grass and into a stand of cottonwoods, leaves flashing in the breeze like coins. The crickets were even worse, raining through the weeds onto our feet.

At the creek, we found Jerry, whose head was so big it looked like it was going to burst. He was older, maybe nineteen, but half as smart. Finn marched right up to him. I didn't like the way Finn was acting, as if he had something to prove. He glanced back at me.

"Come on, he won't bite."

Jerry was breaking dirt clods in his hands.

"Toxic Avenger. Destroy, destroy. Kill, kill," Finn said.

Jerry had been talking to himself while crushing the clods. He looked up, an expression of surprise and joy distorting his pinched features.

"Hi guys!" he cried out with a wave.

His voice was cartoonish and scary.

"You're pretty strong, Jerry, breaking dirt clods like that," Finn said, looking down at him from the crown of the creek's bank. "You're a regular circus strongman."

Jerry didn't get sarcasm. He smiled, proud, let the dirt fall through his fingers while he struck a muscleman pose, arms like weird cobras pointing out from his body, their backs flexing. Jerry had big muscles. He was a man.

"Jerry, this is Jake. He moved in between us and the Hansons."

"Hulk Hogan!" Jerry said, flexing at me. "Hulk Hogan!"

He grrrred and Finn laughed. I smiled, disturbed by the theatrics. I didn't know what was wrong with Jerry. Did he have a disease? Was it something that could be caught in Utah? The breeze picked up and we all closed our eyes for a second while loose dirt was lifted and carried through the air around us.

"Hulk Hogan," Jerry said.

But now Jerry was showing us his dick, which was huge. Swollen like his head. Unnaturally large and standing up on its own, big and red.

"Hulk Hogan," he said again.

In a flash, Finn picked up a dirt clod and chucked it at Jerry's crotch, fast and hard and with remarkable accuracy. Jerry screamed and squirmed away, clutching his big, hurt penis in his hand and crying out over and over. I turned and fled, Jerry's wails chasing me up through the weeds and crickets and cottonwoods. When I reached the BMX track, I slowed down and waited for Finn to catch up.

"Hulk Hogan," Finn said, out of breath and laughed. "He shouldn't do that."

"What's wrong with him? With his head?"

"Hydrocephalus. There's fluid trapped in his skull and it expanded. It's called water on the brain."

"And his...?" I asked, pointing at my crotch.

"What?" Finn asked, cocking his head and smiling at me strangely.

"His dick, too."

Finn laughed out loud.

"Right! Water on the dick," Finn said, punching me in the arm a little too hard. "Funny."

I smiled, unsure of whether he was laughing at me or with me. We stood across the street from the small, unfamiliar house I now lived in. Mustard yellow. Aluminum and bright red brick. Nauseating.

"Listen, I should go home," I said.

"Do you want to come over after dinner?"

"My mom's not going to let me tonight," I lied. "But probably later, maybe tomorrow."

"Well, I'm glad you're here."

"Yeah, me too."

"We're going to have serious fun."

When I got home, my mother was asleep in her clothes on the sofa. I picked up her glass and washed it in the sink, cooked a pizza pocket in the microwave, then watched TV until I fell asleep beside her in the chair.

I awoke the next morning to the sound of the trampoline springs and girls' laughter. My mother cranked open an eyelid, looked at me, then at the open window.

"What the hell is that?"

"Trampoline."

"Mormon girls on a trampoline at…" she looked at her watch. "Nine o'clock. Jesus."

My mother groaned as she rose from the couch, lurched to the window and slammed it shut. Muttering to herself, she lumbered to the bathroom, cursing Utah and my father.

I cooked breakfast and ate it peering out the kitchen window. Four blonde heads rose and fell over the fence line. Long, dandelion-yellow curls bounced in pairs. I finished my microwave popcorn, stuffed the bag in the trash and wiped the butter on my shorts, then made for the back door. I needed a better look at these Hanson girls.

"Not so fast," my mother said, coming out of the bathroom. Her mouth frothed. She brandished a toothbrush like a wand. "The movers are coming in less than an hour."

I pushed the curtains back from the window and looked out on a typical summer day in Sandy, Utah. The neighborhood had exploded with activity. The BMX track across the street was awash with kids, cars passed on the streets, people emerged from their houses and went to work. It was like *The Twilight Zone*. Where had they all come from?

"I'm not joking around."

"Okay, okay." I returned to the living room and changed the channel. The TV was hot to the touch. It hadn't been off since we arrived. Despite the closed windows, I remained tortured by the sounds of squeaking springs and full-throated Hanson girls.

I spent the day carrying boxes of familiar things into the cramped, unfamiliar house. My room was in the basement. Its windows looked out into web-filled window wells. Just a sliver of sunlight penetrated to my depth. On the upside, I had the whole downstairs to myself. Other than my room, there was an empty rec room and a big storage closet. Upstairs, as my mother supervised the movers with a drink in her hand, I unpacked my clothes and toys and games and stuffed them in the storage closet. I hung my Joe Montana and Banzai Pipeline posters on the wall, set my globe and swimming trophies on the desk beside the door, and made my bed with its *Star Wars* sheets and comforter. I stepped back and took a look. The room felt wholly alien.

Upstairs, my mother had returned to the couch. Boxes remained unopened in their respective rooms. I had to climb over three boxes thickly labeled BATHROOM in pen to pee.

"Mom," I asked. "Should we unpack?"

"Why don't you start in the kitchen? When you get enough done, I'll make dinner for us. How's that for a deal?"

On TV, *Simon & Simon* were exchanging witty banter amidst a fistfight with goons. I opened the tops of eight boxes and gazed down at our hoard of kitchen utensils, plates, bowls, knick-knacks and appliances. I studied our new kitchen. There was no way it was all going to fit.

"Mom! There's not enough room."

"Goddamnit Jacob, take what won't fit downstairs and put it in the storage room. Show some common sense."

"You mean the rec room."

"Wrong, mister!" My mother yelled over her shoulder at the kitchen. "I mean the storage *slash* rec room."

"But I don't know what you want to keep up here!" I protested.

My mother's frustration and anger was seeping into my voice as if I were involuntarily mocking her.

"Don't make me come in there!"

Enraged, and because she couldn't see me, I flipped her off with both hands. I kicked the nearest box. A large, metal mixing bowl crashed onto the floor with an ear-piercing clangor and rolled across the kitchen. In an instant, my mother leapt from the couch and stormed into the kitchen, all furious eyes and set jaw. I backed away, an arm up for defense and a stream of swear words pouring uncontrollably from my mouth. She snatched my elbow in one claw-like grip and raised her other hand. I shrugged low, trying to somehow retract my head into my body as her hand leapt from my elbow to my collar. My shirt ripped in her hand as I fell to the dirty linoleum among the boxes. She tried to kick me, but I scurried between two of the boxes, picked up the mixing bowl and held it like a shield. Just as she was about to destroy the entire kitchen in pursuit of me, the doorbell rang. We both glanced in the direction of the front door. She pointed down at me, placed a finger to her lips and pointed at me again for good measure. "Best behavior," she hissed.

As she walked out of the kitchen, I crawled from among the boxes and peeked around the corner to see who was at the door. My mother blocked the gap with her body.

"Can I help you?" she asked with the artificial sweetness she reserved for strangers. Not unlike Finn, I thought.

"Welcome to the neighborhood!" A woman's sing-songy voice reached the kitchen. "We live right next door on this side. My name is Marie Hanson and these are my daughters: Debra, Brenda, Dawn, and Rebecca."

A four-part "Nice to meet you" chimed. I poked my head into the entryway for a look. Framed beneath the portcullis of my mother's arm, I saw one of the girls. She looked about my age. She glanced into the house and saw me. When she smiled, I ducked back into the kitchen, my heart pounding. She was the prettiest girl I had ever seen. Like a girl from TV. And she lived next to me with three of her sisters. I had snuck into their yard, jumped on their trampoline and peered at their underpants through their bedroom window. Cold fear gnawed my gut.

"What pretty girls!" My mother said. "How old are you, each of you?"

I wondered if they could tell she'd been drinking.

"I'm four!" piped a shrill voice.

"You are?" My mother asked in syrupy facsimile. God, I pleaded, please shut her up. Kill her right now so she doesn't say another word to these people.

"Rebecca's the youngest. Brenda and Dawn here are nine."

"Are you twins?" My mother's voice was outrageously condescending and bizarre.

"Yes, ma'am," the twins chirped in unison.

"And this is our oldest, Debra. She's twelve."

"Why, that's my son's age!"

"You *do* have children. We weren't sure. Is he your only one?"

"Yes."

There was a pause, as if Mrs. Hanson was waiting for her to continue.

"Well...I know you must be busy getting settled."

"What pretty girls you are," my mother said again. "Just *dolls*."

"We brought you this," a Hanson girl said. "We made it ourselves. It took all morning."

"Debra!" Mrs. Hanson reprimanded her without anger.

"My word, it did? Well, it's lovely. Thank you."

"Is your son home?" Mrs. Hanson asked.

"Oh, he's very tired right now, but I'm sure you'll meet him soon."

"If there's anything you need, please don't hesitate to ask. In the card, on the cake there, I've put our phone number. I also run a little business out of my home. A hair salon. I cut most of neighborhood kids' hair."

"I'll keep that in mind."

My mother shut the door and walked back to the kitchen. She shoved the cake onto the counter, then ripped open the envelope. Inside there was a greeting card with an angel on it. A smaller business card fell to the floor. She put the greeting card on the counter and picked up the business card.

"Of all the nerve," she said. "Can you believe that? That's a fine welcome to the neighborhood."

"Can I have some cake?"

"Hanson Hair Styles. The audacity of these people."

I cut a piece. Carrot cake. I put it on a plate, then began to eat it with my fingers.

"Use a fork," my mother said, dropping the cards into the garbage and opening the freezer in search of ice cubes.

"Mom, what does 'water on the brain' mean?"

"Water on the brain? I have no idea. Where did you hear that?"

"Nowhere," I said, piling more cake onto my plate.

She took her fresh drink to the living room and rejoined the brothers Simon. The sound of the trampoline springs began again and my mother swore. I peered out the back window, wiping white icing from my lips.

"Don't even think about going out there. You're tired, remember?"

I silently told her to go fuck herself, loudly dropped my dish in the sink, and went into the bathroom. Stepping over boxes, I looked at myself in the mirror. I needed a haircut.

A week after the movers delivered our possessions, awkward piles of boxes still cluttered the house, turning my mother and me into hunter-gatherers. As we fished out whatever we needed on a day-to-day basis, things slowly found their places. The kitchen was equipped for cooking, but we continued to rely on the microwave, a device that still hadn't lost its novelty. Weekly shopping trips consisted of freezer-fillers at the Smith's Food King up the road. My mother visited the state liquor store more frequently.

I hadn't been able to convince her I needed a haircut, despite combing my bangs over my eyes every morning, but I'd managed to see the Hanson sisters a few times during the week. I'd even spoken to the twins once through the fence between our backyards. They'd peeked through a knothole and asked me why our yard wasn't pretty and the lawn hadn't been cut. I told them I didn't know. When they asked me why my Daddy didn't do it for us, I told them that he was in California, firing people. Horrified, they ran back into their house, leaving me squinting after them through the fence slats. I prayed they didn't tell their mother I'd scared them. I wanted to get back on that trampoline so badly I could've died.

Before long, the trampoline coupled to Debra Hanson in my pre-pubescent mind. At twelve years old, I was obsessed with sex, yet ignorant about its mechanics. I spent hours devising elaborate plans involving the trampoline and impressing Debra Hanson. The blood rushed to my hairless penis. To what purpose? Why should anything except urine come out of it? Thanks to a black-and-white pictorial in the health section of the California public library system, I had a general understanding of how the sexual act was performed, but I assumed sex felt just like dry humping my pillow: arid and mildly titillating. When I fantasized about a girl, I visualized buddy-like adventures with long kisses, hand-holding, and deep hugs. Mostly, I associated Debra Hanson with the great, warm, bouncy black mesh in her backyard. The rhythmic sound of the springs haunted me.

I began spending a lot of time at Finn's. His mother was very friendly and always offering food. Plus, Finn's little brothers kept her busy so we could do whatever we wanted. The youngest of the brothers were two and three. The oldest, Peter, was nine and always wanted to tag along. Finn hated Peter, who was creepily quiet most of the time and had a disturbing habit of cowering and kowtowing to his brother, standard traits that Finn shouldn't have held against him, but Finn, like many older brothers, could be exceptionally cruel. Peter was the oddball of the family, and I suspected

Finn resented Peter's originality. Peter had a long, gothic face and raven black hair. He looked like he could play drums for The Cure. Ultimately, none of Finn's scorn was Peter's fault. Finn was just passing on the misery and abuse heaped on him by the community at large. He assured me none of the kids in the neighborhood had permission to be friends with us, an opinion I gathered held some truth. Kids were friendly with us in a civil way, never telling us we couldn't join them on the BMX track or in the pool or down by the creek or at the basketball courts, but never inviting us either. Before long, I enjoyed Finn's humiliation and ostracism of Peter. I even jumped in now and again with a deprecating remark. Afterward, I felt a little rotten about it, but Peter could be maddeningly spineless.

Finn's prized possession was a massive Bolivian bullfrog named Johnny Fank-Fank, who ate crickets like popcorn. We spent a lot of time catching food for him and constructing what we perceived as a Bolivian bullfrog utopia in a plastic wading pool. Johnny Fank-Fank didn't seem to appreciate our labors. All he did was sit wherever we set him and wait for live crickets to be dropped in his vicinity. But once the crickets entered Fank-Fank's Cricket Death World, Johnny transformed into a horrific, murderous creature, befitting his name, which Finn said was the most evil name he could think of. The Hanson sisters were terrified of Johnny. Finn put him in their bags or under their hats where they'd left them on the grass, or even, Finn winked once, up Debra Hanson's dress. I couldn't stand the idea of Johnny Fank-Fank anywhere near my dream girl, but I decided to hate the slave instead of the master. A friend like Finn was a rare commodity.

Yet tending to Fank-Fank's needs was no replacement for the trampoline. I wondered if an ache for God was anything like my ache for the weightless thrill and peace of the trampoline. The sight of Debra Hanson's hair flouncing wildly over the fence, the sound of the springs and peals of angelic laughter, it was all too much for me sometimes. Tormented and over-stimulated, I retreated to my shadowy basement.

When Sunday finally came, I stood breathless in my house's entryway, watching the Hansons pile into their station wagon. The girls wore long, flowery dresses with high necklines and big straw hats. Debra Hanson, hatless, looked grown and beautiful with her hair tied back in a ponytail. Their father, whom I now saw for the first time, was a small, balding man in a light blue suit. He ushered his blond brood into the car. Then, along with every other family in the neighborhood, the Hansons backed out of their driveway and drove slowly to church. The trumpet-blowing angel Moroni capped the temple's enormous spire, which dominated the suburban landscape for miles. The moment the Hansons' station wagon turned the corner, my hand lit upon the doorknob.

"I want the front and back lawns mowed today," my mother said. "The realtor said the lawnmower in the garage is perfectly good."

"But—"

My mother shot me a glance. I whined and sighed and turned around and went to find the mower. I opened the garage door and examined the old, heavy machine. I unscrewed its gas cap and peered inside. Dust. As I filled the mower from a flaking, rusty can of gasoline, the gas spilled over my shoes and dribbled into the driveway, filling the garage with fumes. As I yanked uselessly on the ripcord, Finn materialized at the sun-dappled mouth of the garage, his hands casually stuck in the pockets of his lab coat.

"Ready to jump, amigo?" he asked.

"I have to mow the lawn," I said, kicking at the lawnmower. "But this thing is a piece of shit. It won't start."

Finn laughed. He liked it when I swore.

"You have to prime it, see?"

He reached down and pushed a little rubber button four or five times.

"Now try."

With one yank, the lawnmower coughed a cloud of exhaust and idled with loud chugs. Impressed with Finn's expertise, I killed the engine so we could talk.

"Thanks."

"You sure you can't jump?" Finn asked, poking around our garage.

The thing was, I probably could have ditched mowing. My mother was fairly oblivious to anything outside the house after mid-morning, but I realized I didn't want to associate Finn with the trampoline just now.

"Yeah, my mom's a total bitch."

Finn picked up the gas can, unscrewed its lid, and took a big whiff. The can might have been freshly baked bread. "You ever huff gas?"

I didn't answer straight away. It felt like a trick question. I'll huff and I'll puff and I'll blow your house down, I thought.

He screwed the cap back on.

"Gas is like model airplane glue or spray-paint. It gets you high."

My idea of getting high was a lot like my notion of God. Unclear. A word with no meaning attached to it.

"I'll show you sometime."

"Whatever. I'd better get started," I said, yanking the ripcord and starting the mower.

"Don't forget the bag on the back or all the grass will fly up in your face!" Finn yelled over the engine.

I waved, annoyed by the noise and his inscrutable questions, and watched him saunter to the Hansons' side gate. Huffing gasoline sounded dangerous. High? I picked up the can, unscrewed the cap and smelled the fumes. The inside of my nose burned and my eyes watered. I screwed the cap back on. As I struggled to attach the bag to the rear of the lawnmower. The trampoline springs squeaked plaintively next door.

Finn and I were carrying a boxful of crickets to Johnny Fank-Fank when I talked to Debra Hanson for the first time. She was sitting in the shade of some cottonwoods in her front yard and reading a book as we passed.

"Finn, you don't have Johnny in that box, do you?"

"Not to worry, milady," Finn said, a crooked grin on his face.

"That's good," Debra said, heaving an exaggerated sigh of relief.

"'Tis but a boxful of doomed crickets for Johnny to gobble."

"I hate that toad," she said, screwing up her face in disgust.

"He's a Bolivian bullfrog."

"I still hate him."

"What are you reading?" I asked, desperate to be part of the conversation. Her expression changed from disgust to nonchalance when she looked at me. After a moment, she flipped the cover over. *A Wrinkle in Time*.

"That's a good book," I said.

"I've just started it. You're the new boy next door."

"Jake."

"I'm Debra."

"Come on, Jake. Fank-Fank hungers."

"It was nice to meet you."

She smiled and returned her attention to her book.

As we walked away, Finn reached into the box and crushed a cricket between his thumb and forefinger.

"I hate that bitch," he said, wiping cricket guts on his lab coat.

Finn wasn't what you would call a sports type. It's not that he wasn't athletic. He may have even been athletically gifted. He just didn't care for normal activities. He was exuberantly talented on the trampoline. He performed his flips, flops, twists, turns, pikes, somersaults, and other strange, unnamable contortions with the utmost grace. He was also fixated on lawn darts. He'd found some at a garage sale—six huge, vicious, metal darts fletched with a quarter pound of brightly molded plastic. Darts with serious heft. Not toys. They felt deadly. Like holding my father's service revolver. And they just cried out to be used in an irresponsible manner. Finn's lawn dart game invariably deteriorated into Finn's lawn dart wars, usually at Peter's expense, but occasionally at mine or even his own. We'd hardly finished feeding Johnny Fank-Fank before Finn snatched the lawn darts. He jogged out to the front yard and threw them high into the air one after the other and dodged them as they fell. When each dart sank heavily into the turf, Finn somersaulted like a commando. I ran into the yard behind him, followed by Peter who was beginning to show some confidence due to my vague acceptance of his existence. Finn tossed one high over our heads and yelled, "Incoming!" My eyes searched the sky for a deadly falling needle. Peter looked at me and covered his head with an arm, his lip curled back to reveal his crooked front teeth. I grabbed him and yanked him out of the way of the dart, which sank to its hilt inches from where he'd been standing.

"Goddamnit, Finn!" I yelled.

Peter looked at me with a frightened mixture of respect and devotion. Finn walked towards us, the rapture of the moment slowly yielding to guilt on his face.

"It wasn't going to hit him."

"You could've killed him. More importantly," I said, pushing Peter away, "You could've killed me."

Finn had stopped listening. A new game was afoot. Jerry approached, wandering down the sidewalk with a finger in his ear. The tail of his dress shirt fluttered from his corduroy pants. His body strained its too-small clothes. Jerry looked like a disheveled superhero. I imagined his origin story. Jerry: a mild-mannered, normal boy who was kidnapped and experimented on by an evil crime organization. They used a giant turkey baster to inject serum into his brain cavity, transforming him into a ultra-soldier bent on world domination. Unfortunately, the experiment went horribly awry and the serum that was supposed to uber-ize him distorted his features, inflated his skull, and destroyed his wit.

"If it isn't Hulk Hogan," Finn said.

"Jerry!" Peter yelled out, his voice a garbled mockery of Jerry's. "Jerry! Duhhh!"

Peter danced and crowed like a drunken jester, ecstatic not to be the object of scorn for the time being.

"Hi, Peter!" Jerry called out, a big, happy grin on his face.

He looked pleased to see Peter and I guessed that they were some kind of friends. However, their power dynamic was entirely altered by Finn's presence. I couldn't keep my eyes off of Jerry's crotch, knowing what I did about what monstrous thing lay there. Instead, I busied myself collecting the lawn darts from where they'd landed around the yard.

"Come on, show us your big muscle, Hulk," Finn said. "Let's see it."

Jerry ignored Finn, refusing to be baited. "Peter, do you want to come to the creek?" he asked.

"N-o-o-o!" Peter answered as if that was the dumbest question he'd ever heard in his life. "I don't."

"My brother's not coming down to the creek with you, Jerry. I've seen what you do at the creek. I'm thinking about telling your parents."

"F-F-Finn!" Jerry stammered, his face red and his eyes scared. "Don't talk to me."

Peter clapped his hands. "F-F-F-Finn!" he mimed, cock-eyed, his tongue poking grotesquely from his mouth.

Finn laughed and his little brother glowed in response. When I chuckled, Jerry trained his sad eyes on me, and I suddenly felt a surge of anger. I threw a lawn dart high in the air, then watched it apex, waver, and turn its heavy metal point straight down towards Jerry's big head. Jerry hadn't even looked up.

"Watch out, dumbass!" I yelled.

With a gunshot crack, the dart struck the sidewalk behind Jerry and clattered away. Jerry flinched, startled by the sound. He looked at the dart on the ground and looked at me, creeping toward a realization.

"Jerry! Jerry, dear!"

We all turned to see Mrs. Hanson emerging from her side gate.

"Would you like to jump on the trampoline with the girls?" Jerry's face lit up again.

"Yes, Mrs. Hanson," he replied, shuffle-jogging away from us.

Agog, I watched his bubble butt and bubble head follow her into the Hanson's backyard. Mrs. Hanson glared at me for a long moment, shook her head, and shut the gate. My heart sank. For a moment, I thought I was going to throw up. Shame permeated every cell of my body.

"How do you like that?" Finn asked, shaking his head.

"That guy's a retard," Peter said.

"Shut up," Finn said, shoving Peter in the chest, reviving the boy's simper.

"I'll see you guys later," I said. I dropped the remaining darts and headed for my front door.

"Hey!" Finn said, jogging over and placing a hand on my shoulder. "What's wrong?"

"Nothing," I said, shrugging off his hand. "I just gotta go."

Finn's eyes burned at me as I slipped out of the sun and into the cave of my house.

"Is that you?" my mother called from the living room.

"Who else would it be?"

"Watch your mouth."

I went into the kitchen and poured myself a glass of milk.

"I swear to God, that trampoline, that squeaking, is going to drive me crazy," my mother muttered into her glass.

"Why don't you tell them to stop?"

She glanced over her shoulder at me. "Maybe I will."

This only made me feel sicker. I rinsed my glass and slipped out the back door as quietly as possible. The springs were louder than ever. I saw Jerry's head float over the fence like a great, idiotic balloon, a look of rapture distorting its surface. He began to howl and I noticed none of the girls were jumping. Wondering where they were, I snuck along the side of the house and leaned against the fence. I stopped in my tracks when I realized that Mrs. Hanson and Debra were just on the other side.

"...made some people from a different mold. I want you and your sisters to be nice to him. Do you hear me, Miss?"

"He scares me. I don't like him."

"He is a perfect gentleman. He deserves our sympathy and compassion. Do you understand?"

"Fine."

"I'll be in the salon until four o'clock. If it's something important come get me. But don't disturb me unless you absolutely have to."

"Fine."

Mrs. Hanson crunched down the pea-gravel path that led from the backyard to her salon, which smelled strongly of chemicals and shampoo. I remained perfectly still. The fence shook as Debra scrabbled up it and stuck her head over to look at me.

"You're eavesdropping," she said, pushing blond curls behind an ear and cocking her head.

"I didn't mean to."

"I could have told on you."

"Thanks," I said, "for not doing that."

She eyed me, enjoying her point of view. "I've read books about perfect gentlemen," she said. "Jerry isn't anything like them."

"No, he's not," I said.

"He's imperfect and crude. Like Dr. Frankenstein's monster."

"I don't think it's his fault. The way he is, I mean."

Debra glanced back into her yard. I peered through the slats to see what she was studying. Her sisters sat on a garden bench and watched Jerry jump on the trampoline. The girls held hands tightly as if afraid this strange man-child might leap down on them at any moment.

"Sometimes I feel like Meg."

She was looking down at me again, her beautiful face ringed in a halo of curls. The blue sky above seemed to swim and fume and waver.

"Like who?"

"Meg. The girl in *A Wrinkle in Time*. My whole life, I've tried to fit in. Be like everyone else. Or, you know, be like I thought they wanted me to be."

"Like Meg."

"You know how she gets in fights at school and hates being different, but can't help it?"

"Yes," I said, warming to my lies.

"I feel like I just want to push back at church and with teachers. Even at home, sometimes I hate my sisters. I'm never alone. Is that weird?"

"Weird is normal," I said. "I feel exactly the same way. Living here in Utah? It's like living on a different planet."

Debra smiled down on me and a buoyancy overtook my body, filling it with helium. I almost floated into the sky and kissed her. Debra executed a practiced wink, like Madonna on MTV, before she slowly disappeared behind the fence. To watch her go, I pressed my face against the coarse slats. The splintered wood hurt my face. She sat on the ground a few feet from her sisters and opened her book, but didn't read. Instead, she looked to the trampoline. Together, the three girls watched grimly as Jerry, gibbering like an ape, cavorted on the trampoline above them.

One morning, I watched Finn's parents and younger brothers pile into the family Suburban and drive away. I clambered over the fence and dropped into their backyard. Through the sliding door, I saw Finn seated at a piano, his back to me. I knocked on the glass, but he didn't turn around, so I slid the door open. A flood of music surprised me. It had never occurred to me that people actually played pianos in their homes. The piano in our old house was basically a glorified shelf for knick-knacks. I was at Finn's side before he noticed me. His fluid fingers froze over the keys and the music vaporized in mid-air.

"Geez, Jake. You scared me." He carefully closed the piano's key-lid and turned to face me.

"You're really good," I said.

"I've been playing forever."

"What was that?"

"Chopin."

I nodded. The word meant nothing to me.

"Where did your family go?"

"Hiking in the mountains. Here, I want to show you something."

He slipped off the piano bench and crossed the room. I followed him to the stairs, which we bounded up three at a time. In his room, he dropped to his knees and dug under the bed until he found a wooden cigar box. He undid a tiny brass clasp and opened it.

"Two things, really. First these."

He handed me a pack of cigarettes.

"I stole them. Cool, huh?"

I nodded. It *was* cool.

"And this."

He unfolded a piece of paper and handed it to me. It looked like a recipe for something, but the list included water, Drano, and aluminum.

"What is it?"

"The ingredients for a bomb."

"Where'd you get it?"

"Some guy."

"Who?"

"I know lots of guys. Come on."

I followed him back downstairs and into the kitchen. He pulled an empty two-liter soda bottle out of the trash and told me to fill the bottom with water. As I did this, he fished under the sink and emerged with a bottle of Drano. With the confidence of a chemist, he poured drain cleaner into the soda bottle, mixed it with the water, and replaced the cap.

"Look in that drawer there," he said. "Pull out the Reynolds Wrap and tear off a few feet and follow me."

We went into his garage, which was almost empty. His dad didn't seem to have any tools. Nothing in there but a snow shovel, a lawnmower, a bunch of oil stains, and a boxy, red container with GASOLINE printed diagonally in yellow letters. Finn picked up the container and sloshed the liquid around inside. He unscrewed the top.

"Smell that," he said, swirling the spout under my nose. "Breathe it in."

"Careful," I said, gently pushing the can away. "You're spilling it."

"Gas evaporates almost instantaneously. Don't worry. You want to get high?"

"I thought we were building a bomb."

He nodded and screwed the cap back on the can and grabbed a pair of gardening gloves from a shelf. "You're right. First things first."

We hiked to a plateau above our neighborhood where housing developments hadn't begun in earnest yet. These benchlands consisted of large, flat spaces filled with weeds, dirt clods and vast numbers of leaping crickets. A forest of survey stakes marked the sites of future homes—an entire mini-suburb from the looks of it. Finn amused himself by catching crickets as we walked and dropping them into the bomb. By the time we reached a spot that Finn deemed safe, the clear plastic bottle was filled with dead and dying crickets soaked in our brew. After clearing a test site by tamping weeds down with our feet, Finn gave us each a cigarette. We smoked and made a solemn study of the towering Wasatch Range to the east. I mimicked Finn's technique and found the burn of the cigarette felt good. Manly. What we were doing here on the plateau was serious and cool, I decided. With some ceremony, we ground our cigarettes into the sand and shook hands. Finn put on the gardening gloves and picked up the bomb, addressing it with cold calculation. He eyed the concoction through the green filter of the plastic bottle and nodded, satisfied with what he saw.

"Aluminum," he said.

I handed over the long sheet of foil and he tore it into pieces, balled them up and stuffed them, one after the other, in quick succession, into the bottle. A strange, acrid white wisp emerged as Finn screwed the cap on as tight as he could, shook the bottle wildly, and placed it back on the ground.

"Back away! Back away!" Finn cried. "Hurry!"

I stumbled backwards, startled by the alarm I heard in Finn's voice. When we were about twenty feet away, Finn placed a hand on my chest, stopping me, his eyes never leaving the bottle. It didn't move. Seconds passed. Seconds turned into a minute. Two minutes. I finally relaxed and glanced over at him.

"It's a dud," I said.

"Shhhh," Finn hissed.

"What's happening?" I asked.

"Sodium hydroxide in the drain cleaner. Aluminum."

"So?"

"Hydrogen gas."

The bottle began to swell and harden, filling with white smoke. It shook with frustration and slowly tipped over on its side. Suddenly, a loud, concussive POOM shook the air. The force of the explosion shocked me and I stumbled backwards over my feet, landing on my butt in the dirt and weeds. A salamander of white gas slithered from the bottle and into the sky. Smoking bits of material sailed through the air.

"Time to go," Finn said, a lunatic smile on his face.

We ran all the way back to his house, taking a route through the creek bottom and sneaking at times on our hands and knees so no one would connect us with the scene. When we finally reached safety, fire sirens had begun to wail. Finn had suffered a chemical burn the size of a quarter on his forearm. He treated it with salve without flinching and bandaged the wound. Next, we burned the bomb instructions and flushed the ashes down the toilet. Then we sat in front of the TV and pretended to watch it, sweating and tense, waiting for the authorities to pound on the door. After an hour passed, the sirens were long gone. We began to smile, then laugh, then roll on the floor with exhilaration. POOM! I closed my eyes and saw our genie of white smoke surrounded by swirling chemical fairies and felt proud and overjoyed. At that moment, I didn't think I had ever felt closer to another person in my life. "Friends for life," Finn said, clasping my hands in his. "Friends for life," I promised.

That night I didn't think about Debra Hanson or the trampoline as I fell asleep.

After the bomb, the Fourth of July seemed unspectacular, especially under Utah's strict laws about fireworks. Finn and I sat on the fence, watching the neighborhood kids wave sparklers and ignite black inchworms. From the fence, we could see the street and the Hansons' backyard. To the delight of the congregated Hanson clan, the girls were performing choreographed routines with sparklers. Dressed in red, white, and blue outfits complete with cardboard top hats, they high-kicked to a Sousa march emanating from speakers in the windows of the house. Hunched like a vulture, Finn sneered at the scene next door.

"Of all the lameness."

I nodded vaguely. The Hansons were highly practiced. Even the youngest kept in time. It was obvious they'd been preparing for a long while.

"Come on," Finn said. "Let's get out of here."

"Hold on a second," I said.

Finn hunched further on the fence to demonstrate his contempt for all things Hanson and patriotic. The girls' sparklers whizzed in smart arcs through the air. Blonde curls radiated like platters of sunshine from beneath the Uncle Sam top hats. Tan knees poked from beneath sky-blue skirts at precise angles as they marched, spun, kicked, and knelt. Calf muscles flexed and strained beneath white tube socks. The toes of their shiny black shoes cut through the freshly cut grass, kicking individual blades into the air. As the Sousa March oompahed to a big finish, the girls spun, fell to one knee, doffed their hats expertly, and held their sparklers high in the air, four identical white smiles glowing in the soft dusk light. The Hanson clan erupted into applause, and some of the families on the street glanced toward the house.

"Come on!" Finn said again.

"*Wait*," I said.

The music suddenly shifted and the Pointer Sisters' "Jump (For My Love)" erupted from the speakers. The girls hopped up from their finale kneels and, to the delight of all assembled, ran to the trampoline and climbed on, sparklers in hand.

"Come on, Jake. We've got things to do. We're wasting time."

Finn sprang from the fence and began walking towards his house. I ignored him.

"Do you want to be a part of this mission or not?"

"What mission?" I asked, tearing my eyes away from the Flying Patriotic Hanson girls and their fabulous golden curls.

"You have to come with me to find out," Finn said, continuing into the house.

I watched them for another minute, and with a sigh, ran after Finn.

Finn drew the cigar box from under his bed and opened it with a solemn and official air. "I trust anything I show or tell you is in strict confidence." The lid fell back, and in the box, on a bed of felt lay three ninja throwing stars. They were more beautiful than any jewelry I'd seen and fathomlessly black and wicked as a shark's eye.

"Whoa," I said, reaching for one. "Are they real?"

"Don't touch," Finn said, brushing my hand away. "We don't want fingerprints on them. We only touch stars while wearing gloves."

He grabbed two pairs of ski glove liners from his bedside table and handed me one. I put on a liner and picked up a star. It was heavy.

"Feel the balance?" he asked, hefting the biggest of the three stars. "Finely tooled in Japan. Only one place in the world makes them like this."

"What do they say on them?" I asked, running my fingers over the Japanese characters on the face.

"Death is honor," Finn replied without a moment's pause. "Or death before all."

I nodded, wondering how he knew that.

"Careful. They're as sharp as Ginsu blades."

"Okay," I said, practicing the throwing hold I'd seen in movies.

"Between your thumb and forefinger. Like this. Hyaaah!" Finn said, demonstrating proper technique in slow motion. "Properly thrown, these things can go right through the human body."

I nodded. "I've seen that."

"Really?"

"In a movie."

"But they're more commonly used as messages."

"What?"

"When someone was marked for death in feudal Japan, a ninja hucked one of these and stuck it in the target's front door. As a warning."

"That they were about to die."

"Exactly. The Japanese have always been known for their exceptional cruelty. The target knew he could be killed at any time."

"Who's our target?"

"Our target is a zeek named Troy Coleman."

"Who's he?"

I returned the star carefully to the felt, stood up, and looked in on Johnny Fank-Fank, who'd been surveilling me from inside his terrarium. I still hated him.

"Troy Coleman is the biggest zeek in school. Plus, he sucker-punched me once. Knocked out one of my teeth."

"Which one?" I asked, peering into his mouth.

"It was a baby tooth."

Outside, darkness came in earnest. The street was lined with kids waving sparklers.

"He beat you up?"

"He didn't beat me up. He got one sucker punch in."

"Did you hit him back?"

"He knocked my tooth out," Finn said. "The teacher broke it up before I got a chance."

I nodded and plucked Johnny Fank-Fank from the terrarium. He must have weighed five pounds. I didn't know about Utah schools, but where I came from, getting beat up by the biggest zeek in school made *you* the biggest zeek. Whatever a zeek was. I didn't mention this to Finn. "So what are you going to do?"

"We are going to send a little message."

"But it only takes one of us to throw the star."

"Ninjas always work in pairs."

"I thought they always worked alone."

"You just *think* they're working alone. There's always another one around, backing the first one up."

I replaced Johnny Fank-Fank. He resettled on his haunches, then continued his thousand-yard stare.

"When?"

"Tonight."

"I can't. I told my mom I'd be back an hour after dark."

"Tonight, tonight. We'll sneak out after your mom's asleep."

He was not joking.

Sneaking out was a cinch. My mother was comatose by ten every night. You could light her eyebrows on fire and she wouldn't wake. Wearing my blackest clothes, per Finn's instructions, I eased back the deadbolt and slipped out the front door in a turtleneck, sweatpants, and sneakers. Liberated into the night, I stepped onto the cool, green grass of my front lawn, slipped from one puddle of shadow to another, hunkered down in the hedge and waited for Finn. The street was an entirely different place after midnight, desolate like Sunday, only darker. I was confident I was the only one up and about.

That night, Finn was late. I'd almost gone back to bed when he finally slipped out his front door and ran to the hedge, a black satchel over his shoulder. Wordlessly, he handed me a pair of the glove liners and signaled me to follow him. We made our way from yard to yard, cautious at first, then increasingly reckless.

Drunk on adrenaline and the summer night air, we sprinted, ducking and rolling, leaping and swerving through the yards, crossing the shadowy bridges that linked islands of lamppost light to one another. Whenever a car passed, we dove for cover and lay still, our chests heaving, heads down. Once it was gone, we were back on our feet and running. We looked in on sleeping families, stole the bulbs out of porch lights and smashed them in the street, rang doorbells and brazenly waited to hear movement in the house. We cavorted up one block and down another, over this fence and through that gate. Private property meant nothing to us. We dismantled lawn ornaments and destroyed gardens, terrorized pets and frightened sleepless children. We were boogeymen.

By the time we reached the Zeek's house, we'd been out for hours. We hunkered between two large cottonwood trees in Troy's yard. Finn opened his satchel and withdrew the throwing star in a deeply ritualistic manner. He lifted it in the air between us. Lamppost light glinted off its surface.

"First," Finn whispered, reaching into his satchel and withdrawing two rolls of toilet paper. I snatched one and we leapt to work, webbing the Zeek's trees, his mailbox, the lamppost. The pale tissue hung in shameful fat ribbons that pleased me greatly.

When we finished, Finn positioned himself twenty feet from the Zeek's front door. He withdrew the throwing star and ran his gloved finger over its razor sharp edge. He looked at me and smiled. I gave him the thumbs up, ready to run once it thunked into the door. Finn drew back slowly, his breath measured. His technique appeared flawless. But when he released the star, it sliced sideways through the air and bounced off a glass window with a terrific clap. I was already halfway down the block before the lights snapped on and the yelling started.

The following Sunday, my mother tried to rope me into another morning of lawn maintenance, but I simply walked out the door, pretending not to hear. She yelled my name so loud the Hansons probably heard it in the church pews. I was already sprawled on the warm, polypropylene mesh of the trampoline next door, dozing in the sun. My mother yelled my name one last time before slamming the front door shut. Earlier in the week, I'd heard my mother on the phone, warning my father that I was becoming *unmanageable*. But he was a thousand miles away firing people. I couldn't see the threat.

An hour or so later, Finn joined me on the trampoline and we played a game called Crack The Egg. The egg was one guy wrapped tight in a ball. The other guy bounced him as hard as he could, trying to crack him open. It was a riot. Sometimes the egg bounced three or four feet into the air, sometimes off the trampoline altogether. It was a game of endurance. Finn called it training.

The Hansons' backyard was an Eden on Sundays. When we grew bored with our trampoline games, we dozed side by side on the trampoline or planned night missions or peered through the windows of the house for underpants and other visible taboos.

During the rest of the week, when the gates of Eden were slammed shut by Mrs. Hanson, we lived for the night. While the sun was up, we resented the world with a quiet and knowing arrogance. Who were these kids playing on *our* lawns, in *our* streets, riding bikes down *our* sidewalks?

Meanwhile, the unsavory needs of Johnny Fank-Fank, his despotic rule of the wading pool, began to resemble the dull life of a listless bullfrog. My mother complained that all I did was lie around and sleep. She even threatened to find some camp for me to go to if I didn't "shape up." So I spent even less time at home. I'd get up, cook something in the microwave, and go over to Finn's if only to sit in his backyard and wait for him to finish his chores or piano practice.

As for Debra Hanson, I rarely saw her anywhere but on the trampoline. Of course, she might as well have been jumping on the surface of the moon. I didn't dare climb the fence and wave to her. But if she was jumping I would be close, lounging in my backyard or taking out the garbage or kicking the ball against the side of the house. I prayed she would clamber up the fence and talk down to me again. When she wasn't in the air next door, she vanished.

Eventually I forced my mother's hand by getting gum stuck in my hair. It hadn't been planned, but served my purposes nicely. Brandishing the scissors like a Cossack, my mother had put a huge divot near the crown of my head trying to hack the offending glob out of my hair. The next morning, when she woke up, she'd felt bad enough to call Mrs. Hanson. Holding the receiver of the phone a few defensive inches from her ear, my mother listened to Mrs. Hanson's shrill, cheerful suggestion of three o'clock. I wondered if she remembered the lawn darts incident with Jerry. She didn't seem like the type who forgot such things.

At ten minutes to three, in my nicest shirt, I walked over to the side gate. My mother had looked at me strangely when she saw what I was wearing, but had refrained from comment. The smell on the salon side of the house was a mix of noxious chemicals and nose-crinkling perfumes. I followed the sound of a tinny radio playing pop music to the door of the salon, which was tiny—two chairs in a room no more than twelve feet long and half that wide. An older woman I didn't recognize from the neighborhood sat in the closest chair, a plastic bag over her head. Black grease dripped down her neck from inside the bag. She gave me a kind smile. Mrs. Hanson beckoned me to the far chair.

"Hello Jacob. Don't you look nice. Take a seat. I'll be right with you."

I squeezed past the crone and took a seat. There was nothing to read. My California barber had lots of magazines and comic books in his waiting room.

"This is Jacob, Mrs. Young. He's the boy who moved in next door."

Mrs. Young looked at me as if with an injured neck. I assumed she was trying to prevent the grease-drip from moving further down her neck.

"Hi," I said.

She nodded, eyeing me. An odd smile wedged wrinkles this way and that about her face.

"Mrs. Young is our bishop's wife, Jacob."

"Oh?"

"There," Mrs. Hanson said, making final adjustments to the bag on Mrs. Young's head. "Ten more minutes and we'll rinse."

Mrs. Young closed her eyes as if she were about to immediately fall into some profound sleep.

"What for gosh sakes happened here?" Mrs. Hanson said, running her fingers over my divot. Mrs. Young opened a curious eye.

"Gum."

"I should say so," she said. "Why don't we try to soak it first? *Debra*?"

I heard steps on the gravel outside and I tensed, trying to look cool while her mother fastened an apron around my neck. Debra appeared at the door with a book in her hand. She wore shorts and a tight white T-shirt that highlighted her tan skin and blond curls. I looked at her, then looked away, then looked at her again. She smiled.

"Go get me some of that special detangler we keep in the kitchen, please, hon."

She disappeared.

"She's more beautiful every day I see her," Mrs. Young said, her eyes closed.

"And she's beginning to know it," Mrs. Hanson said.

The women laughed. I stared uncomfortably at a poster of different angular hairstyles. Debra returned and handed her Mom a plain, white bottle.

"My special ingredients," Mrs. Hanson said, shaking the bottle. "Guaranteed to get the gum right out."

"How did you get gum in your hair?" Debra asked.

"I don't know," I said, totally cowed.

"That was dumb."

"Debra, be nice," Mrs. Hanson said, turning the water on in the sink behind my chair and testing the temperature.

Mrs. Young clucked her tongue.

"Yeah, it was," I conceded, trying to absolve her.

Instead of leaving, she leaned against the wall and studied the poster. She pointed at one woman with dark New Wave hair and heavy mascara.

"Do you think she's pretty, Mrs. Young?"

Mrs. Young squinted. "She's very handsome. Her cosmetics, however, are overdone."

Everyone looked at the woman who seemed brooding, angry, tense. I thought she was a knockout.

"I can't wait until I get to wear makeup."

"Well, I hope you show more sense than she did," Mrs. Young said.

"My mom says I have to wait until eighth grade to wear make-up. Just two more years."

Mrs. Young zagged up a puckered eyebrow.

"I said we'd talk about it. I think eighth grade is too young."

"No it *isn't!*"

I was surprised by how young she suddenly sounded.

"What do *you* think, Mrs. Young?" Mrs. Hanson asked.

"No reason to rush out of childhood. Girls have their whole lives to be wives," she answered.

Debra scowled. "I don't want to be a wife."

"Debra!" Mrs. Hanson barked.

Defiant, Debra snatched her book from the counter and walked out.

"I am so sorry," Mrs. Hanson said. "I don't know what's gotten into her."

"Strong-willed child," Mrs. Young said, closing her eyes.

I'm not sure when the poltergeists began. Maybe the first week of August. Although it continued to be deeply satisfying, sneaking out had become almost routine. We moved through the neighborhood like rumors, reaching through open windows to ruffle the hair on the backs of sleeping families' necks, disturbing their dreams. We paid no heed to property lines. I suppose it was a natural progression to breach their walls.

After a long night of sneaking, we found ourselves in a completely new and different neighborhood. We rarely spoke to each other when we were out. We complemented each other's movements in the dark as if telepathic. He climbed the porch of a big two-story white house and before his hand even reached for the knob, I knew we were going inside. The thrill of the invasion, the ease of walking into people's privacies was spellbinding. We moved from room to room, silent, not touching anything. White hallways glowed around us. Relaxed as cats, we strode purposefully through living rooms and into kitchens. In one, Finn opened the refrigerator, took out a cucumber and set it in a dirty glass in the sink. I picked up a photograph from the counter and peered at it in the weak light. Parents, five kids. Nice Mormon family, as my mother would've said. I slipped the photo out of the frame and replaced it backwards. Finn signaled approval with a thumbs up. We moved through the rest of the downstairs rooms, rearranging one or two things. We flipped a seat cushion over, unplugged a lamp, opened a coffee table book to a certain page, inverted flowers in a vase. In one living room, Finn raised a finger to get my attention and plucked a metronome off the top of a piano. I looked around and grabbed the first thing I saw: a small-scale model of the Tabernacle. Then we disappeared out the door, running and rolling, giddy, swerving back the many blocks home. Just before we split up to steal again into our respective houses and lie awake in our beds until the blood stopped pounding wildly at our temples, Finn named our forays.

"Tomorrow night we poltergeist again."

And so we did.

But while my nocturnal life grew ever richer and riskier, my diurnal life encountered increasing harassment from a front I had foolishly considered quiet. My mother decided she was done with drinking. After seeing Jane Fonda, a woman my mother's own age, on a talk show, my mother bought an aerobics video, deciding she was going to lose all the weight she'd gained in Utah. My father, after all, was due to join us the first weekend of September, less than a month away. The Fonda video came with a booklet outlining the caloric values of different foods and drinks. When my mother saw how many calories were in a fifth of vodka, she steeled herself for sobriety. When she got an idea in her head, my mother executed discipline. Unfortunately, her new clarity meant that she was much more conscious of my movements and began to interrogate me to learn what I did with myself every day. When she learned I spent the majority of my time over at the Levy's, eating their food and using their bathroom, she grew a terrible shade of red and blew embarrassment and anger and frustrated sobriety in my face. Shocked by her sudden awakening, I stupidly tried to ignore her and walk out. She responded by slamming me up against the entry closet door and backhanding me across the face. I stumbled down to the basement, shocked tears on delay. A few hours later, I heard the doorbell and my mother's voice explaining to Finn that I was grounded. With unwise cheek, Finn questioned the grounds of my punishment and got the door slammed in his face.

A week passed before I could visit the Levy's again. My mother lost a few pounds and occupied herself with TV and the slow unpacking of a few boxes every day. Eventually, she settled into her new pattern and even formally apologized for hurting me. She gave me a hug to show she was sorry.

In the basement, I spent my time admiring all the items I'd stolen, reliving each theft. My mother never asked about my treasures because she didn't know they existed. She never came downstairs. When I tired of reminiscing, I stretched on my bed and let the sound of the trampoline lull me to sleep. When night fell, my real life commenced.

Not long after my grounding, Finn beat Jerry with a rake. Over the weeks, I'd come to see Jerry enjoyed a great deal of compassion and vocal sympathy in the neighborhood—not just from Mrs. Hanson, but also from many of the parents on the street. When Jerry ambled down the sidewalk, cars slowed and fathers and mothers waved and called out, "How you doing, Jerry?" or "Enjoying your summer, Jerry?" while trying to convince their kids to do the same. I wondered if Jerry felt like a celebrity. Personally, I still didn't like him and mistrusted him after the first incident down by the creek, but I did my best to be civil. Mrs. Hanson was always home whether she had a client in her salon or not, so I controlled my behavior in case she was watching.

On the day of the rake, Finn and I were in the front yard building a mesh cricket-catcher of Finn's own design to facilitate the gathering of food for Johnny Fank-Fank when Jerry strutted up the sidewalk. We stopped what we were doing to watch him approach. He looked immensely pleased with himself, due to, I assumed, the new pair of folding Porsche sunglasses wedged on his huge face.

"Snazzy sunglasses, Jerry!" Finn called out as Jerry approached.

Jerry beamed and paused on the sidewalk. He touched the lenses with his fingers as if confirming the existence of the sunglasses. "They're the coolest," he said. He took off the sunglasses a la Tom Cruise in *Risky Business* and wiped them off on his plaid brown, short sleeve, button-up shirt. "M-my Pop bought them for me." With the sunglasses off, two bright red indentations ran from his nose to his ears where the shades had been cutting off circulation to his face.

"You'll be getting some girls now," Finn said.

"Y-you bet," Jerry said.

Just then Debra and her twin sisters emerged from the side gate, most likely coerced by their mother to be nice to Jerry. They approached hesitantly, so I knew they were on a distasteful mission. I wondered if they were going to invite him to jump on the trampoline again, and I suddenly wished misfortune on him. Why should a retard get their attention? Jerry glanced at the sisters and waved. They waved back.

"Hello, Jerry," the twins chimed.

Debra stepped from the protection of her yard's cottonwoods for a better look at what Finn and I were doing. She held a book as always. Jerry gave us a serious look, then with some difficulty slid the sunglasses back onto his face.

"W-watch this, guys," he said, brushing his hand through the pube-like head-hair. He stepped in front of Debra, startling her. "Hi D-Debra," he said.

"Hi Jerry. How are you today?"

"Do you like my sunglasses, Debra?" he asked, stepping closer.

Instinctively, as if beginning a folk dance, Debra retreated. She lifted her book to her chest in a defensive posture but remained silent.

"My Pop bought them for me," Jerry said.

"They're nice," Debra said.

As if gauging the distance, she glanced back at the side gate of her house.

"They fold up and go in here," he said, pointing to a little black case attached to his belt at the hip. "Like James Bond."

The twins peered from either side of Debra, staring up at Jerry towering over them, their faces meek but filled with an awful curiosity.

"I was wondering, D-Debra…if I…" Jerry began.

Jerry paused and looked back at Finn as if seeking his approval. Finn wore an awful smile on his face. Debra waited patiently, trying hard to be a good, compassionate Mormon girl. Instead of finishing his question, Jerry lurched forward, grabbing Debra by the shoulders. As his grown-man's hands seized her body, Debra's expression flashed from surprise to horror to a terrible blankness, as if someone was turning the dial on a television. The twins ran screaming unintelligibly back to the side gate while Jerry lost control of himself, smothering Debra's face with kisses. He dragged her to the grass and proceeded to rub his crotch against her hip. He slobbered on her ear with the entirety of his mouth, the way a lamprey feeds. Debra only stared into the hot blue Utah sky, praying no doubt. She moved her book to protect her crotch. What could she be thinking? Maybe nothing. Before I could get to my feet, Finn had grabbed a rake from a nearby flowerbed and started whaling on Jerry with the handle. He unleashed a flurry of jabs at Jerry's ribs, breaking the handle into two pieces, then substituted with his feet, kicking until Jerry was separate from the girl. I tried to help Debra to her feet, but she pushed my hands away and rolled over to her knees.

"Don't touch me!" she screamed.

Mrs. Hanson sprinted towards us, closely followed by the twins. A salon customer with wet hair stood farther back, holding the youngest Hanson daughter in her arms. Jerry was weeping, his sunglasses in pieces on the lawn beside him.

"What in God's name is going on here?" Mrs. Hanson screamed. She scowled from Finn to me to Debra.

Dropping her book, Debra reached for her mother and broke into gasping sobs. Mrs. Hanson took her daughter in both arms and lifted her up, half-carrying, half-trotting her across my front yard and through their side gate.

"He went berserk," Finn said, looking at the rake handle. "He attacked her. I think he was trying to rape her."

The wet-haired customer, a woman roughly my mother's age, sent the youngest Hanson girl inside the house and came forward to assess the situation. She studied Finn for a long moment then me. Our faces must have corroborated Finn's story because she then looked down at Jerry.

"Jerry, I think you oughtta go home now and sit with your mama. Someone's going to call you real soon."

Jerry looked. "I-I...," he said, his face contorted and wet from tears.

"Come on now. Get up and go."

Jerry struggled to his feet, bent over, still crying, and collected the fragments of his Porsche sunglasses.

"I don't think you should come around here any more either. Not for a long while, okay? Go on home to your mama now."

Finn picked up the rest of the rake. Instead of watching Jerry's shamed departure, I watched Finn. His chest was still heaving from effort.

"Jacob."

My mother was standing on our porch.

"In the house."

Finn and the wet-haired customer watched me walk back into my house. As I went, I wondered if I'd looked like a coward, freezing instead of acting as Finn had. How had he moved so fast? My mother put her arm around me as I came in and shut the door behind us.

"I knew it from the first moment I laid eyes on him. That boy is dangerous."

I couldn't tell which boy she was talking about and didn't ask.

After Jerry's beating, Finn refined our poltergeists for increased difficulty and risk. Instead of one a night, we began to do two and then three. No longer satisfied with rearranging the details of common rooms, Finn started sneaking into bedrooms, opening drawers and books, upsetting wastebaskets and resetting alarm clocks inches from the heads of sleepers. Finn's escalations redoubled the stress of our invasions. At times, people awoke and stared into the darkness or asked if anyone was there. Once, I watched Finn fetch a little girl a glass of water. She sat up mid-poltergeist and looked right at him through the dark and said she was thirsty. Instead of panicking, Finn carefully put the lampshade he was holding down and slipped out of the room. He returned in moments with a glass of water from the bathroom. The girl sipped, then wiped her lips with the back of her nightgown sleeve. As Finn took the glass back from her, she thanked him and rolled back to sleep. Finn took the glass from that house— that and a newfound desire to interact with people in their dreams. "It's the next logical step," he said.

I loved the feeling of rummaging in other people's lives; I owned them somehow, but I was becoming aware of a looming threshold. Our ratchet clicked toward certain rupture.

Some night, a father would wake up or we'd set off an alarm. A patrolman might spy us hiding in a flowerbed. But I was afraid to vocalize my doubts to Finn, especially after I'd failed to defend Debra. I didn't want to get caught or go to jail, but I also didn't want to lose Finn's respect because I found myself increasingly in awe of him. When I was unscrewing the top of a salt shaker in some stranger's house, I worried the lights would snap on, revealing a middle-aged Mormon with one finger on the switch and another on a trigger, but Finn never balked or hemmed.

Ultimately, our poltergeists ended because our own privacy was invaded. One night in late August, we met at our secret headquarters, the hedge beneath Peter's window. Communicating with hand signals, we agreed to head north towards the elementary school and then work our way east. Together, we hurtled through the neighborhood. As the last of the televisions turned off and the one a.m. patrol passed on Albion, we crossed an empty lot and chose a house to poltergeist.

Finn climbed the porch stairs. But just as he was about to try the doorknob, he froze, glancing into the street behind us. He shook his head and pushed me back. We scuttled around the edge of the house and hid. I stayed very still, trying to hear what had startled Finn. A ragged pant, like the sound of a tired dog, came from the vicinity of a hedgerow across the street. I indicated to Finn that I heard it. As we watched, a pale moon rose over the hedge. A face! We had a stalker, and he'd lost track of us. Finn slipped away and I followed, but instead of running in the other direction, we circled behind the wall and crept upon our quarry.

Finn sprang and threw a hand over Peter's mouth, muffling his little brother's scream. When he was satisfied Peter wasn't going to cry out or run, Finn slowly withdrew his hand. Staring furiously at his brother, Finn zipped his own lips for quiet. Together, the three of us skulked home through the pleasure-less night, hiding from what seemed abundant traffic. A half block from our street, a patrol car surprised us, and it was only by chance that we didn't get caught. Peter was standing in clear sight of the patrol as it passed. I don't know why we were spared. When we separated, I looked back to see Finn shoving Peter roughly home.

The next day, I came out to the backyard with my microwaved breakfast in hand. I found Finn perched on the fence, staring morosely at the mountains. In my living room, my mother was performing leg lifts in time with Jane Fonda. I walked to the fence and stood beneath Finn. He didn't say anything, so I climbed up beside him and continued eating. Looking across my yard, I could see the Hansons' trampoline. It had sat unused since Jerry's attack. The day after the incident, the Hansons had piled into the family car and left on a camping vacation. Neither Finn nor I had even suggested jumping on the trampoline in the meantime. Something had changed.

"He's ruined everything."

"How did he find out?" I asked through a mouthful of bagel dog.

"He saw us from his window."

"What are we going to do?"

"Not much we can do. He threatened to tell if I hurt him."

"We could let him come along."

"We'd get caught in no time."

He was right. "Let's just wait a few more nights until his guard's down and he's falling asleep again."

Finn shook his head. "No, it's over. It'll never work. We'd have to spend too much energy worrying whether he's ratting us out. It would affect our concentration just enough to screw us up," he said. "We're going to do something new today."

"Oh yeah?"

"Yeah. My parents are taking my brothers out to Jordan to visit my grandparents. That takes all day. My grandparents try to convince them to rejoin the church. Come over when you see them leave?"

"Okay," I said, popping the ass-end of my breakfast into my mouth.

Later, Finn was acting strangely when I let myself into his house. Outside, cricket-saturated fields roared under a dry and searing sun. The Levys' air-conditioning raised goose bumps on my arms. Finn was jumpy, lacking his usual self-assured gravity. He led me straight past the piano, through the kitchen, and into the garage. Still carless, it echoed with emptiness and un-use. In the dark, oily garage, Finn bent over a gas can. "Come sit," he said.

I made my way across the concrete, letting my eyes adjust to the gloom. Three small diamond windows cut diagonally in the garage door were the only sources of light. They hadn't been cleaned in ages. I found a spot on the floor without an oil stain and sat cross-legged next to Finn. He unscrewed the lid of the can and sloshed the fuel around some.

"Are you sure about this, Finn?"

"Troy and I did it once."

"The Zeek? The guy whose window you hit with the star?"

Finn shrugged.

"We did it last year, before the fight."

He passed the can to me, and I held it in my lap.

"Put it on the ground and lean over it so you don't spill."

"What's it like?"

"Dreaming *really* hard, but you're awake."

I placed the can on the ground before me and leaned awkwardly over it.

"Put your lips right on the threads. Form a seal with your mouth."

I bent down and the fumes scorched my eyes, so I sat back up. "Just try. It won't kill you. I promise."

I pushed the can over towards him.

"Show me."

He lifted the can, wiping its mouth clean with his hand. He placed his mouth over the threads, forming a seal and took four long gasps off of the can, one after the other, exhaling long and slow. After the fourth hit, his head began to nod and his chin fell to his chest. The gas can began to list precariously, so I took it from him.

"Unnnn…" Finn mumbled, his eyes closed.

I watched him, scared that he was going to pass out. I shook his shoulder and repeated his name. His hooded eyes opened and spotted me in the gloom. He gave me a lazy smile, then closed his eyes again. After a few more moments, he gathered his bearings, ran his hands over his face and sat up a little straighter.

"A thousand helicopters flying through my head, all their blades swishing at the same time. Foosh, foosh, foosh, foosh, foosh." He massaged the heels of his hands against his temples. "It's the craziest thing."

He reached for the can again, but I held it back from him. I wiped off the mouth and leaned over it with my eyes closed. With my lips over the threads, I formed a seal and sucked in. The fumes burned my lungs. I wrenched my head back and coughed.

"Again, again," Finn said.

Steeling myself, I drew three long huffs, exhaling each as quickly as possible. Before I'd finished the third, the garage floor tilted beneath me and I tipped over. A fountain of sparkles erupted from somewhere inside me, prickling and tingling through my body. I could see and hear currents shoot to my fingertips and toes. My head swelled, and for a moment, I feared I was turning into Jerry. I could hear my skull cracking as fluids deluged it. On the ceiling, a movie ran in reverse, the film threaded sloppily in the viewer: a man with wings played the trumpet backwards, the eerie and un-natural music of a distant siren. The angel Moroni saw me and winked just as the film caught in the projector and burned, melting the image grotesquely. When reality returned, Finn was leaning over me, his eyes worried.

"Jake! Jake! Can you hear me?"

It took me a moment to remember where I was and what I'd been doing.

"Sit up, you've got oil all over your back."

When I righted myself, my brain squirmed inside my skull. "My head hurts."

"It'll go away. Let's go outside, get some fresh air."

"No, let me sit. If I move, I'll puke."

"You were really gone. You took too much your first time."

Finn screwed the cap back on the can and set it against the wall. He stood and pressed the garage door opener. The mechanism whined and growled, then laboriously hauled the door up with a medieval clanging, admitting the midday sun-light, which reflected off the white driveway, scouring every last corner of the garage, and blinding me.

Two weeks before Labor Day, when my father was finally going to join us in Utah, the Hansons returned from their vacation. Finn and I were lounging with Johnny Fank-Fank under the sprinklers of my front yard. As the Hansons pulled into the driveway, I made eye contact with Debra, who was crammed into the backseat with her sisters. She looked away as the car came to a stop. The doors flung open and Debra's three sisters piled out and disappeared through the side gate, down the pea-gravel path and into the backyard. Within moments, the trampoline springs' squeaks resounded through the neighborhood once again. I imagined my mother swearing to herself inside the house behind me.

Debra, book in hand, stepped out of the car. She followed her mother into the house without a glance at me. Her father, looking exhausted and happy to be home, began undoing the magpie's nest of rope that held the camping chairs and suitcases to the roof of the Chrysler Town and Country.

"I was hoping they weren't coming back," Finn grumbled, dribbling a handful of sprinkler water over Johnny Fank-Fank's dark, knobby spine.

"Why?"

Something had changed between us. We still saw each other every day, but joylessly. We hadn't snuck out at night since Peter tailed us, and we hadn't even taken advantage of the trampoline while the Hansons were on vacation. Instead, we spent our time wandering the cricket fields or the creek drainage. Finn never suggested the garage again, nor did we talk about what had happened there. Our relationship now felt compulsory. We marched through the summer days, talking less and less.

My mother continued to spend her time leg-lifting with Jane Fonda and snacking on soda crackers in front of the TV.

She managed to whittle the number of unpacked boxes to one or two in each room. Our house was beginning to feel a little like a home, and my mother became a lot nicer to me as well, treating me more like an adult. Maybe she sensed a change in me, a seed of maturity in the weariness and anxiety I'm sure I radiated. Regardless, I avoided her and most everyone else, as much as possible. Sitting alone in my room was the most comfortable place for me. At one point, I even told my mother to tell Finn I was sick when he came over. Instead of going home, Finn tried knocking on my window with a stick. I ignored him until he went away.

A few days after Debra's return, something fell into my window well. I stirred from my funk and worked to open the grimy window so I could pluck the envelope out of the well's Byzantine network of spider webs. The lavender envelope was from Debra. Inside, Debra asked me to meet her down by the creek the next day at four o'clock. The note was written in big, purple cursive letters on unicorn stationery. I smelled the paper. No perfume. No hearts nor Xs and Os. Not even a 'dear.' A perfunctory note stating time and place. I spent the rest of the day on my bed, tracing the words and numbers with my fingertips. What could she possibly have to say to me?

The next morning, Finn's mother, screaming at her son, shattered our neighborhood's calm.

"Griffin Levy, what in the world have you done? He's your brother! How could you do something like that?"

Curious, I jumped the fence into Finn's backyard and walked towards the sliding glass door. From the patio, I could see into their dark living room. Finn was sitting on the piano bench and looking out at me, his face drained of all emotion. The shrill, congested steam whistles of Peter's asthmatic lungs coughed and sputtered in blubberings from an upstairs window. Mrs. Levy, noticing me, turned around and furiously slammed the sliding glass door shut, effectively sealing the drama off from the neighbors' ears. Through the glass, she stared me down and pointed at my yard. I retreated and remained there until I heard the garage door go up and heard the Levys' car leave the house. Soon, the front door slammed shut and Finn slipped over the fence into my yard, a backpack on his shoulder.

"Jesus, Finn, what in the hell did you do?"

He dropped onto the grass, wiped his hands off and re-shouldered the pack.

"I'm leaving. Do you want to come?"

"What do you mean?"

"I mean I'm leaving."

"Running away?"

"Are you coming?"

"What did you do?"

"Got my brother back for ruining everything."

Finn's voice chilled me.

"Where'd your mom go?"

"To take him to the hospital. I chucked the throwing star at him—I just meant to scare him, but I missed. He needs stitches in his face." Finn took Johnny Fank-Fank out of his backpack. "You need to take Johnny. He can't come with me."

I shook my head. "I don't want him."

"Then come with me."

I shook my head again.

"Why not?"

"I've got something to do."

"Like what?"

Johnny Fank-Fank and his abiding stare remained perched on Finn's outstretched hand. Both owner and bullfrog seemed to be accusing me of something.

"I'm meeting Debra," I said.

"Debra Hanson?" he said. "*She's* why you won't come with me? What happened to undying brotherhood? What happened to our oath?"

"Nothing," I tried, lamely.

"You have no honor, Jake. And that's the worst possible thing I could say to someone. Goodbye."

Finn satcheled Johnny Fank-Fank again and walked to the fence.

"What are you going to do?" I asked, following a few feet behind him.

He clambered onto the fence, straddled it and looked down at me, the backpack hanging from his shoulder. "I'm gonna let Johnny free in the creek and then I'm leaving."

"Where will you go?"

Finn disappeared over the fence.

Debra was seated cross-legged in the dirt beside the creek. She picked up a dirt clod and broke it apart, dropping the chunks into the lap of her dress, which was stretched tight between her knees. The dirt bounced on the taut fabric. "It's like a trampoline," she said, without looking up.

I sat down next to her.

"And we're like the dirt," she said. She laughed, but it wasn't really a laugh. It was a mean sound. A sarcastic exhalation. Suddenly I felt afraid. She said, "Some seed fell on stony ground, where it had not much earth, and immediately it sprang up, because it had no depth of earth, but when the sun was up, the seed was scorched, and because it had no root, withered away."

A fat fly landed on Debra's cheek, then backrolled into the air. She didn't seem to notice. Flies circled Debra's head like a halo and visited the dirt in her lap, their buzzing a grim melody amid the static of the crickets' drone. They circled her head like a halo. They visited the dirt in Debra's lap.

"You're going to ruin your dress."

"Do you think bad things are meant to happen to bad people?" Debra asked. She broke another dirt clod onto her lap. "Or do people become bad when bad things happen to them?"

I looked away instead of attempting to answer. Below us, just at the waterline of the creek, a thick horde of flies swarmed two flat rocks, blanketing a dark mass of skin and blood and intestines. I leaned forward for a better look. Johnny Fank-Fank lay smeared across the exposed sides of the two rocks. He was very much smashed to death. I eased down the bank and scraped Johnny Fank-Fank's carcass from the stones as best I could, but only made a bigger mess. Finally, I pushed the two flat stones into the water. They sank heavily to the bottom, each creating a new series of ripples on the creek's surface.

I looked around for Finn, but didn't see him.

"The thing is dead," Debra said. Her voice was almost lost beneath the roar of the crickets in the fields around us.

"Finn said he was going to let him go. He would never do anything to hurt Johnny."

"You don't know anything," Debra said.

"What?"

"I said you're dumb."

At the shore, flecks of bloody skin and intestine lay here and there. Flies continued to greedily gorge themselves, one spot to another.

"Go back to where you came from," Debra said. "You and your pathetic lies and your drunk mother and your crudeness."

The roar of crickets and flies deafened me. Debra glowered from where she sat on the crown of the creek's bank.

"Right," she finally said.

She stood up. Dirt fell from her dress, revealing bloodstains and chunks of Johnny Fank-Fank sticking to her lap. She waited for me to say something. When I didn't, she smiled and in that smile was a cruelty I had never supposed existed, least of all in a twelve-year-old girl. I watched her walk away, parting the flies and crickets as she moved.

I turned to the creek and, for a long time, hours maybe, I watched the water flow over the rocks. Insects fattened themselves on what remained of Johnny Fank-Fank. When at last I walked home, the ground felt exceptionally baked and hard. It had no bounce to it. None at all.

The Moth Orchid

Fifteen degrees below zero. The hothouse glowed like an ember in the false light of another winter morning. Miniscule leaks in the dome blew jets of steam into a monochromatic landscape—white birch, black spruce, white snow, black night, white stars. The steam curled and writhed in the frigid air before dissipating in the fathomless sky. The dome: a great, foggy cataract, stared in all directions but saw nothing. Within, a riot of red and purple orchids, of white fabric and fluorescent light. Long tables set in rows and loaded with a descending spectrum of Phalaenopsis Blume from a deep bruised purple to a tangerine red. Swaths of muslin hung sporadically from the ceiling like fragments of a Bedouin tent, creating the indirect light shade-loving orchids need. Fans whirred from the corners of the room, circulating the warm air in Zephyrus currents. The space was filled to bursting with rich heat and light, with dizzying vibrancy and the smell of earthy life.

Alasa Memnov slept on a cot surrounded by the orchid-laden tables. Pale and raven-haired, she blocked the humming fluorescent light with a sleeping mask. Her single, sweaty sheet clung to her body like a film, provoking a terrible, constricting dream. A lifeless, three-pound fetus had grown in the stomach of a four-year-old girl. A team of doctors operated on the girl's swollen stomach. As they worked, the doctors discussed how it was possible. A rare congenital defect, the fetus had grown inside the girl when she herself was just a fetus in her mother's womb. With mouthless masks and piercing eyes, the doctors probed the unborn mass. Alasa recognized herself there, embedded at the girl's core. The alarm clock beside her bed shrilly bleat six a.m., and Alasa was torn from the body of the unconscious girl and lifted into consciousness by the cold grip of forceps. She awoke into a fierce and cleansing light.

Alasa untangled the sleeping mask from her hair and swatted the clock silent. The dream receded. She re-closed her eyelids and nearly recaptured the dream, but it slipped away into the abstraction before she could grab its wriggling tail. Resigned to wakefulness, Alasa kicked the sheet off and dragged her underwear from a nearby chair, wishing, as she did every morning, for a shower.

The hothouse was constructed of polytetrafluoroethylene-coated glass, a cloth woven from fine glass filaments and stretched across the dome's geodesic frame. Beyond: an unhuman darkness. The sun wouldn't brush the land for hours. Alasa had grown up in Alaska, but far to the south, near the ocean. The Interior, here in Fairbanks, was different. Back home, storms blew down from the Aleutians. Winter raged and blustered, gnashed and stomped, but eventually moved on. In Fairbanks, a bell jar of winter descended. Beneath it, nothing moved, not even the air. Snow piled twelve inches and higher on branches and power lines. Daylight died to a dusk near high noon. Winter sun arrived through a slit of cracked open sky, sprinkling photons across the tundra like seed on barren ground before darkness ruled again.

Alasa drowsed to a fogged wall and wiped condensation from the glass and drenched the forearm of her long underwear. Bright, crisp stars shone like tiny holes poked in oilcloth, as if the night sky had been draped over an adjacent world made of blinding light. She imagined gutting the sky with a skinning knife, letting all the golden light in the universe pour over the world like hot butter. Sealing everything in eternal warmth.

The glass fogged again, and her own features confronted her. She still looked young. Limited exposure to the sun had its upside. She pushed the slithering black eels of her hair around with both hands in a half-hearted effort to put it in place. Alasa noticed a strand of gray and plucked it from her head. Gray hair unsettled her. Hair is made of proteins. Neurotransmitters are made of proteins. Bioelectricity propagates because of proteins. Receptors, too, function on proteins. Hair and memory are linked. We inherit both and can't control either. Alasa didn't like to think about it.

She crossed the space of the dome to her bathroom: a gray water bucket. She removed its lid and, without acknowledging its contents, squatted and relieved herself. From the sound in the bucket, she knew she had to empty it soon. From the acrid smell, she knew she needed to drink more water. "Drink more water," she said, and the sound of her own voice startled her. She addressed a row of orchids on a nearby table. During the night, their petals had begun to wither. She inspected the gauges affixed to a support at the center of the hothouse. Eighty-one degrees. Good. Humidity read twenty percent. Not good. Her orchids were thirsty.

Vexed, Alasa navigated the labyrinth of tables and long swaths of hanging muslin to reach the humidifier. She slid the water tray from its base. Dry. Dusty. She hissed at herself. Not a simple thing, to keep orchids thriving in the arctic. Each step in the regimen was vital, and she had been missing some. Last night, the humidifier. She tried to remember falling asleep but couldn't. She *did* remember a fetus within a little girl. She yanked the humidifier's water tray out, refilled it from a five-gallon can of water and replaced it. Moist air once again puffed gently from the machine's snout. She could almost hear her flowers sigh.

Amid the remaining orchids, Alasa found one too close to the hothouse wall, its petals black and withered. She took her time amputating the blighted bits with paring shears. When she finished her rounds, it was nearly nine-thirty. She was late.

Alasa drove from the wooded hothouse road to the George Parks Highway. She hit ice fog just after the ENTERING FAIRBANKS sign. The fog enveloped her truck, forcing her to slow. Ice fog. A Fairbanks specialty. The frozen exhalations of thousands of chugging tailpipes. An immobile, cotton candy ball of smog trapped by the temperature inversions of the Fairbanks basin. Months could transpire without clean air. Alasa loathed the ice fog, along with trips to town.

Fairbanks proper was a floe of hotels, churches, bars, and other businesses, each exulting itself as the "Farthest North" of its kind. The New Horizons Assisted Community claimed no such distinction. Her mother's nursing home was a nondescript three-story building downtown. Alasa found a parking space nearby and left the truck's engine running so it wouldn't freeze. Standard practice in Fairbanks. She plucked the orchid bag from the seat beside her and hurried across the parking lot, through two sets of sliding doors, and into the reception area. A nurse's aide looked up from a book, *Winter Blues: Seasonal Affective Disorders and You*, as Alasa approached.

"Ms. Memnov. So wonderful to see you today."

"Hi, Jill. Is my mother ready for church?"

"Marne saw to her at ten."

"Thank you."

Alasa repeatedly punched the elevator button. On the ride to the second floor, she unzipped the orchid bag and peered inside. The blanketed flower remained upright and intact. The elevator opened, and she hurried down the hall to her mother's room. On the far side of the bed, her mother sat —or had been set—in a wicker chair. She faced a lit television. Her hands rested as if placed in her lap and her back seemed too straight, almost propped. She had been dressed in an olive-green cardigan, burgundy wool pants and a pair of institutional yellow socks, the kind with grip tape on the soles. She looked costumed, clownish. Bebe Memnov was sixty-one years old. She looked much older. Her blank expression aged her, as did her gray hair. Alasa didn't like to visit her mother, but as soon as she admitted this to herself, she felt guilty.

"Good morning, Mom," Alasa tried to be cheerful. She walked around the foot of the bed, set the orchid bag down, and kissed her mother's gray head. "I brought you an orchid." She unwrapped the flower from its various layers of protection and set it on top of the television. She fussed with its petals until she was satisfied they looked perfect. A flower that could win prizes. Bebe continued to stare at the flickering television. Her favorite show was on. *The Sunday Morning Silver Screen Gem*. This morning it was *Cleopatra*. Before the disease, Bebe could have recited lines verbatim from this one.

"This orchid is from my new batch of clones. I'm getting closer, see? Almost the same hue as the dress. Remember that spring dress you'd wear when I was little? I loved that dress. Oh, sorry."

Alasa stepped back from the TV so her mother could watch Elizabeth Taylor sail the Nile on a golden barque. Shortly, a nurse came in with an armful of fresh towels. A good nurse, Marne. Alasa was always impressed with her care and efficiency. She was Swedish, with an accent both sing-songy and dour like a northern dirge. In practiced motions, she set the towels on the bed, opened the closet, withdrew a long coat, draped it over her arm, and approached Alasa's mother, placing a hand on each shoulder.

"Up, Mrs. Memnov. Up, now."

And Alasa's mother, like a charmed serpent, stood and moved two steps to the left under Marne's direction.

"You're running late this morning," Marne remarked.

"A special strain of my orchids is finally blooming. I lost track of time."

"Is this one of them?" Marne lifted the orchid and admired it in the light. "It's wonderful. It's a miracle you manage to grow these here."

"You should have that one."

"Oh, heavens no," Marne said. She set the flower down and nearly knocked it from the television set. Alasa quashed a reflex to leap to its rescue.

"You take good care of my mother. It's the least I can do." She tied a scarf around her mother's neck and pulled her hat further down over her forehead. Her mother's face pinched into the face of a shrunken apple doll. She didn't look comfortable, but frostbite could set in without her mother so much as whimpering. Not an inch of her skin could be exposed to the air for long.

"But it's a gift for your mother. You brought it for her."

Alasa wheeled the chair toward the door and into the hall-way as Marne began to make her mother's bed.

"Marne, she'll never know it was here."

"Don't be so sure. Your mother, she's got a secret life. She comes and goes."

Marne unfurled a clean white sheet across the mattress and expertly tucked its corners.

"Does she ever speak to you?" Alasa asked.

"Not with words. Sometimes she's…her spirit—"

Marne cast blankets and pillows through the air and they found the bed with a neat, sentient precision. She tucked her surplus towels under an arm. "It's more just a feeling I get sometimes, Miss."

Beneath her parka, Alasa was already beginning to sweat. She worried her mother might be overheating, too, before she took her outside, but Alasa found herself suddenly angry. She realized she resented Marne, not because she spent so much time with her mother and not even because of what she said about her mother's supposed secret life. The nurse knew so much about them and Alasa knew nothing about the nurse. "Explain what you mean," she said, just shy of snappish.

"I often feel like she's somewhere else. Somehow watching me from some other part of the room while I feed or dress her. Even walking out the room. Leaving her body behind all together."

"Ms. Memnov?"

The man's voice broke the spell of Marne's chilling words. In the hallway, Alasa faced a small man wearing a black down jacket that threatened to swallow him. Straight dark hair, dark skin. Latino or Native, she assumed. He had a hawkish nose and wore thick glasses.

"You are Ms. Alasa Memnov?"

"I am."

Alasa shook his hand as Marne excused herself and squeezed past them. Alasa watched her go, then pushed her mother's wheelchair down the hallway in the opposite direction. The man followed, almost jogging to keep up.

"I'm sorry," Alasa said as they reached the elevator, "I'm very late. Whatever you want is going to have to wait."

He slipped in front of her and thumbed the elevator button. "I am Dr. Rene Funes."

Latino, then. "Are you new? I don't recognize you."

"I don't work for this facility, Ms. Memnov. I drove from Anchorage to speak with you."

"I'm sorry to be rude, but this just isn't a good time. Today's the theophany. We're late."

Dr. Funes followed Alasa and her mother into the elevator. He punched the button for the first floor and sealed them into the box together. Noticing a bead of sweat on her mother's forehead, Alasa cursed. She loosened the scarf to allow air in.

"Theophany?" Dr. Funes said.

"The Feast of the Epiphany. My mother is Russian Ortho-dox. What do you want, Doctor?"

When the elevator reopened, Alasa rolled her mother out backwards, swung her around, and headed across reception. Again, Dr. Funes trailed. "I'm principal physician and re-searcher at the University of Alaska's Center for the Study of Alzheimer's."

"My mother has already seen a lot of doctors. Honestly, I don't know if it's worth bothering her with more."

"Actually, I traveled all this way to talk to *you*."

Alasa pulled up short before the first set of front doors. Outside, the ice fog hazed with a weak and distant dawn. "If this is about billing, you'll have to contact my insurance company directly."

Dr. Funes, slightly winded, unzipped his jacket and withdrew a manila. "No, it's nothing like that." He ran his hand along the edge of the folder. "This is difficult. I don't know how to begin."

"Out with it, Doctor. My mother needs to get to church."

He handed her the folder. "Your results."

Hesitant, Alasa took the folder. "Results of what?"

"Can we sit?" Dr. Funes tugged at his collar and gestured to the lobby chairs. "Your mother submitted your material to us on December 29th, 1972. It's rather extraordinary, actually."

"*What* is?"

"Your mother's foresight. Her faith in the program."

Alasa's name was written across the folder's tab. A label was affixed to its face. THE LOWE PROGRAM IN MOLECULAR MEDICINE AND HUMAN GENETICS. UNIVERSITY OF ALASKA, ANCHORAGE, ALASKA. 99504.

"She was involved in a study that became a genetic analysis of early-onset dementia. The gene was isolated last fall."

"And she submitted my genetic material?"

"A lock of hair."

Alasa thrust the envelope back at him, and he flinched.

"You're saying this folder will tell me if I'm going to end up like my mother?"

Dr. Funes tried to smile, but instead he just looked ill. "There are some other things as well. Personal effects. Things your mother left with us to give you when the time came. Perhaps I should have called first."

Dr. Funes refused to retake the folder, so Alasa stuffed it under her arm and pushed her mother towards the door.

"Wait."

Alasa paused but didn't turn around. She'd triggered the door's automatic opening. Buffer air from the artic entryway blasted the three of them.

"I'm sorry. That was tactless, indelicate. I'm a research physician. I have no experience with this type of thing. Can we meet later? Let me explain why I've come."

Alasa sighed and looked down at her mother. "Look me up under orchid growers. I'm the only one."

Alasa pulled into the small, crowded parking lot of her mother's church. Its hipped roof, painted a dull gold, glimmered through the ice fog in the mid-day dawn. Alasa slid from her truck and plugged its block heater into the spot's outlet. The sound of an organ and the congregation singing in Russian poured from the church as one of the ushers jogged out through the cold to help Alasa with her mother.

The priest was delivering the Sermon of the Theophany. The congregation stood. A pair of children to the rear rocked back and forth on the balls of their feet, tired and antsy. Alasa parked her mother in the aisle, and a family shuffled quietly aside to make room for her. "And the sons of the prophets that were at Bethel came forth to Elisha, and said unto him, knowest thou that the Lord will take away thy master from thy head today?" The priest stood before a golden Iconostasis laden with three rows of Orthodox icons. His voice resonated high in the church eaves. "And he said, Yea, I know it. Hold ye your peace."

Alasa's eyes wandered to the dark, somber icons of saints behind the priest.

"Faith! When we have faith, there is no fear of oblivion for there is no oblivion to fear. By faith, Enoch, in the Book of Genesis, walked with God: and then he was not, for God took him."

Alasa studied the icon of John the Baptist's severed head upon the plate.

"He was translated that he should not see death, and was not found, because God had translated him."

Alasa's gaze traveled the concavity of the ceiling, high into the eaves where dim light shone through a tiny window.

"Enoch walked so close to God, that one day he crossed into eternity."

When the service concluded and the congregation had filed out, Alasa waited. Her mother held a vacant stare toward the altar. Smiling, the priest approached and knelt before her. He was an old man, much older than Alasa's mother, but he was nimble and there was clarity in his eyes when he spoke. Alasa couldn't help feeling a little jealous and awed.

"How are you, Bebe? I'm glad you could come. You look wonderful today." Wryly, he looked up at Alasa. "I wish you'd taught your daughter Church Slavonic, though. Her mind wanders during my sermons. And she gets tired of standing."

Patiently, the priest helped Alasa shepherd her mother outside again, into the cold, into the truck. "The fog gets worse every winter," he said.

"More people, more cars, more ice fog."

"Or maybe our view of the world just grows hazier. Drive careful, okay?"

Alasa shut the passenger door and hurried to the driver's side as the priest shuffled quickly back towards the church.

Exhaust billowed from the tail of a jacked-up truck in front of Alasa at a stoplight. The traffic signal hung like a fuzzy red disc in the air. Alasa glanced at her mother, checked her seat belt as the light changed. The truck ahead of her revved and spewed exhaust, obscuring Alasa's vision. She plowed through the cloud toward the city limits, turning off near the Chena River. She followed the narrow road down through the grade of black spruce. Bent, drunken, desperate trees clung to the permafrost. She slowly crept the truck down the bank and onto the thick ice of the Chena. The truck's headlights speared the patchy fog, illuminating the warped topography of the frozen river. Alasa and her mother sat, idling, staring out the windshield. Alasa's breath punctuated the silence. Before them, the frozen river ran like a heavenly road to nowhere. Everything was still.

Alasa stamped on the gas. For a moment, the wheels spun before finding traction. The truck jumped, its engine roaring violently. They fishtailed wildly across the ice, and Alasa yanked the steering wheel to the right. The force of the turn pressed her up against the window. Her mother leaned, too, straining against the seat belt. The truck completed a circle and slid to a stop. Alasa clutched the wheel with both hands and stared out forward again. The truck's engine coughed and died. Alasa screamed. She pounded the wheel with the heels of her hands. Her mother only leaned awkwardly against her own seat belt. Outside, headlights illuminated the silver band of frozen river.

At the nursing home, a fresh-looking orderly Alasa had never seen before materialized from behind the reception desk to wheel her mother back to her room.

"Welcome home, Mrs. Memnov, how was church?"

"Don't ask her stupid questions."

The orderly—just a boy really—hesitated, blinking away his surprise. "I'm new here. That's what they train us to do."

"Figures," Alasa said. She handed her mother off and sped to the hothouse.

When she awoke the next morning, Alasa found the manila folder atop her alarm clock. She cast aside her sleep mask and took the folder into the hothouse's arctic entryway, the foyer between her orchids and outside. Shutting the door behind her, she slipped into her down jacket, stepped into her fur-lined boots and opened the outermost door.

Steam burst into the dark sky as Alasa shut the door behind her. The exposed skin of her legs brittled, as if transformed to porcelain. Her face crackled with cold. Her breath was painful and shallow. It was always at this moment, when her lungs felt like two Ziploc freezer bags, that Alasa marveled at the resilience of the body. For an impossibly complex and fragile bag of blood, bones and flesh, it seemed too forgiving. The cold stung like needles, but made her feel undeniably present. Overhead, laser green light slipped and swirled and eddied in the sky. Emerald smoke blown across the stratosphere. The mystery of the northern lights gave Alasa some comfort when the months rose like torpid bubbles through the cold oil of winter. The university's lauded Geophysical Institute had spent years firing rockets loaded with gauges and instruments up into the lights. Not long ago, Alasa had seen a headline in the local newspaper that read, $16 MILLION LATER, GI STILL DOESN'T KNOW WHAT MAKES LIGHTS GLOW. When her skin finally became so cold it stopped stinging, Alasa went back inside.

The telephone rang. She couldn't remember the last time she'd heard the phone ring.

"I was wondering if it wasn't too much trouble, what your schedule was today."

Dr. Funes. She had not opened the folder. She'd merely run a finger along its flimsy spine, worrying whether she would have to open it in order to get on with her life.

"This morning then," she said. "Do you need directions?"

"I can find my way."

She boiled water for tea and returned to her orchids. The spectra of color splashed across the hothouse in waves of purple to red—a violent beauty, this floral hemorrhage. And her creation. No denying that. Yet it mystified her. Alasa looked in the manila folder. Inside: a map of her hometown, Lotus, Alaska; a photo of her as a teenager, her arm around another girl, Lucy Chandras, her best friend from high school; and an odd, charcoal drawing of a small girl curled up, sleeping in the snow. She'd looked at the drawing for a very long time, wondering who had drawn it. And if *she* had drawn it.

Alasa was heating a knife over a Bunsen flame when Dr. Funes arrived. She examined the blade to ensure it was red hot before cutting the orchid on the table beside her. The exterior door creaked open and Dr. Funes knocked to enter. Bundled against the cold and carrying more folders, the doctor staggered under the drastic rise in temperature.

"The door, PLEASE!" Alasa ordered.

Dr. Funes hurriedly pulled the door shut. "My, but it's so very—good lord." He took off his steamed glasses and squinted around at the orchids.

"Take something off before you have a stroke."

Dr. Funes stripped without grace to his shirt, suspenders, and wool pants. "This is remarkable. You live here?"

"Yes."

"It's like the tropics. What are the cloths?"

"They filter the light. Orchids don't like direct sun."

Dr. Funes approached and looked over her shoulder. "May I ask what you're doing now?"

"Topping this strain to make clones. The flowering node is cut above the internode." Alasa severed the stem with her knife, then tweezered a tiny triangle of material on the cutsite. "I cover the dormant growth with a sheath."

"Blinding it."

"Protecting it."

"And what trait, precisely, are you trying to isolate?"

"A very specific color."

"I see. Yes."

"What percent of people who carry the gene develop the disease?"

"One hundred, of course. If they live long enough," Dr. Funes said.

Alasa set the tweezers down.

"I'm sorry, let me restate that. Just because you carry the gene doesn't mean you'll experience early-onset dementia. You might be sixty, even seventy years old before it affects you."

"But my chances of getting it earlier are high."

Dr. Funes wiped sweat from his gleaming forehead. "Yes."

Alasa turned to the sink and filled a glass of water. "It could start in my thirties, couldn't it? It could have already started."

"Have you been experiencing lapses of memory? Mood swings? Disorientation? Hallucinations of any kind?"

Alasa handed him the water. "No."

"Thank you. Do you remember exactly when your mother began to exhibit symptoms?"

"In Lotus, where I grew up. She said it started a few years after my father disappeared. I wasn't much older than a baby."

"Your father, Ms. Memnov. Where is he now?"

"Dead."

"Ah. I'm so very sorry." As if toasting her dead father, Dr. Funes drained half the glass and set it on the table, then wiped his forehead again and squinted at the fluorescent lights. "How, may I ask, without seeming rude?"

"He was first mate on a halibut vessel that sank off Kodiak."

"A brave man. You must miss him."

"I never met him. I miss my mother more."

"You and your mother were close?"

"Inseparable. What are the folders you've brought with you?"

"The data," Dr. Funes said, pleased. He waved the folders at her. "I've brought—"

"I'm not interested in the data unless they contain a cure. I think you're finished here."

Dr. Funes opened his mouth to speak but said nothing. He wiped the sweat from his face and began again to dress himself in layers. "I've made a terrible mess of this. I truly am sorry," he said, putting his hat on and zipping up his parka.

"Stop apologizing. You could have just sent the results in the mail. I suppose I appreciate what you've done, delivering them by hand. It was a nice gesture."

"I wouldn't for a moment lead you to believe I have a cure, Ms. Memnov, but I have been developing a proactive cognitive regimen. Memory exercises. A program of action."

Alasa stroked the petal of an ailing orchid. She plucked it from the plant and let it fall to the floor. She inspected the row of orchids. Petals fell like a train behind her.

"A problem with your flowers?" Dr. Funes asked, his voice startling Alasa.

"Are you still here?"

"I apologize one final time. Good night. Or morning, rather. If you have any questions or concerns, I'm at the Best Western until tomorrow morning."

"For the last time, *shut that fucking door.*"

In his wake, Alasa flopped on her cot and stared at the ceiling. The sky was a shade lighter than pitch black. The sun was coming up in its slow, hazy, tortuously wintered way. Like an incomplete thought. She tried to imagine the sun's warmth. Summer. Green leaves. She couldn't. How long since summer? Years. This winter was lasting five or ten. Alasa clenched her hands and lurched from the cot, nearly upending the nearest table. Wracked by claustrophobia and despair, she snatched an orchid and smashed it on the ground. Next, she spiked the alarm clock like a football. Finally, she wheeled on the gentle, puffing humidifier and kicked it. Her fury sent plastic parts across the hothouse. The machine stopped breathing. The hothouse was silent save the humming of the fluorescent lights. On the floor amidst the contents of Funes' manila folder, she saw the charcoal drawing of the little girl asleep in the snow.

Alasa had been drinking in a bar next to the Best Western for an hour before Dr. Funes joined her in the booth. He ordered coffee. She re-upped her whiskey.

"I want to know how my mother got involved with you people."

Dr. Funes showed her a map of the Bering Sea with labels written in Cyrillic. A small island near the center was circled in red. "In the late 60s, I was part of a project researching a diaspora." He turned from the map to copies of old immigration paperwork, photos of two people, a man and a woman in their mid-twenties dressed in their finest blacks, their hair as inky as their clothes. The woman wore a dark headscarf. Somber expressions. The poor quality of the photos rendered their eyes depthless and opaque. They appeared as if they'd been arrested returning from a funeral. A third photo captured a baby just a few months old, yet the baby stared at the lens of the camera with a startling clarity. "These are your grandparents. The baby is your mother. They arrived in Alaska in 1947. As you probably know, only a few cases of standard Alzheimer's appear to have a strong genetic basis. There is much nobody knows. We can't predict whether any given relative of an Alzheimer's patient will develop the disease."

Alasa tore her gaze away from the infant's.

"Early onset dementia, on the other hand," Dr. Funes added, "runs in families and is thought to have a significant genetic component."

"I know this."

"Of course," he said. "But what you might not know is that the dementia your mother suffers from is so rare, it's almost unheard of outside of this one place." Dr. Funes tapped the circled island. "In the middle of the Bering Sea. Where it occurred in eighty-five percent of the Caucasian population."

Alasa had begun to feel nauseated, but she did not interrupt.

"Now these," Dr. Funes said as he revealed more old photos, "are photographs taken by the cultural anthropologist Anton Barbeau who studied the community in the years leading up to the Second World War."

He handed her a beautifully composed shot. Grim-faced children shepherded adult men and women in dirty white cassocks across a rocky windswept hillock lined with partially submerged, bunker-type houses. Tied together with a rope to keep them from straying, the adults looked insane. One's mouth and eyes were wide as if he were singing or yelling. Another raised her arms and kicked out her legs goofily. A few others appeared wholly emotionless. The children each held one end of the rope that looped around the adults' waists.

"The children served as primary caregivers." He passed her the next photo. At a long wooden table in a dim, low-ceilinged room, children used large, carved spoons to feed the adults. "The unaffected tended to the essential activities: agriculture, animal husbandry, hunting." Dr. Funes flipped through more photos depicting adults at work in rocky, windswept fields, tending flocks of sheep, and fishing and hunting from sealskin kayaks.

"So, you tracked down my mother," Alasa said, plucking the photo of the infant from the table.

Dr. Funes fidgeted with his mug, turning it about. "Actually, she was referred to us."

"By who?"

"The State of Alaska." Dr. Funes said. "Your mother was a single parent, no family to speak of."

"You paid her?"

"She was compensated to participate in the study, yes. Thanks to her we've identified mutations in several genes that predispose a carrier for early-onset Alzheimer's."

Alasa reached for the map and Dr. Funes slid it to her. The circled island was in the middle of the Bering Sea. As remote a place as any on the planet.

"The island's name?"

"Today it's called St. John's."

"Eighty-five percent of the population. More than five to one."

"Originally, yes. But this ratio changed when the Cold War necessitated a military presence on the islands. The gene pool was diluted by Soviet soldiers and later by emigration."

"What about the natives? Didn't they mix in, dilute things further?"

"There's little record of a native population. The island is extremely remote and its winters almost unbearably harsh. The island was, of course, strategically important to the Soviets. If it wasn't for government food drops, I don't think year-round existence would have been possible. Aleut hunting parties stopped over but there were no permanent native settlements on St. John's, nor any instances of miscegenation as far as we know."

"Whoever wound up there inbred like royalty, embedding the gene deeper and deeper into the community."

"Apparently. There are no records."

Alasa drained her glass and set it down, crunching an ice cube between her teeth. She leaned back, exasperated, and buzzed. "Remarkable."

"Yes."

"This is a nightmare."

"I recognize how unsettling this must be—"

"Save it. You can't fake empathy. What else have you got?"

"A suggestion. Would you like to hear it?"

Alasa signaled the waitress for another drink.

"Go back home," he said.

Alasa picked up her refill, and a little spilled over the rim, pouring down her hand. "Right after I finish this, I think I will." She shot the glass dry.

"I meant to Lotus. Where you grew up."

"Why?" Alasa croaked. Her esophagus burned from the drink and she winced. "Why would I do that?"

Dr. Funes leaned forward. "As a cognitive exercise. It will help us gauge the effects, if any, on both long- and short-term memory simultaneously."

"Us?"

"My interest isn't altruistic, or not entirely. I'm hoping to advance the science."

Alasa swam through her drunkenness to a realization. She had no idea about this doctor. Was he even a doctor? Who *was* this man who knew so much about her and her family?

"Ms. Memnov." Dr. Funes leaned even closer. Alasa smelled coffee, mint, and licorice on his breath. "My research has convinced me this disease is combatable, but the patient must be proactive. There is no way for me to truly empathize with how you must feel. I will not even attempt it. But I have spent my life fighting this disease and I want to help you. Moreover, I think you want my help. Why else would you call me tonight?"

"I've been forgetting things."

"We all forget things."

"My orchids are dying. I'm forgetting things I don't forget."

"Such as?"

"I lose sense of what time it is. Day or night. What month it is, even."

"When the sun is up for only a few hours a day—"

"This isn't some seasonal disorder. I'm Alaskan."

Dr. Funes sipped from his mug for some time. He finally said, "I can provide no guarantees other than a promise that action is far preferable to inaction." He placed cash for both of them on the table, then picked up his coat. "You know where to reach me."

At the nursing home, Alasa eschewed the elevator for the stairs. She climbed them two at a time, unzipping her parka and taking off her hat as she went. Sweating, she rushed down the hallway and into her mother's room, which was empty.

But from the bathroom, she heard someone. A woman humming something familiar. A waltz. "Blue Danube." Alasa flung her layers on the bed and entered the bathroom. Naked, Alasa's mother sat in a plastic chair in the shower. Steaming water poured over her body. Marne, who had been humming and scrubbing with a loofah, stopped. She turned off the shower and took a large towel from a hook. Alasa's mother gazed dreamily at the gleaming tiles. She rocked back and forth as if still listening to a tune while Marne dried her body. Alasa walked out and sat on the bed. The orchid she'd left on the television was wilting. Alasa's mother, swathed in a bathrobe and a towel around her head, soon emerged from the bathroom. Marne guided her to a chair.

"Sit down," Alasa said. "Please."

Marne sat on the far side of the bed. Flawless skin, a marble surface. Alasa wondered briefly how old Marne really was—younger or older than herself? Alasa had assumed the latter but suddenly she was unsure.

"Tell me what you meant the other day," Alasa said. "About my mother. You said my mother goes places."

"I've been a nurse for twenty years, Ms. Memnov. I've taken care of people like your mother all my life. When the disease reaches a certain stage, the soul gets cast loose. Some people get taken by surprise."

Alasa watched a petal from the orchid atop the television float languidly to the floor.

Marne said, "Years ago, there had been an old couple. They lived together as husband and wife in the same house for forty-five years. They did everything as a couple. They even developed Alzheimer's together. They remained in their home long after both had lost their senses and had become dangers to themselves. At this point, their son and his wife removed them from the home and placed them in a nursing facility. Not long thereafter, the son put the house on the market. A young couple purchased it almost immediately and moved in. But the old couple was still there. Not physically, of course. Their bodies had been carted off, but their souls —the energy that made them *them*—remained. The barrier between consciousness and this other state had become permeable to them. Their energy remained in that house. Their bodies resided with a nurse in a facility miles away. Their energy went about its business in the home—watching TV, cooking, doing the laundry, gardening—and somehow also manifested physically in the real world. For the young family, the result was terrifying. Televisions, lights, appliances turned on and off mysteriously. Doors opened and closed by themselves. The young couple managed to rationalize these things for weeks, until they decided to update the living room curtains, which were an old and unfashionable color of orange. As young people do, they mocked the tastes of others, laughing at the curtains' dated ugliness while taking them down and stuffing them into garbage bags. They returned from purchasing new curtains to find the old ones shredded into strips and the metal curtain rods tied savagely into knots. The house went back on the market and remained there until the old couple died. They passed away together, too. Within an hour of each other. Sweetest thing I ever saw."

Alasa's head felt heavy and sluggish from alcohol. The nurse's ghost story had exhausted her.

"Are you okay, dear?" Marne asked, placing a hand on her shoulder.

"Where does my mother go?"

"Sometimes she goes no further than the other side of the room. Other times I sense her downstairs or in other rooms of this building or even in other parts of the city. Often I get the feeling she's a long way away from here."

"Farthest North Best Western," said the tired voice of a female front-desk clerk.

"Dr. Rene Funes." Alasa plucked an eraser off the nursing home reception desk and picked at it with a fingernail.

"Room number?"

"I can't remember it."

"Just a moment."

"Yes?" Dr. Funes.

"I'm sorry to call so late."

"Ms. Memnov."

Alasa pictured him sitting upright in bed, his bony chest and eyes squinting in the light of his bedside lamp.

"I've been thinking about your suggestion. Is tomorrow too soon?"

"Not at all. What about your orchids?"

"They'll be fine. Tomorrow then?"

"Tomorrow."

In the hothouse, the orchids were dying. Petals darkened with blight and stems lolled at sick angles. Drunken ghosts of muslin lay across the floor and tables. Alasa stood beside her cot, packing a duffel bag with clothes. To his credit, Dr. Funes didn't ask what happened. He said nothing as he watched her turn down the dial of the temperature gauge and turn off the fluorescent lights.

Alasa threw her duffel bag into the back of Dr. Funes' SUV and climbed into the passenger seat. She looked only forward as they drove off the hill and turned south.

"We'll stay in Anchorage tonight and continue on to Lotus in the morning," Dr. Funes said.

Alasa bunched her jacket at her shoulder and rested against the window. White birch, black spruce, snow, and rock flashed past outside.

"I have to stop by my office tomorrow morning if that's alright," Dr. Funes continued.

Alasa studied the reflection of her own eye in the window until the glass steamed up.

When she awoke, they were approaching Denali National Park. The sun's dim rays illuminated the enormous moon of Mt. McKinley, rising up from the tundra. It glowed the light pink color Alasa planned for her next spectrum of orchids. The mountain's summit cut a slit in the belly of the sky and divided the jet-stream wake of frozen air for miles.

Halfway to Anchorage, they stopped for gas. Dr. Funes came out of the mini-mart with two cups of coffee. Alasa rolled down her window and took hers from him. A bearded, shivering hitchhiker stood in front of the market. Alasa waved him over. Joyous with relief, the hitchhiker jogged over to the SUV, took off his backpack, opened the rear passenger door, and hopped in. Dr. Funes started the engine and pulled back onto the highway without saying a word about their new passenger.

"Oh man. Ahhhhhh, my face," the hitchhiker said.

A young man. With his hat off, he looked almost childlike.

"You'd think this beard would be good for some warmth, but it isn't." He rubbed his face with his hands. "I owe you folks big time. I can't tell my head from my ass in this cold. My whole body is numb. You saved my life. That bastard kicked me out of the store. Wouldn't let me wait inside any longer."

"He should be arrested," Alasa said. "He endangered your life."

"That's true, that's so goddamned true. I'm Tom."

He thrust his hand over Alasa's shoulder for a shake.

"Alasa. This is Dr. Funes."

"How you doing, Doc?"

Dr. Funes didn't take his eyes off the road. Rude, Alasa thought. Maybe Tom made him nervous. Could be he didn't like hitchhikers or was just a careful driver. Tom, in any case, didn't seem to notice. He was a good-looking guy under all his hair and wool.

"How long were you waiting?" Alasa asked.

"A while. You're the first car going south in a long time. I got a ride in a road sander from," he said, rubbing his head furiously, "...excuse me, Alasa, but this hat is just itching my head to death....from the Talkeetna turn-off. Started from Fairbanks this morning. Trying to get to Anchorage for a wedding tomorrow." He couldn't keep his fingers away from his head.

A siren distracted them and they turned to watch an ambulance appear on the highway behind them. Dr. Funes pulled to the side as the ambulance overtook them on the icy road.

"Looks like an accident," Tom said.

"Where's the hospital?" Alasa asked, as the flashing lights disappeared around a bend ahead.

"There are little trauma centers in many small communities," Dr. Funes said, as he pulled back onto the road. "Serious cases require a medevac down to Anchorage."

Tom was scratching his head again and looking at his nails as if he expected to find something beneath them.

"Are you okay?" Alasa asked.

"Fine. My head just itches and I'm, you know, feeling a little tired."

"Get some sleep. I'll wake you when we're in Anchorage."

Tom reclined his head, then lifted it quickly and reached to hold the back of it. His eyes widened as if with a bad memory, but when he saw Alasa watching him, he tried to cover with a smile but only managed to look sick before he reclined his head again.

The SUV rolled down East Fifth past Merrill Field and into Anchorage. The lights of the city played on Tom's sleeping face as Alasa reached back and gently shook his arm. "Hey, kid. We're here."

Tom's eyes cracked open and yawned. He was cute alright. Alasa thought how nice it would be to wake up next to him.

"I was having the weirdest dream," he said, as he realized where he was. "Oh."

Alasa understood his reaction, or believed she did. She despised Anchorage. It combined everything she hated about the lower forty-eight with everything she hated about Alaska. "Do you know where you need to go?"

"Uh, drop me off anywhere."

The SUV stopped at a downtown red light. The Macy's skywalk ran between two buildings overhead. Scratching his head again, Tom grabbed his pack and hat and exited the car. Alasa rolled down the window. The air felt almost warm. The temperature was probably hovering around zero, but a positive fifteen degrees since Denali made a difference. Tom stood dazed on the corner.

"You sure you're okay? Where are you going?"

The light turned green and Dr. Funes drove away. Tom waved, then turned and began walking up the street, still scratching the back of his head. Rolling up her window, Alasa erased him with a thin barrier of glass and ice.

Dr. Funes emerged from the office of the Anchor Arms Motel and handed Alasa her room key. Alasa was exhausted. She dragged her duffel bag down the row of doors toward her room. Inside the room, she left the bag just inside the door and stripped for a shower. How long since she'd taken one? She reeked, but had to wait for the water to heat up. She noticed a black blotch on her shoulder. Dirt? A bruise? Some kind of rash? She approached the mirror for a better look. A tattoo. A black orchid. With numbers beneath it. A date: 12/29/72. Panicking, she tried to wipe it off.

"What is this? What is this?"

In the shower, she scrubbed the tattoo until it hurt, rubbing two hotel-sized bars of soap into the black ink to no avail. Her skin burned hot and red. She gave up, slumping down in the shower and wept in frustration and fear, letting the scalding water anoint her head.

The Chugach were already backlit at nine the next morning. Alasa had forgotten how beautiful these mountains could be. Sunlight crowned the skyline—beatific sunlight. The tundra of the Interior was so flat and still while the Chugach jutted into the sky like cathedrals. Buttressing the Gulf of Alaska, these mountains gathered more than six hundred inches of snow a year. Ten times more than Fairbanks.

They stopped first at Dr. Funes' office near the university. Needing to use the bathroom, Alasa followed him into the hospital. Nurses, patients, orderlies, and family members crowded the hallways. Dr. Funes unlocked a door labeled

LOWE PROGRAM IN MOLECULAR MEDICINE AND HUMAN GE-
NETICS.

Alasa hurried down the corridor, passing a sign: CRITICAL
CARE – AUTHORIZED PERSONNEL ONLY. She turned where Dr.
Funes had directed her. No bathrooms in sight. Just a series of closed doors. She stepped cautiously through an open
door at the end of the hallway, hoping to find someone familiar with the hospital's layout. Inside, beneath an oxygen tent,
lay a bearded young man with a bandaged, shaven head and
two sunken, blackened eyes. Tubes protruded from his mouth
and nose. Beside him, a respirator wheezed, and a heart mon-
itor beeped.

"Ma'am, visitors aren't allowed in critical care. You'll have
to leave." The nurse who spoke sat in a chair just inside the
door.

"What happened to him?"

"Car accident on the Parks. He was medevacked in around
ten or so. He's in an induced coma." She urged Alasa out and
shut the door in her face.

The name on the paperwork beside the door: Thomas Port-
man.

Dr. Funes found Alasa crying in the women's bathroom by
first calling in to her. After a few moments, he entered and
knocked politely on the bathroom stall.

"What are you doing in the women's bathroom, Doctor?"
Alasa asked. She flushed the toilet, wiped the tears from her
face, and exited the stall with as much dignity as she could
muster.

"I was concerned."

"The boy from last night. He's in a coma. In this hospital.
The critical care ward." Alasa washed her hands in the sink.
Warm water poured through her outstretched fingers.

"What boy?"

"The hitchhiker."

"I don't know who you mean."

"TOM. The boy with the beard! The kid who rode in your backseat for four hours from Denali to Anchorage! We dropped him off downtown."

Dr. Funes placed a hand on Alasa's shoulder and looked into her eyes. "There was no one."

Alasa shook badly, then wiped away tears, desperately trying to regain her composure. "Let's go," she said.

"Are you alright?"

Alasa left the bathroom with Funes following. No, Alasa thought, I am not alright.

"A dream. You must have dreamt of a boy similar to the one in the hospital," Dr. Funes said.

"Not similar," Alasa said. "Not just similar."

They drove south past Turnagain Arm, Alasa hypnotized by the shifty, bobbing ice floes that sparkled in blinding brightness. An hour later, jagged peaks, fjords, and crystallized lakes dominated the landscape. A fairy kingdom. A world made of glass and light. As they approached a tunnel, Alasa said, "This is the first time I've ever driven to Lotus."

"They just finished tunnel. It's the longest highway tunnel in North America now. Two and a half miles."

"I liked the ferry."

They pierced the heart of the mountain range, and the tunnel sang a strange doppler tune, a three-note warbled melody that sounded like how her mother used to call her name when she played outside in the summer. She saw a four-year-old girl watering flowers in the yard of a beautiful house. An enormous sapphire-blue castle wall of glacier encircled the town. Alasa's mother appeared at the front screen door. She was young, in the prime of her life. She wore a light spring dress the color of Alasa's special orchid, a complex color that seemed both festive and bloody, ripe and bruised.

"Alasa," her mother called, opening the screen. "Alasa! Come in, dear!"

She set her watering can down beside her flowers and ran across the yard, burying her face in the fabric of her mother's dress.

"Wash up for lunch."

Her mother followed her into the kitchen and brought lidded bowls to the table from the stove. Warm bread and a fresh salad graced separate plates beside the stew.

"Go ahead," Alasa's mother said.

They bowed their heads.

"Great is our Lord, and great is His might, and of His understanding there is no measure. Take care of my Daddy in heaven and my Mama and me down here on Earth. Amen."

"Amen."

The mother lifted the lid from the girl's bowl. Full of snow. A tiny child's hand thrust up, cold and bloodless and blind. It bloomed before her eyes like an arctic flower, ice-blue and impossible.

"Alasa."

Alasa opened her eyes. Emerging from the tunnel, she was thrust into bright sunlight on the southern side of the mountains. The Lotus Glacier, a mountain of sapphire-blue ice, tumbled headlong into the sparkling waters of the Sound. At its base, distinguished solely by a few hundred smoking chimneys, nestled the town where Alasa had grown up.

"Welcome home," Dr. Funes said.

Lotus was quaint, rugged, buried in snow. By December, the town would disappear beneath fifteen-foot drifts and be transformed into a labyrinth of claustrophobic corridors. Only the main drag, a quarter-mile strip that ran from one end of town to a large community parking lot, would be plowed. Access to cars and therefore to the outside world meant a rented space in that lot. Snow machines and walking sufficed for local transport. Most of the shops closed for the winter, but the bars and a few other essentials stayed open year-round. The off-season population was five hundred, but it quadrupled in summer. With the influx of tourists came change—buses and ferries full of tourists from Anchorage and the place exploded with money. Docks swarmed with commercial and recreational fishermen. Glacier tours, adventure tours, whale watching tours. In winter, things were different. In winter, Lotus hunkered down and people lived like rodents in a warren. They dug their own little bit of the labyrinth out and generally stayed put. As they idled silently down Lotus' Main Street, Alasa, wanting time alone, asked Dr. Funes to stop in front of the Green River Bar & Grill.

"I made reservations at the Lotus Lodge," he said.

"Park down at the end of this street. You're gonna have to pay twenty bucks or so. There will be guys there to shuttle our bags down to the lodge on snow machines, but it's not far."

"I'll leave a key for you at the reception."

Alasa nodded, exited the car and shut the door behind her. It opened back up and Dr. Funes thrust her parka out at her.

"Your coat."

Alasa snatched the parka and climbed over the snow bank in front of the bar. It was embarrassing, forgetting your parka in Alaska. She pulled open the heavy door and walked into the Green River. Inside, a half-dozen men lined the dim bar. All but one sat in front of drinks and stared up at a commercial for deodorant on the television screen. The sixth was reading a book. George Thorogood played from a jukebox. A pool table squatted like a green sarcophagus behind them, taking up a lot of space. Except for the motion on the flickering screen, the physical stillness was so total that Alasa felt she could have been looking at an oil painting. She took a seat beside the reader and watched the television until the bartender made his way to her.

"Whiskey on the rocks and a glass of water."

"I'll get that," the reader said.

The bartender looked to Alasa for an okay. When she shrugged, he went about making and serving the drink. Only coffee before the reader, who placed a marker in his book, rested it on the bar, and lit a cigarette.

Alasa lifted the drink in thanks. He cheers-ed her with his coffee.

"Just passing through?"

She nodded.

"Good idea."

"You come to bars to read and drink coffee?"

"My therapist says I need to socialize. So I sit at this bar with these numbskulls for an hour every day and read."

"Fuck you," said a man at the end of the bar without taking his eyes off the television.

"The conversation keeps me coming back."

The reader was good-looking, but not in an Alaska way. He was young, but balding, and he wore glasses. Alasa liked his jawline. She liked that he didn't drink. In Alaska, sober meant trustworthy. Alcohol ruined ninety percent of all eligible men in this state. Alasa liked to drink. She just didn't like the men

91

she slept with to drink. She finished the whiskey, took a sip of the water and stood.

"Thanks for the drink."

He placed his burning cigarette in the ashtray and reopened his book. "Hey," he said.

Alasa turned, afraid she'd left her wallet on the bar.

"You should stop by the library some time," he said.

"Why?"

"Because I'm the librarian."

Alasa followed a series of high-walled snow corridors to the waterfront. In some places, people had sprayed arrows and names on the walls to indicate where junctions led. Street names. Business names. Sometimes just the words "This Way" or "Do Not Enter." As she approached the waterfront, the corridors shrunk and finally disappeared all together near the pier. It was four p.m., already past sunset and the Lotus Glacier towered over the town in the gloaming, plunging its icy teeth into the sea. As a sliver calved from its face into the water, profound rumbling chased a gunshot crack across the water. The glacier was always slowly moving, growing out, expanding towards the town. Or maybe it was shrinking. Alasa couldn't remember which. It no longer seemed to matter.

Her mother had learned her husband's fate while standing on this very pier. Alasa, fetal at the time. Yet her mother had told her the story so often that she retained it as her own memory. Family members of the crew had waited for the Coast Guard to return from the site of the wreck. *The Lotus May* had exploded and sunk off Twoheaded Island days prior. A liquid gas line broke and ignited when gas met galley stove.

The Coast Guard commander wrung his hat with worry as he addressed the expectant crowd.

"The sea took all souls, folks, I'm sorry."

The sea took all souls. The gray metal of the Sound rippled in the wind. A hothouse-sized chunk of ice floated not far from shore. Alasa's pangs turned to anguish. She'd abandoned her orchids, her beautiful sanctuary. What of the struggle, the long hours, the frustration, the years it had taken her to build her farm into a business? Was it even a business? She'd never sold any orchids. For a living, she did something for the university. Yes. Didn't she?

Panic gripped her. She turned from the water and hurried back into the labyrinth. It was much darker now. She sprinted the corridors, not slowing until she had regained Main Street. Safe among the storefront lights, she doubled over before an optometry shop and let her aching lungs recover and grow warm. She saw through the window an optometrist, who could be her peer. The woman was fitting an older man with glasses. The customer twisted his face under a newly applied nosepiece, and the optometrist didn't appear to care. She looked bored and irritated, smoking through the interaction. She fiddled with the glasses and handed them back. Another attempt by the customer. Another drag on the cigarette by the optometrist. She met Alasa's eyes and Alasa turned away headed towards the lodge.

Alasa covered her tattoo when Dr. Funes arrived with dinner at her room. Soda and fried halibut with tartar sauce. They sat on her bed, using newspaper as a tablecloth, and ate the greasy halibut with their fingers.

"How does it feel to be home after so long?" Dr. Funes wiped his mouth with a napkin and sipped up his drink.

"It's like I'm dreaming about someone else's life," Alasa said. "But I saw someone I recognized."

"Someone you know well?"

"I think she was my best friend in high school."

"What did you talk about?"

"We didn't."

"Well, you must, of course."

"Why?"

The ball of greasy newspaper in her hand reminded her of things within things, not-yets within not-yets. She recalled a woman and an infant, a fetus within that infant.

"This is why we are here."

"What would it prove? I'm a different person than I was then."

"Your shared history with people like this friend is the key to strengthening re-cognition. The mind is a muscle. It must be flexed. We must send your memory to the gym. It must do bench presses and curl dumbbell. It must, as they say, get ripped."

She laughed, in spite of herself.

The next day, Alasa returned to the optometry shop.

"Oh my god. Alasa Memnov!"

Alasa approached the counter. She caught a glimpse of herself in one of the dozens of mirrors in the place. She took her hat off and ran a hand through her hair. "Hi Lucy."

"Hi Lucy? Are you fucking kidding me? Just like that? The mysterious Alasa Memnov walks in the door after what—two decades? Hi Lucy."

Alasa shrugged.

"Alasa goddamn Memnov, the vanishing girl. Honest to God, I can say I never thought I'd see you again. How the hell are you?"

"I've been better. Yourself?"

Lucy gestured at the shop, the street outside. "Lotus, you know? Still living in the maze. Never managed to escape. Nothing much ever really changed for me. I'm married, I guess. Got two kids."

"Congratulations."

"It's not really what I signed up for, to be honest."

"Life is like that."

"Damn straight." Lucy suddenly brightened. "Hey! Let's go get a drink. Give me ten minutes to close up here."

"Are you sure that's okay?"

"Sure I'm sure! I'm the damn boss."

This woman had been her best friend? Alasa couldn't believe it.

So close to the shop, the Green River caught them. Lucy knew everyone there. The librarian, again reading at the end of the bar, lifted his coffee in greeting to Alasa. Lucy pounded the bar and demanded drinks for her and her "long lost best friend."

"Ten pounds every ten years, they say. Look at me, Ally. How much would you say I've gained?"

"You look great."

"Bullshit. I look like the tourists we used to make fun of. Remember? Remember how we'd get high and laugh?"

"Sure." Alasa did not remember and affected a smile.

"Those fat, pasty, middle-aged bitches with the little dogs under their arms and their bratty children and drab little husbands?"

"Every summer," Alasa said.

"Well," Lucy drained another drink and slapped the bar. "I got the brats and the fat, but my dog and husband sure as hell ain't little. They're both huge. They kind of look like each other. The Rottweiler's better looking, actually. Better hung, too. And what about gorgeous you? What's your story?"

"Nothing much to speak of. A few flings now and again over the years, I guess."

Even fortified by alcohol, Alasa could not match her gaze. Lucy began to cry childlike tears and just as rapidly apologized through them. "Why did you go?"

"I don't know," Alasa said.

"You just left me."

"It was so long ago. I was young."

"We were like sisters, you said."

Dumbstruck, Alasa grimaced as Lucy patted her hand, leaving it moist with tears. Alasa fought the urge to wipe her hands with a napkin.

"It's not your fault. I'm glad you made it out. I'm just...so unhappy, Ally. After you left, everything kind of went to shit. You meant so much to me." A crude oil of mascara and tears dangled in droplets from her lashes.

"I should have written." Alasa spoke to the drink between her hands. "Things have been tough. They haven't been good."

"Don't apologize," Lucy said, collecting herself. She laid a twenty on the table for the drinks. "I have to go back to work now."

"Why don't we order some food or something, take a walk?"

"It's way too late for that, but don't you worry about me, baby. I can take care of myself."

Alasa watched her go, her old best friend whom she remembered not at all.

"You're a real people person, aren't you?" the librarian asked, taking Lucy's empty seat.

"She's going back to work," Alasa said.

"Don't fret. She won't blind anyone. A half dozen kamikazes are just a warm-up. I've seen her drink every man in this bar under the table."

"Comforting."

"Fortunately, your eyes appear perfect. Black as night and deep as an abyss, but perfect."

"You're a real charmer. Tell me, how did you become the dusty old librarian of this backwater?"

"You make it sound so exciting."

"It's exciting?"

"Damn straight. The librarian is the most powerful person in *any* community."

"How's that?"

"We're the keepers of the collective memory, the only ones who can ever really remember."

The librarian led her, stumbling and laughing, to the small, but high-ceilinged library. The wooded structure was burnished to a warm glow. Alasa walked past the reference desk admiring the tall wooden shelves filled with books, the hardwood floors, and the wrought-iron staircase, which wound to an overhead balcony. "It's like a church in here." She hefted a book from a shelf. The volume felt good. Solid and real.

"That's because it used to be a church."

For an instant, Alasa heard a chorus in the balcony, saw a bearded priest sermonizing from the reference desk. "Russian Orthodox," she said. "I must have come here with my mother. When I was a little girl. She was devout."

"So you *are* from Lotus."

Alasa didn't answer. Instead, she wandered into Fiction, running her hand along the spines.

"The state acquired the building in the late seventies. When the congregation dwindled," the librarian said.

"To where?"

"Passed away, mostly. Kids move out of Lotus first chance they get. So, where we once had a church, now we have a library."

He took a book from the shelf and moved it to its proper space, aligning spines along the way.

"So are you a God-fearing librarian?"

"I'm good with God. You?"

"I forgot he existed."

"What reminded you?"

"Death."

She leaned against the stacks and grabbed the librarian playfully by the belt as he approached.

"Death?"

"Or something very much like it."

She took off his glasses and kissed him.

"It's been a long time," he said.

"Some things," Alasa assured him, "you don't forget."

While the librarian slept in the loft, Alasa crept down the wrought-iron staircase and found Borges in the stacks. She plucked *Labyrinths* from the shelf and took it to the loft to read, hoping it would put her to sleep, but it engrossed her instead, as it once had long before. She forgot about the librarian until he woke and beckoned her close. He examined the book, almost seemed to caress it. "You like it?" he asked.

"One story in particular. It's about this young guy who falls from his horse and afterward he can't forget any experience—

real or imagined—from the present or the past." She opened to a page. "'His perception and his memory were infallible,'" she read aloud. "'He knew by heart the forms of the southern clouds at dawn on the 30th of April, 1882, and could compare them in his memory with the mottled streaks on a book in Spanish binding he had only seen once.'"

"That's some memory," the librarian murmured.

"'The present was almost intolerable in its richness and sharpness. As were his most distant and trivial memories.'"

"The old gift-that's-really-a-curse trick."

"He drowns in memory."

"Hm."

"He goes insane."

The librarian ran his hand along her thigh and her hip, up her back and across her shoulder. "What is this? A black dahlia?"

"Orchid."

"And the numbers? What are they—a date?"

"I don't remember," she said angrily.

"Apologies. I didn't mean to pry."

Alasa stood and began to dress as quickly as she could.

"Where are you going?"

Alasa slipped a sweater on and faced him, alarmed and vulnerable on the couch.

"If a doctor appeared and told you that you were going to start losing your mind. What would you do?"

"What?"

"If he had studied your DNA and found out you carried a gene that stole your mind and then turned you into a hat stand. What would you do?"

"I'd be pretty pissed off."

"After that."

"I don't know. What could I do? It's my mind. I can't shore it up with a two-by-four."

Alasa donned her boots, grabbed her parka, hat, and gloves and heaved the library's heavy door open and slipped into the cold. Overhead, the cranes' heads of streetlights bowed over the labyrinth of snow. Orange shadows dogged her as she moved.

The northern lights in the magenta of her mother's spring dress rippled and swayed above. If only that color would pour down into her orchids. Unsure of where to go, Alasa paced a few circles like a wolf before lying down in the middle of the street and resting her head in the snow. She allowed the aurora to transfix her and felt not in the least bit cold.

"No peudo olvidar nada," said the black-suited Funes beside her. All around then, the ice-blue of glaciers, the blinding whiteness of snowfields, and at their feet, the moraine lake of unknown depth and extent.

"You remember *everything*?"

"Todo," Funes said. His sapphire eyes: gimlets into her own. "Me hace insano."

"Soon, I won't be able to remember anything."

"Esta niña. Esta afuera. Ella va helarse. Hace muy frio. No tenes frío."

Alasa cocked her head, bewildered. A bitter wind suddenly blew across the lake. Alasa turned her back. She grimaced and folded her arms over her chest, shielding her body from its bite. Clouds blocked the sun. It grew dark.

"Alasa!"

Whose voice? She turned again toward the lake. Funes had gone.

Stripped to her long underwear, Alasa awoke in her hotel bed. A half-dozen heavy blankets weighed her down, and she groaned as she pushed them off her chest. Groggy, she stumbled into the bathroom and vomited, only to re-emerge to Dr. Funes curled in a chair by the door with her parka over him.

"How do you feel?" he asked.

"Hungover."

Dr. Funes approached and laid a hand on her forehead.

"Very, very dangerous. Ten more minutes and I would be treating you for hypothermia. You're lucky I happen to be a night owl. I found you by accident. I was taking a walk before bed."

"I want to see the house where I grew up."

"Rest first."

"I'm running out of time."

In a tight section of the maze, snowdrifts towered overhead. The corridors were narrow and poorly maintained. Alasa would never have found the house without the marker of its spray-painted number. A grotesque, gothic knocker adorned the door. A gargoyle of some kind, resembling, Alasa realized, Funes the Memorious. She knocked. The insulating berms of snow ate the noise, reducing the knock to a sound like a fingernail clicking against a tooth.

No one answered.

Alasa climbed the snow to look into a high window of the house. All dark, perhaps abandoned. Yet nearby she spied a crude, steep staircase carved into the snow. Alasa mounted it and struggled up the side of the twelve-foot wall.

"Where are you going?" Dr. Funes called from below, but Alasa let the question drift away without a reply.

At the top, she pulled herself into the sparkling white topography above the maze. The upper stories of houses dotted the landscape around her. Towards the water she could see the cavern that was Main Street. Smoke rose from chimneys. In the distance, a pod of snow machines ferried guests from the lodge. Behind her, the Lotus Glacier loomed. Alasa grew a little dizzy, dazzled by the vastness outside the maze and her proximity to the sun.

A post-holed trail led from the ladder to the back of the house. The evident freshness of the trail puzzled her. The house was obviously vacant. Probably for the rest of winter. Why would anyone be up here? Possibly a caretaker of some kind, checking the pipes or the meter. The postholes were deep, but Alasa managed to follow them. She had to rest every few steps. Sweat ran down her back. She stripped off her parka and left it hanging off the gutter of the house. At the trail's end, Alasa paused at the edge of a deep well in the snow. She expected to see a fuse box or a water main near the back door. But no. Something else. Someone had dug a huge square in the snow. It plunged all the way down to the ground. Hidden in the shadowy murk, some kind of marker, some kind of stone. Alasa found steps in the inner wall of the well. She tried the first one, but it collapsed and set her tumbling, shrieking, into the well. She struck the ground hard and rolled with a groan onto her back. Overhead, a square of blue sky.

It was peaceful down here, Alasa decided. But she'd landed on something and crushed it. Its remains jabbed at her. She arched up and extracted a dead, potted orchid. She stroked its skeletal stem and set it down. She crawled across the bottom of the well to a gravestone and wiped the snow from its face with her bare hand.

IN LOVING MEMORY
GOD'S PRECIOUS ORCHID
ALASA MEMNOV
SEPT 2, 1968 – DEC 29, 1972

Alasa's breath hung before the stone, lingering between them. Finally, she turned and clawed her way up the ladder, out of the snowy well, away from the child's grave.

Dr. Funes waited for her on the roof of the house. He would remember this, too, as he remembered everything.

"I don't understand," Alasa said when she reached him.

"The mind creates gentle, if elaborate ways to tell us the worst kind of news." He handed her *Labyrinths*. A scrap of newsprint marked her place.

TODDLER DIES OF EXPOSURE, MOTHER HELD

A local girl died of exposure Tuesday after her mother accidentally locked her outside the house overnight, according to the Lotus County Coroner's Office.

Neighbors discovered Alasa Memnov, 4, at 8 a.m. Wednesday morning on the front step of her own house. She was partially buried in the overnight snowfall.

Time of death is yet to be determined, according to Sheriff Carl Roy. An autopsy is underway.

"At this time, we are ruling the child's death a terrible accident. Her mother appears to suffer from dementia. It appears she should not have been entrusted with the care of a child," said Roy.

The mother, Bebe Memnov, 33, of Lotus, had been diagnosed with early onset dementia.

"I would say the system failed her, but from what her doctors have said, the symptoms manifested far quicker than anyone expected," said Roy.

Memnov remains under guarded supervision at St. Peter's General Hospital in Lotus and will be transferred to an institution in Anchorage, according to Dr. Samuel Clowe.

"Mrs. Memnov is lapsing in and out of catatonia. She is aware her daughter has died, but she does not appear to remember the incident."

A public vigil will be held in Alasa Memnov's memory on Jan. 1 at the Lotus Library.

The combined glare of sun and snow overwhelmed Alasa. She shut her eyes. When she reopened them, she and Funes waited beside the empty bed of her mother's room at the nursing home.

"How do you feel?" he asked.

"Ready," she replied.

Funes lifted the sheet. She climbed into bed.

"Has she forgiven you?" he asked.

Bebe Memnov rested her head on the pillow.

"That remains to be seen," she said.

Funes tucked the old woman in the bed and turned off the light.

"The important part is that you have forgiven yourself," he said.